Public Governance and Strategic Management Capabilities

T0291202

"This book fills a gap in comparative information on public governance by providing evidence of what is happening in the Gulf States."
—*Richard Boyle, Institute of Public Administration,*
University College Dublin, Ireland

This is a book about the modernization of public governance and the development of strategic states. It focuses on six Gulf countries (United Arab Emirates, Oman, Qatar, Bahrain, Saudi Arabia and Kuwait) and presents research findings from quantitative data analysis and comparative analysis of the trends and developments of the six Gulf states.

The book analyses the workings of the governments of the Gulf States, including the way that they have tackled national development since the mid-1990s. This includes how their strategies for economic diversification have been reflected in trends in revenues from "oil rents" and whether they are still rentier states or not. Evidence is presented on key topics such as government strategies and long-term strategic visions. Careful consideration is given to reputational evidence and to the strategic process capabilities of the governments: integration and coordination of government machinery, mobilizing public and private stakeholders, evaluating, and adapting—all defined as strategic process capabilities. This examination of government is also used to study their performance in strategic results areas: the economy, the natural environment, and the happiness of their citizens. The countries emerge from this analysis as far from identical in terms of capabilities or in term of performance.

Paul Joyce is an Institute of Local Government Studies Associate at the University of Birmingham, an Affiliated Researcher in the Department of Public Management at the Solvay Brussels School of Economics and Management (Université Libre de Bruxelles) and Visiting Professor at Leeds Beckett University.

Turki Faisal Al Rasheed is Visiting Professor at the Department of Agriculture and Bio-systems Engineering, College of Agriculture and Life Sciences, University of Arizona, USA and a Visiting Research Fellow at Liverpool John Moores University, UK.

Routledge Critical Studies in Public Management

Edited by Stephen Osborne

For a full list of titles in this series, please visit www.routledge.com

The study and practice of public management has undergone profound changes across the world. Over the last quarter century, we have seen

- increasing criticism of public administration as the overarching framework for the provision of public services,
- the rise (and critical appraisal) of the 'New Public Management' as an emergent paradigm for the provision of public services,
- the transformation of the 'public sector' into the cross-sectoral provision of public services, and
- the growth of the governance of inter-organizational relationships as an essential element in the provision of public services

In reality these trends have not so much replaced each other as elided or co-existed together—the public policy process has not gone away as a legitimate topic of study, intra-organizational management continues to be essential to the efficient provision of public services, whilst the governance of inter-organizational and inter-sectoral relationships is now essential to the effective provision of these services.

Further, whilst the study of public management has been enriched by contribution of a range of insights from the 'mainstream' management literature, it has also contributed to this literature in such areas as networks and inter-organizational collaboration, innovation and stakeholder theory.

This series is dedicated to presenting and critiquing this important body of theory and empirical study. It will publish books that both explore and evaluate the emergent and developing nature of public administration, management and governance (in theory and practice) and examine the relationship with and contribution to the overarching disciplines of management and organizational sociology.

Books in the series will be of interest to academics and researchers in this field, students undertaking advanced studies of it as part of their undergraduate or postgraduate degree and reflective policy makers and practitioners.

Innovation in City Governments
Structures, Networks and Leadership
Jenny M. Lewis, Lykke Margot Ricard, Erik Hans Klijn, and Tamyko Ysa

Public Governance and Strategic Management Capabilities
Public Governance in the Gulf States
Paul Joyce and Turki Al Rasheed

Public Governance and Strategic Management Capabilities

Public Governance in the Gulf States

Paul Joyce and
Turki Al Rasheed

Routledge
Taylor & Francis Group

NEW YORK AND LONDON

First published 2017
by Routledge
711 Third Avenue, New York, NY 10017

and by Routledge
2 Park Square, Milton Park, Abingdon, Oxon OX14 4RN

First issued in paperback 2018

Routledge is an imprint of the Taylor & Francis Group, an informa business

© 2017 Taylor & Francis

The right of Paul Joyce and Turki Al Rasheed to be identified as authors of this work has been asserted by them in accordance with sections 77 and 78 of the Copyright, Designs and Patents Act 1988.

Library of Congress Cataloging in Publication Data
A catalog record for this book has been requested

ISBN 13: 978-1-138-33999-6 (pbk)
ISBN 13: 978-1-138-92634-9 (hbk)

Typeset in Sabon
by Apex CoVantage, LLC

Contents

List of Figures and Tables   vii
Preface   ix
Acknowledgements   xi

PART I
The National Level   1

1   Challenges for the Gulf States   3

2   Transitions in Public Governance   21

3   Contingencies and Variations   39

4   Constitutions and Institutions   60

5   Reputations for Governance and Competitiveness   80

6   Becoming Visionary and Strategic   93

7   Governing for Results   132

PART II
The Supranational Level   151

8   The Gulf Cooperation Council   153

PART III
Commentary and Conclusions   163

9   Summary and Conclusions   165

Index   181

Figures and Tables

Figures

1.1	Thematic Groupings of Challenges	19
3.1	Hypothesis: Economic Growth Rates Vary by Type of Industrializing Elites	42
3.2	Paths to More Effective Government	47
3.3	The Three Building Blocks of an Effective Public Sector According to the World Bank (1997)	49
3.4	Doing the Right Things Effectively	50
3.5	Causes of Government Budget Transparency	53
3.6	A Synthesis of Theories and Models Important for the Effectiveness of Public Governance	58
4.1	Constitutions and Government Effectiveness	61
4.2	Public Governance in Saudi Arabia	65
4.3	Governance Institutions at Federal Level in the United Arab Emirates	72
5.1	The Gulf States' League Table of Government Effectiveness (Perceptions)	86
5.2	The Gulf States' League Table of Global Competitiveness Rankings 2015–16	89
7.1	Strategic Process Capabilities	135
7.2	The Gulf States' League Table of Strategic Process Capabilities (Hertie School of Governance Database)	138
7.3	Fluctuations in Oil Rents in the Gulf States, 1995–2014	145
9.1	Modernizing Public Governance—the Strategic State in a Context of Globalization	170
9.2	Barber's (2007) Model of Effective Government	177

Tables

1.1	Total Population	5
1.2	Percentage of Population Aged 0–14 (% of Total)	6
1.3	Employment to Population Ratio (15+, %, Modeled ILO Estimate)	6

1.4	Oil Rents (% of GDP)—Selected Countries	7
1.5	GDP at Market Prices (Constant 2005 US$) (000,000,000s)	7
3.1	An Institutional Approach to the Comparison of Public Governance	44
5.1	Public Governance—Key Dimensions in 2000 and 2014 (Percentile Rank Scores)	81
5.2	Public Governance Indicators in 2014 (World Bank Data)	83
5.3	Government Effectiveness Estimate—World Governance Indicator	87
5.4	Government Effectiveness (World Bank) and the Global Competitiveness Rankings 2015–16	89
6.1	Oman and its Diversification Strategy	97
6.2	Objectives and Strategic Bases of the Eighth Development Plan	105
6.3	Private Sector Share of Real GDP and Private Investments in Saudi Arabia	108
6.4	A Composite Picture of the Visionary and Strategic Pattern	123
7.1	Strategic Process Capabilities (Hertie School of Governance 2014)	136
7.2	Strategic Process Capabilities and Generic Economic Outcomes for the Gulf States	139
7.3	Strategic Process Capabilities and Generic Social and Environmental Outcomes for the Gulf States	141
7.4	Oil Rents (% of GDP)	144
7.5	Long-Term Strategic Visioning and Evaluating and Adapting	148
9.1	Transparency International Corruption Index	167

Preface

We wrote this book because we thought between us we might do a reasonable job of casting a fresh eye over the challenges of public governance in the Gulf states. We both felt that this would require us looking with an open mind at the data and any evidence that we could find on what has been happening over the last twenty years. Our aim was to be as objective as we possibly could be and to make as much use as possible of ideas drawn from public management, especially those dealing with the application of strategic management. Another intellectual debt of this book is to the work done by the OECD in a whole series of countries where it has carried out public governance reviews. We have been particularly inspired by the OECD idea of a strategic state and the discussion of strategic-state capabilities. As we finish this we recognize that there is still much more to be found out and understood about how good public governance comes about and is maintained in the Gulf states. We have found the experience of studying governance in the Gulf states an enlightening process. We have done our best to keep some focus on the application of ideas to produce better and more useful (we hope) understandings of public governance.

Paul Joyce and Turki Al Rasheed,
August 2016, London and Riyadh

Acknowledgements

We are grateful to the people in the Gulf states who gave us their time for this project, who talked to us or gave us written views on public governance in the Arabian Peninsula. We should also acknowledge the extensive use we made of the studies contained in *Power and Politics in the Persian Gulf Monarchies*, which was edited by Christopher Davidson. This book was an invaluable source of insights into the history, constitutional developments, and economics of the countries in the Arabian Peninsula.

Part I
The National Level

1 Challenges for the Gulf States

Public Governance and Gulf States

This is a book about public governance and national leaders' attempts to deal with the economic, environmental, social, and political issues of their countries. Public governance might be generally defined as the use of government action and power, although narrower definitions can be offered for specific purposes. This book is concerned with public governance defined as the work of societal maintenance and societal development by government, involving government decisions and actions deploying and committing economic and social resources. This definition was inspired by one proposed by the World Bank (1992) some time ago—arguably at the dawn of a post neo-liberal period in countries such as the United States and the United Kingdom.

In this book we look at the public governance of six countries that are members of the Gulf Coordinating Council, which was set up at the beginning of the 1980s. These countries were Bahrain, Kuwait, Oman, Qatar, Saudi Arabia, and the United Arab Emirates. In this book we explore the circumstances and records of the six countries and assess the idea that strategic-state capabilities (OECD 2013) are the basis of successful public governance. We are asking: do Gulf countries in the Arabian Peninsula manage better when they make use of strategic thinking, long-term strategic visions and plans, and strategic capabilities?

It seems right in this exploration of public governance in the Gulf that we should draw on ideas and theories developed to understand public governance throughout the world. The effects of globalization are seen as all pervasive these days and the wisdom of looking at individual countries, or even small groups of countries, in isolation without an appreciation of what is happening elsewhere in the wider world seems likely to be a mistake. In any case, it is our intention to place the Gulf states in a wider context from time to time during our analysis of the data. This in effect will serve to keep the analysis of the six countries in perspective—showing how they compare with countries in Europe, East Asia and elsewhere.

We shall be continually considering variations between the six Gulf countries and using comparative analysis to study government actions and consequences. We draw data and evidence from and have been influenced by a variety of evidence sources, including (especially) published databases and interviews and we make use of analysis and comparative analysis. There are, however, limits to what can be shown through tabular analysis and our approach to each chapter reflects our desire to get as close as possible to these limits. So, we use our analysis and synthesis of evidence to draw together what we have found out and at the end of the book we also provide a summary that is deliberately more judgmental than elsewhere in the book. We think of the final chapter of the book as more of a commentary to make sense of what the evidence may be showing us rather than an analysis as such.

The theoretical concerns of the book include: (i) assessing the usefulness of the concept of a "rentier state" when attempting to explain public governance in the Gulf countries, (ii) the assessment of strategic-state actions and consequences, and (iii) the conceptualization of key attributes of strategic capabilities used within public governance systems. On the latter point, we have in mind the following strategic capabilities when thinking about governance processes: the development of long-term thinking and visions, the integration and coherence of administrative machinery, the development of implementation and delivery capacity, the engagement of citizens to get their support for national development strategies, and government interactions and partnership with organizations in the private sector business world.

In this book we will offer our perspective on the state of public governance in the Gulf countries and our judgments on how changes in public governance relate to modernization and improved government effectiveness in economic, environmental and social policy domains.

Introducing the Six Countries

The Arabian Peninsula is located in the southwest part of Asia and it has important relationships with the United States, Europe, and East Asia. The six countries of the Gulf Coordinating Council are all geographically close neighbours on the Arabian Peninsula. They are Bahrain, Kuwait, Oman, Qatar, Saudi Arabia, and the United Arab Emirates. Saudi Arabia is by far the largest of the six, both in terms of land mass and population.

All the six GCC countries are traditional monarchies, with the state playing a visible role in economic activity. Kuwait and Bahrain have relatively open political systems, including a written constitution, a parliamentary electoral system, and a free press. Though the formal structures of the other four members are less well developed, these countries have made progress in strengthening political pluralism and participation in recent years. According to Held and Ulrichsen (2012, 15),

> In the late-1990s and early-2000's all six GCC states embarked on processes of significant political change . . . These aimed to introduce a measure of political pluralism and a participatory dimensions, and renew

the legitimacy of ruling elites while co-opting oppositional groups in a carefully managed top-down process of incremental change.

One aspect of the situation in the Gulf is the dichotomy between political development, where institutions remain quite traditional, and economic ambitions, which can be benchmarked against the most sophisticated economies in the world. Increased political participation in some of the Gulf states has led to a balancing act between the customary consensus-building approach to decision-making and a desire for more vigorous policy debates on key issues (Bank 2010).

They have a variety of demographic, economic, social, and cultural characteristics in common. Their total populations have each grown very rapidly between 1995 and 2015 (see Table 1.1). Saudi Arabia had the smallest population growth—still very large in absolute terms at 67 percent—and Qatar had the largest population growth—standing at 346 per cent. All had a falling proportion of children and young people (ages 0 to 14) in the population. Apart from Kuwait, all tended to have a higher ratio of employment to population in 2014 than they did in 1995. The data showing this is presented in Tables 1.2 and 1.3.

All six countries have in the past been characterized as having unusually large oil sectors in their economies. In fact, there has been some use of the concept of a 'rentier state' to characterize the oil-rich economies of the Arabian Peninsula. This concept has been used in acknowledgement of the fact that all six countries have had large volumes of government revenues from their exploitation of oil resources. In a sense the concept is deployed to explain or recognize that the oil resources have had profound implications for their societies in terms of economics, politics, and social matters. It does not take much imagination to derive from this concept the proposition that a rentier state is engaged in managing the exploitation of a 'natural advantage' and also faces the challenges of allocating a plentiful revenue stream to

Table 1.1 Total Population

	1995	2000	2005	2010	2015	Population change 1995–2015 (%)
Bahrain	563,730	666,855	867,014	1,261,319	1,377,000	+144
Kuwait	1,637,031	1,929,470	2,263,604	3,059,473	3,892,000	+138
Oman	2,191,864	2,239,402	2,506,891	2,943,747	4,491,000	+105
Qatar	501,019	593,453	836,924	1,765,513	2,235,000	+346
Saudi Arabia	18,853,670	21,392,273	24,745,230	28,090,647	31,540,000	+67
United Arab Emirates	2,350,192	3,050,128	4,481,976	8,329,453	9,157,000	+290

(Source: World Development Indicators, The World Bank).

Table 1.2 Percentage of Population Aged 0–14 (% of Total)

	1995	2000	2005	2010	2015
Bahrain	30.3	30.7	26.8	19.7	21.5
Kuwait	30.0	27.6	26.2	23.6	22.3
Oman	39.7	37.2	34.0	26.5	20.5
Qatar	26.5	25.9	23.5	13.5	15.5
Saudi Arabia	41.5	37.3	33.5	30.4	28.6
United Arab Emirates	26.7	25.2	18.2	13.3	13.9

(Source: World Development Indicators, The World Bank).

Table 1.3 Employment to Population Ratio (15+, %, Modeled ILO Estimate)

	1995	2000	2005	2010	2014
Bahrain	62.6	62.7	63.1	68.0	67.2
Kuwait	66.1	67.1	66.5	66.4	66.5
Oman	56.0	50.8	51.0	55.2	61.5
Qatar	79.6	74.8	79.1	86.0	86.4
Saudi Arabia	49.8	46.3	47.7	48.7	52.1
United Arab Emirates	73.9	74.5	74.2	74.9	77.6

(Source: World Development Indicators, The World Bank).

Note: Final year shown is 2014 because of data availability.

the various needs of consumption and investment in a manner that is seen as desirable and acceptable. The concept has been used to provide a theoretical understanding of the distinctiveness of the Gulf states caused by their oil resources. This emphasizes their differentiation from other countries which have economies reliant on the production of goods and services and the search for economic success through competitiveness and productiveness.

During the twenty years after 1995, the six countries were not unique in having oil industries; other countries that had a lot of oil included the United States, the Russian Federation, Brazil, and Venezuela. But even so, the six Gulf states stood out for the extent to which oil dominated their economies (especially Kuwait and Saudi Arabia, see Table 1.4) and the extent to which oil revenue was a major source of public revenue.

They all had a good economic growth rate in the years after 1995 (see Table 1.5). Saudi Arabia was the fastest growing between 2000 and 2014, more than doubling its GDP at market prices. Bahrain and Qatar were just behind, both nearly doubling the size of their economies between 2000 and 2014. Oman was the slowest growing but managed to increase its GDP by about half over the same period. To some extent, the growth of populations and the increasing rates of those in employment to population should have helped to increase the economic growth of the Gulf states. Another possible driver of economic growth between 2000 and 2010 might have been

Table 1.4 Oil Rents (% of GDP)—Selected Countries

	1995 (%)	2000 (%)	2014 (%)
Bahrain	16	18	15
China	2	2	1
India	1	1	1
Kuwait	40	49	53
Oman	29	50	28
Qatar	28	37	20
Russian Federation	7	20	13
Saudi Arabia	32	42	39
United Arab Emirates	17	20	19
United Kingdom	1	1	1
United States	0	0	1
Venezuela	19	23	(24)

(Source: World Development Indicators, The World Bank).

Notes: Final year shown is 2014 because it was most recent for which data was available. Oil rents can be defined as the value of crude oil production minus the total costs of production. The values are based on estimates of world prices of units of oil and estimates of average unit costs; the values are calculated using these estimates and the physical quantities of oil produced by each country. The data for Venezuela shows the oil rent for 2012 in the last column.

Table 1.5 GDP at Market Prices (Constant 2005 US$) (000,000,000s)

	1995	2000	2005	2010	2014	% change in period 2000 to 2014
Bahrain	10.1	12.4	16.0	20.9	24.4	97
Kuwait	49.6	54.4	80.8	85.6	99.6	83
Oman	25.2	29.8	31.1	41.2	46.6	56
Qatar	—	30.1	44.5	104.4	135.0	96
Saudi Arabia	227.8	258.6	328.5	425.2	524.2	103
United Arab Emirates	106.2	139.1	180.6	203.4	249.6	79

(Source: World Development Indicators, The World Bank).

the relatively high price of crude oil on world markets, but, as Table 1.4 suggests, the biggest changes in oil rents as a percentage of GDP seemed to occur in the late 1990s. Anyway, these Gulf state economic growth rates looked very respectable when compared to those of the largest global economies, although not as impressive as China's remarkable rate of economic growth, which was more than 700 percent (measured by GDP in market prices) over the years 2000 to 2014.

Sometimes the concept of the rentier state seems to be used in a way that implicitly conveys the idea that economic success is unearned and undeserved. If it is said that the export of oil may be seen as creating a financial windfall for rentier states, we can suggest that the implication that economic success is undeserved is contained in the word "windfall". Sometimes, it can be argued, the concept is applied with insufficient appreciation of the stresses and strains created by oil income within societies that are oil-rich and have rentier state characteristics. These stresses and strains are, for example, a byproduct of oil's fluctuating global market. Rulers and governments face challenges in anticipating and adapting to changing oil prices.

Challenges for Saudi Arabia

In 2010 a branch of the UNDP (United Nations Development Program) drafted a document about the work it was doing supporting the government of Saudi Arabia (Al-Rushaid 2010). The document referred to a number of underlying challenges facing the Saudi government in relation to national development. These included unemployment, women's empowerment, competitiveness, equitable regional planning, and so on. The UNDP document also suggested that "the single most significant challenge facing resource-based economies everywhere is to diversify for the sake of sustainability and to avoid the 'Dutch disease' when revenues from national resources lead to structural distortions in manufacturing industries" (Al-Rushaid 2010 10).

The UNDP listed a number of challenges that had already been identified in the Saudi Government's Eighth Development Plan (2005–09). These were in in addition to the challenge of economic diversification that Saudi Arabia's ruler and government had set for the future of the country. The challenges in the Development Plan were:

1   Fast population growth and a high dependency rate with implications for basic public services such as education and health
2   Equitable economic growth across regions
3   The run-down of natural resources (including water)
4   The poor competitive capabilities of certain sectors (especially after Saudi Arabia joined the WTO in 2005)
5   Human resource development
6   The high pace of globalization
7   Impacts on Saudi foreign trade activities by the emergence of international regional economic blocs and free trade zones
8   Harnessing science and technology for competitive advantage
9   Changes in the basis of competitive advantage (from raw materials to knowledge)
10 Competition with other countries to attract capital and foreign direct investment

The UNDP document also referred to national aspirations that posed challenges of strategic intent. It was reported that Saudi Arabia wanted a different kind of future, summed up as "a future that's more inclusive, expansive, sustainable and integrated on both economic and social levels to become one the world's top 10 most competitive economies by the end of 2010" (Al-Rushaid 2010, 10–11). The UNDP reported that Saudi Arabia was currently ranked the thirteenth most competitive economy in the world.

The Saudi government seemed to be interested in much more than GDP growth. The Eighth Development Plan was in part a plan focused on results, with intended results including economic diversification, repositioning the Saudi economy in upstream development, human resource development, and greater productivity, technology, and innovation. In other words, the Saudis wanted to transform the situation by diversifying and modernizing the national economy. In a way, it might be said that the strategic direction implied a shift from thinking about national development in terms of quantitative GDP growth to thinking about qualitative strategic changes in the Saudi economy and the country's human resources. The ambition was to build a different economy and society, one less reliant on exploiting oil resources and redistributing the benefits of oil income through the state.

Further reading of the draft UNDP document revealed the existence of process challenges, meaning challenges to how national development was governed. The national development process from 2003 onwards was becoming more long-term and more closely modeled on strategic planning as an institutional form for development planning. The Saudi Long-Term Strategy 2025, which the Eighth Development Plan (2005–09) said could be published in 2005, was meant to direct four successive five-year plans and would thus cover a 20-year period from 2005 to 2024. The Eighth Development Plan claimed that the first of the five-year plans had been significantly influenced by the strategic planning approach.

The Long-Term Strategy 2025 also made it clear that follow-up and implementation systems were crucial if the policies in the Eighth Plan were to be implemented effectively. Paragraph 4.2 of the Long-Term Strategy 2025 was unequivocal about the difference that a follow-up and monitoring system would make to the delivery of the long-term strategy (Kingdom of Saudi Arabia paragraph 4.2):

> It is said that what gets measured gets done. Thus, follow-up and monitoring are an essential part of designing a strategy. An effective monitoring and evaluation (M&E) system creates desirable incentives for converting ideas into action. Without effective follow-up, the proposed long-term strategy is likely to become yet another exercise in only generating good ideas.

The Ninth Development Plan (2010–14) methodology was also presented as important for ensuring alignment of the five-year plan with the Long-Term Strategy 2025. Each government agency was said to have developed its own long-term strategy based on the national long-term strategy.

As a result of these developments in the processes of national development in Saudi Arabia, there was a logical need for new capabilities in government in some key respects to make the new, more strategic process effective. The Ministry of Economy and Planning began work on capacity development in 2005. (The Ministry of Economy and Planning had been the Ministry of Planning before 2003, when it was restructured.) The capacity development work was expected to end in 2011. The capacities to be developed included: sectoral and strategic planning, regional decentralized planning, and plan monitoring and implementation. It was intended to continue capacity building under the Ninth Development Plan by arranging meetings and workshops.

The UNDP expressed concerns about the individual and organizational capabilities of (what we will call) the centre of government. First, it appeared that there was a very high turnover among staff with relevant qualifications, experience, the right connections, and acceptability. High turnover was an issue for government capacity in respect of expertise in strategic planning, financial management, macroeconomics, econometrics, and statistics. The UNDP document stated (Al-Rushaid 2010, 14): "Consequently, capacity development, at the individual level, has always been difficult to sustain in the long-term."

Second, there was possibly an organizational capability issue arising from the government's structure. The UNDP document referred to a report prepared in 2002 by Rabbi Royan, which, in effect, implied that the Ministry of Planning did not have sufficient authority in the government's structure. The Royan report argued (Royan 2002):

> if planning is still perceived as an important tool to guide economic agents throughout the economy and also steer sectoral Ministries to work towards national objectives, there may be a case for the elevation of the Ministry of Planning towards a Central Agency status that reports directly to the Head of State. Such a status will provide more clout and independence to the planning and monitoring function, which now resides with the Ministry.

In more recent terminology, popularized by (among others) the OECD in its public governance reviews, Royan was arguing to consolidate the structural position of the Ministry of Planning into the "centre of government". Possibly reflecting a weakness in the power base of strategic planning within the Saudi Government, there was also mention by the UNDP document of another problem with obvious consequences for the Saudi Government's strategic capabilities; this was "the dilemma of planning without control on budget allocation" (Al-Rushaid 2010, 15). This particular dilemma was said by the UNDP document to be a factor in the present situation. The importance of this point for the impact of planning was probably critical: strategic plans depend for their impact on the alignment of budget with the strategic plan and the use of performance monitoring and reporting systems to ensure the plan is being delivered and the strategic plan refined and improved. For the UNDP to detect a dilemma in respect of the control of budget allocations could be taken as suggesting that planning to deliver national development was seriously compromised. This may have been caused by a very weak linkage between planning and the public finances.

In a vote of confidence in the more strategic approach being adopted, the Saudi Arabian General Investment Authority (SAGIA), which had been set up under a Council of Ministers Resolution, linked the state of the economy—stable and robust—to the use of long-term visions and strategic planning by Saudi rulers (SAGIA 2015):

> The Kingdom of Saudi Arabia is undergoing an exciting transformation. One of the most enterprising nations in the Middle East, Saudi's vast natural energy combined with the long-term vision and strategic planning of its rulers has helped to create today's stable, robust economy.

The publication of a new long-term strategic vision for the Kingdom of Saudi Arabia in 2016 was also accompanied by a continuing commitment to improving public governance. One specific initiative this time was the planned setting up of a strategic management office (under the Council of Economic and Development Affairs), with responsibility for coordinating government programmes, ensuring their alignment with the new National vision, and ensuring the development of sectoral strategies. A second planned initiative was a Decision Support Centre at the Royal Court, with the stated intent of providing analytical and evidence-based support. The implication was that developing the government's capacity for public governance based on strategic planning and management remained a continuing commitment—and presumably an ongoing development challenge.

More Challenges

So, Saudi Arabia faced many challenges, including developmental challenges in regard to government capabilities. Consideration of the experiences and circumstances of the remaining Gulf states enables us to add quite a few more challenges—some political, some economic, and some that represent other types of challenges. This cannot pretend to be a scientific or systematic list of challenges, but we hope it provides some insights into the situations (past and current) faced by state leaders in Gulf countries.

Factions within Ruling Families

Factions can exist within ruling or royal families. Indeed, there was a very long power struggle between one faction based around the Prime Minister of Bahrain and another based around Bahrain's Crown Prince. The latter faction was identified with modernization and reform of both the economy and the political system. The King eventually assigned to the Crown Prince the overarching authority to make decisions regarding the economy, and the Crown Prince had quite a power base in the Economic Development Board, which he chaired. As circumstances change, so does the relative power of different factions. As a result of developments in 2011, the year of the Arab Spring in the Middle East and North Africa, the balance of power in Bahrain tipped towards the conservatively inclined faction of the Prime Minister and away from the economic reform agenda championed by the Crown Prince.

Kuwait's Internal and External Threats to Security

Kuwait appears to have been beset by national security issues going back more than fifty years. In the 1960s and early 1970s Iraq was a problem for Kuwait national security. Later, in the 1980s, a post-revolutionary Iran was seen as posing a threat to Kuwait's security. And probably most famously, Kuwait was invaded by Iraq's military in 1990, and it took the United States and a large coalition of other countries to come to the aid of Kuwait and expel Iraqi forces from Kuwait. Because of the Iraq invasion as well as fears of terrorism, Kuwait's state and people may have felt very insecure, but arguably all six of the Gulf states may have, at times, felt that they were located in a region in which instability and risk of war were far too likely. Even in 2015 and 2016 the region was suffering from major military conflicts in Syria and Iraq—conflicts that had involved many nations joining in.

Internal security issues have occurred from time to time in Kuwait. In 1985 there was an assassination attempt on the Emir of Kuwait, as well as a series of bombings. In more recent years there have been government concerns about terrorism. In June 2015 there was an Islamic State attack on the Imam Al-Saqed Mosque, leading to 26 deaths and the wounding of 227 people. Also in 2015, three people identified as a terrorist cell were arrested (Reuters 2015):

> Kuwait authorities seized a huge arms cache smuggled from Iraq and hidden beneath houses near the border, arresting three suspected members of a militant cell that was plotting to destabilise the country, local media said.
>
> Majority-Sunni Muslim Kuwait has been on alert since an Islamic State suicide bomber blew himself up at a Shi'ite mosque in the capital Kuwait city in late June, killing 27 people.

Loyalty of the Members of Bahrain's Shia Community

It has been estimated that the Shia community in Bahrain could be as much as 60 percent of the population—that is, a majority. However, the state's leadership in Bahrain is Sunni. Concerns about the loyalty of the Shia community arguably go back as far as 1979 and the Iran revolution. Following the revolution there were suspicions that Iran would be seeking to claim

Bahrain territory as its own and there were some pro-Iran demonstrations. Although it occurred long ago, in 1981, it can be noted that the Bahraini authorities arrested some 73 people who were suspected of preparing a coup and were seen as having links to a pro-Iran organization led by an Iraqi religious cleric. Part of the concern about the Shia community appears to have been based on perceptions that religious authority based in Iraq and Iran has had influence in the community.

Constitutional Disappointments in Bahrain

It has been claimed that, in 2001, the population of Bahrain became hopeful of getting an improved constitution. In fact, a new constitution was put in place in 2002, changing the country from an emirate to a kingdom and reinstating a parliament. This new constitution came on the back of a 2001 referendum on the National Action Charter, which appeared to offer political reforms. The referendum proposed a new bicameral parliament with the elected chamber having the power to pass legislation while an appointed chamber would function as an advisory body. Some 98 percent of those who voted (in a high voter turnout of 90 percent) voted to ratify the National Action Charter. Although a number of reforms were implemented afterwards, there was some disappointment at the new 2002 constitution. The appointed chamber was not confined to an advisory function but also had some involvement with the legislative process. The disappointment led to arguments about whether there should be participation in the Parliamentary process set up as result of the new constitution.

Troublesome Parliaments—Bahrain

The ruler of Bahrain dissolved the country's Parliament in 1975. This seems to have been a response to difficulties in the relationship between the ruler and the Parliament. Various matters became contention issues in the eyes of the Parliament, including the budget, the presence of the United States' military in Bahrain, legislation on internal security, and land reform. It is possible that Parliament's disagreements with the government about the budget were partly fueled by the substantial rise in revenue from the oil industry, which followed the actions of OPEC in 1973. When the parliament was re-established in 2002, it was designed to have more limited powers than the 1970s Parliament. Bahrain never went to a fully elected parliament. The powers of members of Parliament were significantly weaker than they had been in the previous parliament of the 1970s.

Kuwait's Parliament Blocking Reforms

Kuwait has been perceived as being relatively democratic in terms of its public governance arrangements. To this might be added the comment that in Kuwait the parliaments have been relatively assertive and there have been periods of tension between Parliament and the government. Parliament, because of these tensions, was dissolved on three occasions in the 2000s: in 2006, 2008, and 2009. There was a precedent for this since the Emir of Kuwait had dissolved Parliament in 1976. One consequence of this tension may have been the long delays in progressing legislation that has been seen as important for national development.

This Kuwait story is disappointing for anyone wishing to believe that democracy is part and parcel of a modern and modernizing state. It is disappointing from the point of view that it might be hoped that a lively parliament could be seen as invigorating public debate. However, in the case of Kuwait, matters seemed to ease after elections in 2009 and Parliament seemed to become a more cooperative institution. In this period, immediately after the 2009 election, an economic stimulus package was agreed and privatization legislation was passed. The latter legislation had been held up for many years because of the problems in the relationship between the government and Parliament. The easing of tensions was short-lived and by late 2010 a more uncooperative approach by Parliament was back in place. There have also been reports that Parliament delayed the government's delivery of Kuwait Vision 2035 by two years or so, and it was only in 2013 that onlookers started to think that there was a chance that it might progress because Parliament was no longer blocking it.

Political Movements in Bahrain, United Arab Emirates, and Kuwait

Political ideas and movements have evolved over the years in Bahrain. The 1940s and 1950s were years in which there was a fair amount of interest in Arab nationalism and anti-colonialism among the people of Bahrain. During the 1960s and the early 1970s Bahrainis were influenced by new political ideas. Islamist political attitudes began to increase. And in recent years nationalism receded in importance and political movements tend to be Islamist ones. In the case of the United Arab Emirates the nationalist movement did use to be important but by the late 1960s had tended to fade away. In Kuwait the 1950s were years in which nationalism was a growing movement but by the 1980s nationalism was fading, to be supplanted by a rise in Islamist attitudes among the people.

Closing Down Political Protest in Bahrain and in United Arab Emirates in 2011

In response to the Arab Spring discontent of 2011 Bahrain security forces began to control protest and close it down. Saudi Arabia and the United Arab Emirates provided security forces to support the government of Bahrain. Attempts to repress protest included the dismissal of workers who had participated in strikes and other protests during 2011. Expatriate workers were recruited to replace dismissed workers.

The government's response to the discontent attracted adverse comments internationally and some would argue that it did some damage to Bahrain's international reputation and economic prospects. It was subsequently argued that investors were being deterred by political unrest inside Bahrain. It was no longer being seen as a "safe, stable financial hub" (Trenwith 2015).

There were also some reports of problems during 2011 in the United Arab Emirates. In March of that year there was a petition calling for an elected parliament. A small number of the signatories of the petition were put in prison.

Inclusion of Women in Political Life

At the end of the 1990s the emir of Kuwait tried to enfranchise women. But the rulers' efforts failed as a result of Parliament rejecting the initiative when it first met again after dissolution in May 1999. Islamists within Parliament rejected enfranchising women on the grounds of their principles. Some members of Parliament objected on constitutional grounds. Some, apparently, rejected the move to enfranchise women because they were concerned about who would look after the children while women were voting.

Despite the initial setback in Kuwait, progress is being made in ensuring women are participating in political life in the Gulf states. For example, representation through Oman's Consultative Council (Majlis al-Shura) was opened up to women in 1997—meaning they could vote and they could stand for election. In the case of Qatar, Sheikha Moza bint Nasser Al-Misnad, wife of the Emir of Qatar, directed a committee with a mandate to encourage women citizens to vote and participate in the 1999 Municipal elections. In 1999 six of the 248 candidates were women. Further rounds of elections were held in 2003 and 2007. Incredibly, most of the voters (around 70 percent) in 2007 were women. Another example is the case of Saudi Arabia. Very recently (2015) a number of women were successful in standing for municipal elections in Saudi Arabia. Nevertheless, it is clear that there is still a long way to go in terms of women feeling fully included in political life.

Increasing Reliance on Immigrant Workers

Saudi Arabia and the other countries in the Gulf have in recent decades seen a rise in the number of foreign workers being employed in the labour markets. In the case of Saudi Arabia the foreign workers rose from about 30 percent in 1975 to almost 60 percent in 1985. In fact, the percentage of foreign workers peaked at two-thirds of the workforce in 1989 and then fell back until 2004. The data suggests that the peak inflow of foreign workers into Saudi Arabia was between 1975 and 1988. In 2008 only about half of the residents of Bahrain were nationals. In the case of the United Arab

Emirates it was estimated that nationals made up only about 10 percent of the national workforce.

Foreign workers entered a dual labour market in Saudi Arabia. Foreign workers were employed in the private sector and Saudi nationals worked in the public sector. A similar dual labour market situation was to be found in Bahrain. The fact of dual labour markets may be linked to calls for action on human resource development, as suggested in the following comment on the situation in Qatar (Wright 2011, 132):

> Yet the challenge remains one of human development as there is a need for a greater proportion of nationals to become involved in the private sector, since Qatar faces a similar problem to the other Gulf states as the majority of its national population is employed by the public sector.

In late 2015, the Emir of Qatar, Sheikh Tamim bin Hamad Al-Thani, spoke at the opening of a session of the Advisory Council. In the speech he encouraged young people in Qatar to consider more diverse career paths. This drew the following observation from one commentator in the news media (Staff Writer 2015): "His comments come as all Gulf states continue to try to tackle the shortage of nationals entering the private sector, preferring instead to take government jobs which generally come with higher salaries and more flexible hours."

The call for human resource development can also be related to unemployment problems as well as the existence of a dual labour market. For example, there have been large numbers of Emirati adults who were unemployed and it has been argued that many of these nationals were capable of working but were living on public benefits.

In the last decade, Bahrain made attempts to reform its labour market and attempted to reduce the use of foreign workers. Foreign workers are generally paid much less than their Bahraini counterparts. This inequality of pay for foreign workers and nationals could be a problem for governments wanting to see the employment of nationals increase in the private sector.

Economic Crisis in Dubai—2008 and 2009

Dubai appeared to prospering economically just before an international financial crisis struck in 2008 to 2009. Tourism was doing well. In 2006 Dubai was experiencing a real estate boom. Towards the end of 2008, and as a result of the global crisis, there was a massive slump in the stock market of Dubai. By the end of February 2009 Dubai could no longer service its major debt renewals that were due to take place in 2009. It was to all intents and purposes bankrupt. There is an estimate the Dubai stock exchange needed to refinance nearly $4 billion worth of debt. In late 2009 the Dubai economy crashed. Dubai turned to Abu Dhabi for assistance. Abu Dhabi came to the rescue of Dubai and through the UAE central bank made available a $10 billion five-year bond. So Abu Dhabi became a creditor to Dubai.

Fluctuations in the Price of Oil

Oil prices can be volatile. For example, oil prices dropped by about 15 percent between 1981 and 1983. Periods of high prices can alternate with long periods of low prices. The price of oil was much higher in the first part of the 1980s than it was in the next 15 years. In the early 2000s oil prices boomed again and then in June 2014 the price of oil slumped.

The rollercoaster pattern of oil prices is a challenge for public finances. With the big drop in the price of oil in the 1980s, government spending was much reduced in the second half of the 1980s. Personal finances are hit, too: for example, real average incomes of people in Bahrain were much lower in the second half of the 1980s. Attempts to maintain the level of government spending in periods of falling oil prices lead to budget deficits for the government. This was shown by the example of Kuwait, which had a budget deficit in 1981.

As just mentioned, a number of years of booming oil prices in the 2000s were followed by a serious drop in oil prices in mid-2014, creating a slide into a crisis in public finances in 2015 and 2016. When Kuwait's Amir Sheikh Sabah Al-Ahmad Al-Sabah spoke at the opening of the new parliamentary term in late 2015, he reported that Kuwait was losing an incredible 60 percent of its revenues. This led to projected budget deficits because government spending was still continuing. Of course, Kuwait was not the only country that faced fiscal difficulties because of the slump in oil prices.

So, to sum up, when oil prices drop massively, the negative consequences can include budget deficits, stock exchange crashes, and so on. Governments face the challenge of considering large debts and government spending money to prop up companies.

Slow Development of the Importance of Non-Oil
Revenue during the 2000s

Despite what has already been said that about the immense oil resources of Saudi Arabia, Kuwait, and other Gulf states, there is a general assumption in government circles that there is a need for diversification to reduce dependence on oil. This can be seen in the long-term vision statements and development plans produced in the last decade. There is even a feeling around that the governments were more long-term in their thinking during the 2000's than they had been in earlier periods of high oil prices. Nevertheless, by 2015, it was clear that this long-term thinking had not created a successful way of countering the negative effects on public finances of a sudden slump in oil prices; public finances were still very vulnerable to oil price volatility, as shown by the consequences of falling prices for government revenue. The need for economic reforms was as urgent as ever, raising a big question mark over the delivery of strategic reforms aimed at economic diversification. Had strategic change to non-oil industries just been too slow?

And what was holding up economic reforms to bring about economic diversification? Was part of the problem the existence of large reserves of oil? With such large reserves of oil did citizens really find it difficult to see the urgency of reform? This could be a problem for Kuwait because members of Parliament may find themselves promising high spending and low taxes in order to get elected. The "rentier mentality" could be deeply rooted in people's thinking. By this is meant that ordinary people expect to pay little in the way of taxes and yet to receive generous benefits. In essence, Kuwait's government could find it difficult to refocus on investment and production of wealth rather than public services and consumption. This could well be a problem for a country with such oil reserves, finding the country gradually being left behind economically.

Summary

The six countries of the Arab Peninsula are oil-rich countries. Some of them expect to carry on being oil-rich for some time. Others have had to think about economic strategies of economic diversification as a more urgent requirement. The challenges of being an oil economy appear well understood among the leaders in Gulf states. Public finances are vulnerable to oil price changes. Leaders worry that the oil resources create a false sense of security and thus create slowness to invest in education, management, R&D, new technology, and so on. Saudi Arabia has been pursuing a development policy of economic diversification since 1970.

The six countries may appear to be societies with strong traditional aspects and in which religion looms large. But all have been engaging with a need to think ahead and think long-term—to become more strategic. And, even if they have all approximated more or less to rentier states, they have all been contemplating the national development of a different type of state.

All the societies face problems and challenges. Many but not all of them are economic in nature. These issues include: population growth, dependency on state benefits, ensuring economic growth is widespread across all regions, depletion of natural resources, globalization pressures (including trading blocs), competitiveness, and people development, investing in and using science and technology, and attracting foreign direct investment.

Among the big issues and challenges facing the Gulf states in 2015 and 2016 included: the slump in oil prices, slashed government revenue, public spending cuts, economic reforms (diversification), terrorism, and regional conflicts. Thinking about all the challenges, some of them having been around over many years, we can suggest grouping them into five key strategic areas—as shown in Figure 1.1.

As we reflect on the challenges briefly outlined in this chapter, many of them are issues of public governance. It is to the concept of public governance we next turn.

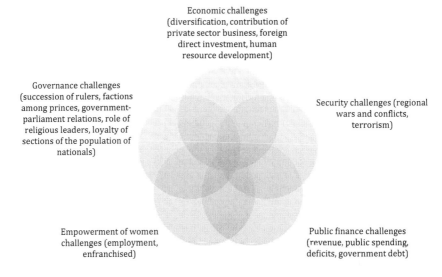

Economic challenges (diversification, contribution of private sector business, foreign direct investment, human resource development)

Governance challenges (succession of rulers, factions among princes, government-parliament relations, role of religious leaders, loyalty of sections of the population of nationals)

Security challenges (regional wars and conflicts, terrorism)

Empowerment of women challenges (employment, enfranchised)

Public finance challenges (revenue, public spending, deficits, government debt)

Figure 1.1 Thematic Groupings of Challenges

Reference List

Al-Rushaid, W. (2010) Strengthening of National Capacities for National Development Strategies and Their Management: An Evaluation of UNDP's Contribution, Country Study—Saudi Arabia. [July 2010]. Evaluation Office, United Nations Development Programme. Accessed 12 July 2016. Available from: http://web.undp.org/evaluation/documents/thematic/cd/Saudi-Arabia.pdf

Bank, T. W. (2010) *Economic Integration in the GCC*. New York: The World Bank.

Held, D. and Ulrichsen, K. (2012) Editor's Introduction: Transformation of the Gulf. In: David Held and Kristian Ulrichsen (editors) *The Transformation of The Gulf: Politics, Economics and the Global Order*. London and New York: Routledge. Pages 1–25.

Kingdom of Saudi Arabia (probably 2005). Long-Term Strategy 2025. [online] [13 July 2016]. Available from: http://www.readbag.com/undp-sa-sa-documents-ourwork-pr-long-term-strategy-2025

OECD (2013) *Strategic Insights from the Public Governance Reviews: Update. GOV/PGC(2013)4*. Paris: OECD.

Reuters (2015) Kuwait Seizes Arms, Arrests Suspects in Militant Plot. [online] [19 August 2015]. Available from: http://www.arabianbusiness.com//kuwait-seizes-arms-arrests-suspects-in-militant-plot—602716.html

Royan, R. (2002) Planning Methodology in the Kingdom of Saudi Arabia: A Quick Review for the Way Forward. In: Evaluation Office, United Nations Development Programme (editor, 2010) *Strengthening of National Capacities for National Development Strategies and Their Management: An Evaluation of UNDP's*

Contribution. National Development Strategies and Country Study – Saudi Arabia. Accessed 12 July 2015. Available from: http://web.undp.org/evaluation/documents/thematic/cd/Saudi-Arabia.pdf

SAGIA (2015) Why Saudi Arabia? [online] [13 June 2015]. Available from: Source of note: https://www.sagia.gov.sa/en/SAGIA/What-We-Do/

Staff Writer (2015) Qatar Cannot Be Built without You Emir Tells Country's Youth. [online] [21 December 2015]. Available from: http://www.arabianbusiness.com/-qatar-cannot-be-built-without-you-emir-tells-country-s-youth-611068.html#.Vne6UYSWHQM

Trenwith, C. (2015) FOCUS—Bahrain's Fiscal Tightrope: The Island State's Battle to Regain Lost Ground. [online] [19 August 2015]. Available from: http://www.arabianbusiness.com//focus-bahrain-s-fiscal-tightrope—island-state-s-battle-re-gain-lost-ground-602661.html

World Bank (1992) *Governance and Development.* Washington, DC: World Bank.

2 Transitions in Public Governance

Introduction

There has been discussion for at least twenty-five years about the precise meaning of governance when considered in relation to the public sector (Kooiman and van Vliet 1993; Frederickson 2004). This book is primarily concerned with government actions and how government strategies and actions can create positive consequences (economic, social, and environmental) for countries. We provide an overview here of the historical context that we hope will provide the best possible basis for the definition of public governance, because, in a sense, it is a definition provided, then, on an experiential basis. The history provides a possibly valuable input to the more tacit aspects of the definition of public governance.

For some scholars, governance is a generic term for interaction patterns and might include hierarchical transactions, exchange transactions and network transactions. As will be seen in the chapter, we are not taking an analytical or abstract approach to the definition. For us the definition of "public governance" does not rule out hierarchical elements or top-down coordination – and nor does it rule out the use of contracts to govern partnerships and cooperation between government and private businesses. This is because our preference is for a definition rooted in the historical evolution of government action—and, at the present time, governments combine top-down actions and the search for nationally based integration and coherence with seeking to foster the support and participation of citizens as well as partnerships with private and voluntary organizations based on commercial contracts. Key to our understanding of modern public governance is the exercise of government power on the basis of setting priorities (selectivity), maintaining focus over time, long-termism in thinking and planning, and interactions and partnerships with citizens and stakeholders in the formulation and implementation of strategies.

In this chapter we provide a summary of the ideas of Margaret Levi (2006), who we think is important in her championing of a "human agency" dimension to the theorization of the making of more effective governments. As will be seen, she does not consider an approach to issues of government effectiveness based solely on institutional models to be an adequate one. It should be noted that she is not concerned with examining government effectiveness only in Western democracies but appears to be trying to develop a more "universalist" view of government effectiveness. Her view is that leadership, among other things, matters alongside institutional and constitutional design.

Public Governance: Diversity and Complexity

There are times when economic thinking dominates and overshadows the way we think about public governance to such an extent that the state is seen as best designed to complement the requirements of the economic system. For example, certain right-wing philosophies, which we may call economic liberalism or laissez-faire thinking as a shorthand label, say that a government's scope should be cut back and restricted to a minimum and that the relationship between government and individual citizens should be based on maximizing individual freedom. In fact, an extreme version of this economic liberalism holds that the only thing a state should do is the protection of the rights of individuals (Dewey 1927). Left-wing philosophies, at least in the early and mid-twentieth century, wanted a system in which economic exploitation of workers was being eradicated and this led to a belief in centralized economic planning by the state. The minimalist state and the centralized planning state offered two very clear alternative options for how people should be governed and for defining the scope and power of the state. With reference to the mid-twentieth century, the choice of system seemed to be exemplified in practice by the United States and the Soviet Union. For a long while it might be thought that the competition between these two systems was a competition to decide which of them was the best form of state for the future of humanity, and which of them would therefore come to dominate the future. Of course, the institutions of the United States and the Soviet Union could not be actually reduced to their one-dimensional characterizations, as sometimes portrayed in political debate and public opinion. In practice, the United States had a government at the federal level that did intervene in significant ways at times and not everything in the Soviet Union was controlled through centralized economic planning (Cole 1947).

If we concentrate too much on laissez-faire governments and governments with centralized economic planning by the state, we are in danger of overlooking the great diversity of political institutions that have existed internationally, now and in the past. We can briefly note some other examples here, for example, the political situation in a country created when political rule is based on military invasion and absorption of a country into an empire (such as the case of Britain during its Roman period) or into a kingdom (such as Britain after the Norman invasion of 1066). At such times, presumably, the concerns of the state and its system of officials and public action are quite distinctive to that type of situation, and there is an element of continuing enforcement of rule though military means (that is, soldiers). Or to take another example, there have been states that although they have had rulers, these are rulers that have had very little impact on the day-to-day lives of most ordinary people and, in effect, the rulers enjoy a certain ceremonial respect rather than far reaching powers to regulate what goes on in a country (Dewey 1927). Yet another example is the theocratic state in which much of what transpires in the interactions between rulers and the governed concerns spiritual issues and matters of social custom compatible with religious teaching. These examples all seem to offer a warning that public governance is a rich phenomenon that cannot be reduced to simple polar opposites.

In the case of Europe, a hybrid of laissez-faire society and socialism developed in the 1950s and 1960s. We can name this social democracy. It was a compound of electoral democracy and "free enterprise". It was a bold experiment to develop government institutions and public policies that offered security and fairness to people generally without going down the route of centralized state economic planning. If there was planning, as in the case of France, it was indicative planning by the state, which depended on the support and voluntary cooperation of businesses that remained free to ignore the planning. This social democracy produced governments of varying party political complexions that were prepared and able to spend a large part of the gross domestic product on public services and social security. These governments appeared to correlate with, in many cases, high trade union density in the private sector, centralized trade union movements, centralized collective bargaining, and electorally successful centre-left political parties. One interpretation of how this pattern of governance worked suggested that the increasing importance of public spending and publicly funded social welfare meant that issues of security and fairness were handled through political rather than economic institutions. It was believed that this had shifted the focus of interest group conflicts away from the economic arena of society, and specifically away from expression in industrial strike action and collective bargaining, to the political arena of party politics and parliamentary processes. Again, one interpretation of the consequences of this type of public governance in the context of strong trade unions and successful centre-left political parties in the political arena was that it permitted the creation of lower unemployment and faster economic growth.

Douglas Hibbs (1978, 165), for example, made use of such ideas in his study of industrial conflict:

> My principal assumption is that [. . .] strike activity is one manifestation of an ongoing struggle for power between social classes over the distribution of resources, principally (though not exclusively) national income.

The core of the argument is that long-run changes in the volume of industrial conflict are largely explained by changes in the locus of the struggle over distribution. Strike activity has declined dramatically in nations where Social Democratic or Labour parties assumed power in the 1930s or just after the Second World War and created the modern 'welfare state'. In these countries an enormous fraction of the national income now passes through the public sector, and the 'social wage', in the form of collective consumption and personal transfers, looms large in relation to the private 'market wage' in determining the economic security and well-being of a great part of society. The political process dominates the final allocation (though not necessarily the initial production) of the national product. Put somewhat differently, political competition and conflict between left-wing and right-wing parties in the electoral arena (the political marketplace) has to a great extent replaced industrial bargaining and conflict between labour and capital in the private sector (the economic marketplace) as the process shaping the final distribution of national income.

Social democratic governments in Europe came under considerable strain in the 1970s, when there was much discussion of a return to a period of economic difficulties (partially caused by the consequences of oil price rises in 1973) combined with fears that social democratic societies were becoming ungovernable. It also seemed that many ordinary people in European countries were feeling some disenchantment with social democracy and the welfare state, maybe because the tax burden on ordinary people had increased substantially over a 20-year period. These new conditions appeared to make it more possible for political parties with very right-wing agendas to achieve electoral success in various European countries.

And so, the 1970s were a period in which there emerged a persuasive right-wing view of how society should be organized and how the private sector should be freed up in order to recreate the conditions for economic success. This involved a resurgence of the idea of the individual and the importance of freedom. These ideas were to prove popular during most of the 1980s, and continued to be fairly popular in many societies well after the 1980s. The same new thinking appears to have influenced policies on international aid and their impact was extended to many countries around the world based on a requirement that governments would undertake reforms based on these ideas in exchange for financial aid.

These 1980s' ideas were then contradicted by a new wave of thinking which was clearly evident by the mid-1990s, and which appeared to become the conventional wisdom for a decade or more thereafter.

Neo-Liberal Philosophy of the 1980s

Hayek (1944) wrote a very influential book, which he considered a political book and not a book on economics. It proved to be very influential with key politicians in the UK during the 1970s and 1980s. Interestingly, in the reprinted book's 1976 preface he argued that the old socialism that was inclined to make use of centralized economic planning and nationalization might seem to be different from a newer type of socialism that brought about societies in which there was a welfare state and redistribution of income through taxation, but that they were actually quite similar in their effects. He thought that the consequences emerged more slowly in societies with welfare state and income redistribution but that the same outcomes were produced as in the case of centralized planning and nationalization. So, his basic stance was as a critic of socialism.

Hayek believed that the nineteenth-century ideas or the principles of laissez-faire were important in Britain up until the First World War. He was not particularly primarily concerned with political democracy. He was arguing for economic freedom, believing that without freedom in economic matters then personal and political freedom could not exist. This freedom in economic affairs was seen as an individual freedom. He argued that the Renaissance in Europe had created an individualist civilization. He, however, saw a need to rescue the idea of individualism, which he thought had become wrongly tied to ideas of egotism and selfishness. For him, individualism entailed people having their own views and tastes and having the ability to develop individually. The opportunity to grow freely, he said, had become the foundation of the social and political life of a number of countries in Europe and was the result of the spread of commerce. He emphasized that it was the growth of commerce that had created the possibility of individuals having choices in how to live their lives. To sum up, Hayek defined liberalism in terms of individual freedom, including the freedom to have your own ideas, to make choices, and to develop individually. And he claimed it had emerged because of the growth of commerce—a development that commerce made possible despite European society having been very hierarchical.

Hayek identifies liberalism with individualism and socialism with collectivism. This either/or categorization denies, at least implicitly, the idea that individuals may develop more as a result of opportunities created collectively. This possibility of the opposition between individual and collectivity being transcended was advanced in the 1990s with the arrival of "Third Way" politics, and the specific claim that people may be enabled by society to realize themselves as individuals.

In the 1970s, 30 years after it was first published, Hayek's book was being read by right-wing thinkers. Among them was Sir Keith Joseph, who went on to be a minister in the Thatcher government that came to power in Britain at the end of the 1970s. It was often said that Margaret Thatcher's beliefs about markets and governments had been strongly influenced by Sir Keith Joseph.

Like Hayek, Sir Keith Joseph was a fierce critic of socialism (Joseph 1978, 100):

> Our troubles stem, I believe, from two world wars and the mood they produce. Wars expand the role of government; in a sense socialism has as much in common with the militarisation of society when you come

to think of it, with its hierarchy and subordination. Wars create great expectations and the belief that government can do almost anything, yet simultaneously they leave the country very much poorer.

Sir Keith Joseph also presented an analysis in which a set of delusions was a powerful factor in the situation he saw around him. In this respect, his posture resembled that of Hayek, implying that there was a set of beliefs that were harmful for the country and should be rejected. He listed them in the following statement (Joseph 1978, 100): "This set of delusions has taken the form of encouraging demand—by full employment policies, by subsidies, by indiscriminate benefits—while discouraging supply—by anti-enterprise attitudes, by vindictive direct taxation, by overmanning and restrictive practices backed by the strike-threat."

While he suggested that governments could intervene beneficially in economic life, he saw this as meaning that governments could in some ways help an economy to realize "its own logic and potential" (Joseph 1978, 101). But, essentially, he was opposed to active government in relation to an economy. He thought government interventions might disrupt the economy's "chains of interaction" and create side effects. He did not quite say that the market is a "natural phenomenon" and that it was not amenable to purposeful and conscious intervention by government, but it is hard to avoid the conclusion that he was thinking that government should mostly avoid "meddling" in the market and should not disturb the "natural" working of market forces.

It was not that he thought governments had bad intentions. He considered that they were intervening to try to deal with problems. But, as he saw it, government policy was under the influence of pseudo-Keynesian thinking, meaning that government tried to use public spending to create a high level of domestic demand. He quoted Hayek and other economists as suggesting that government spending to increase demand would not have positive effects. The problem was that the spending made the state bigger and, in his analysis, the big state is a burden on the private sector. So, an increase in public spending meant placing a bigger burden on the private sector. He believed that the intervention of politics in the market economy based on Keynesianism and the welfare state were rupturing the relationship between earning money and spending money. And if public spending increased too much it became too heavy a burden for the private sector to bear without it being severely harmed. He took the view that if the state sector was more than 40 percent of the whole economy, it could mean that it was too big. Pushing up public spending might create jobs in the short run, but in the long run it was creating problems for the vitality of the private sector, leading to a slowdown in the private sector.

He warned that government then reacted to the signs of the damage to the private sector by further increasing public spending. He was implying the existence of a vicious cycle in which public spending rose and rose. As a result of the draining of the vitality of the private sector, government would finance increasing demand by debt. While intending to create more economic growth, government efforts to solve problems would lead to further problems, including price rises and deficits in the balance of payments, leading in turn to pressures on the exchange rate. Presumably, Sir Keith Joseph had in mind some of the events of the later years of the 1960s when the Prime Minister of Britain, Harold Wilson, had to devalue sterling, and the years of stagflation in the early 1970s, a period which culminated in the British Chancellor of the Exchequer negotiating a government loan by the International Monetary Fund.

According to him, the government also made possible the damaging effects of trade unionism. His judgments of trade unionism were very severe (Joseph 1978, 103–104):

> Unions could afford to ignore restraint, not only wage demands, but also in opposition to efficiency, in frivolity and cantankerousness, in anti-management luddism, in opposing modernisation because they had formed the impression that government would bale them out come what may.

Arguably, his problem with socialism was in part its push for egalitarianism. To put his position in context, we can look at what other famous thinkers said about differentials of wealth and income in society. From the days of Aristotle's work on politics, one of the biggest issues in public governance has been managing the tensions created by the coexistence of rich and poor people within a society, which Aristotle thought to be the case in all known societies. Even Marx did not envision that the eradication of income differentials would be possible in the earliest stages of his projected path to a new kind of society—he thought differentials of pay would persist in the first socialist stage of transition to a future better society. The existence of rich and poor in society may be omnipresent but this does not mean that everyone in society will be reconciled to this state of affairs. Much as Max Weber, the German sociologist, argued, we might expect that the poor strata of society will look to government to compensate it for its inferior benefits and opportunities. Perhaps it might be thought that the welfare states of social democratic societies in the 1950s and 1960s went some way towards achieving "compensation" of the poor through higher taxation, better public services, and generous welfare benefits. (Although, social democratic politicians might even argue, at the end of the 1960s, that they had much work to do before equality had been achieved.)

Sir Keith Joseph had a point of view on this ages-old debate about the rich and poor in society. We might say that he considered that the existence of differentials was crucial for the proper functioning of the private market. He was a believer in the importance of incentives and he argued that egalitarianism would create problems for the economy by lowering the incentives that were needed. He said that while it might not be possible to eliminate the differences between classes, that people should have the opportunity to find the best scope and market for their talents. So, opportunity in the market was what he thought should be offered—not compensation of the poor through taxes, public services, and welfare benefits. He categorically believed that it was important to make the case against egalitarianism.

So, Sir Keith Joseph was in no doubt, as he made his arguments in the 1970s, that a combination of pseudo-Keynesian action by government, trade union action, and socialism was proving lethal for the private sector. He saw all three as interfering with the proper working of the market. He wanted changes in how Britain was governed to protect the spontaneous dynamism of market forces, which he saw as at the core of processes of national wealth creation. He felt the new governance agenda was clear: government should pursue reduced inflation and should refrain from any action that might create excess demand. If a government kept its spending down, this would solve the problem of inflation. With inflation beaten, other problems of society could be tackled.

So, the ideas of nineteenth-century liberalism were being interpreted by a British politician in a way that, arguably, reflected his views of the experiences of the 1960s and the 1970s—especially the problem of inflation, which reached very great heights in Britain of the 1970s. According to this neo-liberalism of the 1970s and 1980s, government needed to be creating a positive environment for the economy and the business community, it needed to be desisting from taxing and then spending very much public money, and it needed to desist from trying to lessen or eliminate inequality created by market forces.

This neo-liberalism was not confined to Britain. It was also found in the rest of Europe and became very important in the United States with the election of Ronald Reagan as President at the beginning of the 1980s (1981–89). There were also claims that donors of foreign aid had sought to induce governments in poor countries to adopt neo-liberal policies.

It may be that there was at least one respect in which Sir Keith Joseph's neo-liberal project for government succeeded. In Britain, inequality increased sharply in the 1980s and remained much greater in the next twenty-five years. This was true in many other countries as well. According to the OECD (2013b, 5):

> Inequality has been on the rise since the 1980s, posing new challenges for governments. In the two decades prior to the onset of the crisis [2007–9], real disposable household income increased across the OECD, but most OECD countries experienced a growth of income inequality, which appears to have accelerated since the crisis. The crisis also exacerbated pre existing [sic] regional disparities, which combined with often significant differences in fiscal capacities, deepened inter regional differences in services for citizens and businesses. This has implications for public governance, in terms for example of dealing with reforms to address issues such as social resentment and political instability.

The Turn to Governance as Opposed to Hierarchical Government

The rise in new thinking about modern governance can be dated as occurring during the 1990s. The new thinking appeared in books, notably Osborne and Gaebler's (1992) book on reinventing government, and in international forums provided by bodies such as the OECD. It also appeared in the change of strategy by the World Bank. Whereas in the past financial aid to poor countries may have encouraged a neo-liberal governance agenda, by the late 1990s the new thinking suggested that active government was essential to maximize the effectiveness of aid. Good governance was needed (World Bank 2000, 1):

> The latest work on aid effectiveness points out the risks of lending to countries with bad policies and poorly performing public sectors. Just as it became evident in the 1980s that potentially good projects often fail in poor policy environments, so it became evident in the 1990s that policy reforms are less likely to succeed when public institutions and governance are weak.

Recent commentators on the governance reforms needed in the public sector and in government often stress the development of networks and cooperation in place of hierarchy and command and control. In the light of their comments, a prediction made back at the beginning of the 1970s may one day prove very prescient. Cleveland (1972, 13) wrote:

> The organizations that get things done will no longer be hierarchical pyramids with most of the real control at the top. They will be systems—interlaced webs of tension in which control is loose, power diffused, and centers of decision plural. "Decision-making" will become an increasingly intricate process of multilateral brokerage both inside and outside the organization which thinks it has the responsibility for making, or at least announcing, the decision. Because organizations will be horizontal, the way they are governed is likely to be more collegial, consensual, and consultative. The bigger the problems to be tackled, the more real power is diffused and the larger the number of persons who can exercise it—if they work at it.

We can compare this with a summing up of the "strategic-state capacity" that is needed in modern public governance, a concept offered by the OECD based on a number of reviews of national government. The following is taken from the review of Poland's government (OECD 2013a, 11):

> In this Review, strategic-state capacity means the extent to which the central government can set and steer a national long-term vision-based strategy for the country, identify and address internal and external

challenges to implementing this strategy correctly through enhanced evidence-based decision making and strategic foresight, strengthen efficiencies in policy design and service delivery to meet these challenges, and mobilise actors and leverage resources across governments and society to achieve integrated, coherent policy outcomes that address these challenges effectively. The strategic-state concept emphasises leadership and stewardship from the centre, integrity and transparency, the importance of networks and institutions both inside and outside government, the need to draw inspiration from sub-national initiatives and from citizens, and the importance of effective implementation of strategy in support of positive outcomes for a country's economy and society.

We can note that, as in the prediction by Cleveland, the old command-and-control model of hierarchical governance is not to be seen in the OECD concept of the strategic-state capacity now needed, and there is the same emphasis on problem-solving through consultation and multiple power centres. There are vital differences, too, between the two quotes immediately above. Very importantly, the OECD's concern is for strategic government— the strategic state—and for the development of processes and capabilities that deliver integration, coordination, and coherence. This type of governance is strategic, long-term and based on interaction with society and stakeholders.

Why did this rethink occur in the 1990s? There is no shortage of possible causes of the 1990s as a period of reflection on, and rethinking of, the role of the state in society and in economic affairs (World Bank 1997). The Soviet Union's apparently powerful centralized state seemed to crumble almost overnight in the early 1990s. The Soviet Union was actually dissolved in December 1991, through the decision of the Supreme Soviet of the Soviet Union. The President of the Soviet Union, Mikhail Gorbachev, had resigned the day before the dissolution. Other momentous changes, also in the early 1990s, included the reunification of Germany and the break-up of Yugoslavia. All of these events may have caused people to look again at the state and recognize that the state could not be taken for granted. On the other hand, the presumptions of the neo-liberal orthodoxy were being implicitly challenged by the successes being achieved by economies in East Asia. The World Bank, in one of its World Reports, made the following judgment (1997, 27): "East Asia's experience has renewed interest in the state's role in promoting markets through active industrial and financial policy."

The World Bank began to articulate a model for how government should become active in economic affairs. First, the state needed to be involved in ensuring the provision of basic services, such as primary and secondary education, which needed public funding. But in ensuring the provision of public services it could make use of public service providers from the private and voluntary sectors. It did not have to be a provider itself. This, of course, echoed the arguments of Osborne and Gaebler (1992). Second, the World Bank recommended the cooperation of the state and private business to further the development agenda and achieve higher rates of economic growth. Third, at various points in the World Development Report (1997), the World Bank commended long-term visions for countries, such as those developed in Japan and Malaysia. Long-term visions contained or produced strategic priorities for the countries.

There was no doubting the way that the World Bank had been impressed by the examples and lessons of East Asian countries which had pursued a long-term approach to national development and had evolved their institutional capabilities and private sector support (World Bank 1997, 83):

> Several East Asian leaders have formulated long-term visions for their countries; examples include, in postwar Japan, the Liberal Democratic Party's declared aim to catch up with the West, and more recently, in Malaysia, Prime Minister Mahathir Mohamad's Vision 2020. They have then worked to create the institutional arrangements needed to translate their vision into a highly focused set of strategic priorities. Powerful elite central agencies have been delegated the authority to develop policies that will achieve the leaders' long-term objectives. Although relatively autonomous, these agencies' deliberations have always been embedded in processes such as public-private councils that provide input and oversight from private firms.

The World Bank's remarks about states in the Middle East and North Africa were much less flattering. They were said to have taken on substantial economic responsibilities in the 1960s and 1970s. The overall assessment was that "regulation is excessive, as is state involvement in economic activity, and delivery of public services is inefficient (World Bank 1997, 166)."

If anything it seems that the crisis of 2007 to 2009, that affected so many countries around the world, led to even greater interest in, and commitment to, reforms to public governance to make it more strategic. Coincidentally, in 2007, the OECD began a series of reviews of public governance commissioned by national governments. Its reflections, in 2013, suggested that the context, including the crisis and its effects, was having an important impact on public governance (OECD 2013b, 4):

> The context in which governments operate is associated with increasing complexity, overlaid since 2008 by the fiscal and economic crisis. Most of the reviews have been conducted in the period since 2008. There have been important developments since the launch of the first review in 2007, with significant effects on the nature and future of public governance, the public service and its employees.

The immediate impact of the crisis was dire. There were crashes in stock markets, governments spent public money bailing out banks, economic output fell, unemployment increased, tax revenues dropped significantly, and governments that were attempting to absorb the crisis found themselves pushed into big deficits. In due course, governments were then found to resort to austerity measures, triggering declines in public services and cuts in public employment. There were pressures to cut social welfare benefits. Some commentators, such as the OECD, pointed out that there had been problems in the public governance systems and that the problems had been highlighted by the crisis in 2007 to 2009. There was also some evidence of a tendency for national responses to the crisis to reflect the characteristics of their public governance systems.

This last point about national variations emerged from an analysis carried out by Kuhn (2010). Making use of governance data collected in 2005–07, Kuhn reported, for example, that Germany and the UK had very different governance profiles. Germany had a pattern of coalition governments, ministerial autonomy, and state (sub-national) autonomy. Germany's federal chancellery was said to be weak in terms of monitoring line ministries. All this suggested serious weaknesses in the strategic capabilities of the German federal government. The United Kingdom was reckoned to have good steering capacity, was well resourced in terms of central strategic advice, but was weak in terms of engaging citizens and partners in civil society. Kuhn considered that the US government scored well in terms of strategic planning, the role of the White House in coordinating activities, and informal consultation beyond government. To, repeat, the main finding of Kuhn (2010) was that how a government responded to the 2007–09 crisis tended to reflect its existing pattern of public governance.

The OECD took the view that the context of the post-crisis world required more coordinated and more integrated action by governments. Strategies had to be coherent across ministries and up and down levels of governance from international to local level. It was a call for what Osborne and Gaebler (1992) had called more "holistic" government. The search for more integration and coordination across ministries led to the use of terms such as "whole of government" and a view that the "centre of government" needed to be skilled and resourced to enable government to be more integrated in its organization and more coherent in its thinking and strategies. And in terms of multi-level governance, this logically had to be based on interaction and partnership rather than simple top-down direction by the national level or simple bottom-up decision-making by the local level. Holistic government in this concept of public governance is a complex totality brought into unity around selectivity, focus, interaction, and cooperation.

One final point was the broadening of the policy agenda within the discussion of how to reform and modernize public governance. The talk is no longer of just economic and social affairs, as can be seen in the following comments on the need for horizontal and vertical coordination in tackling a "green growth" agenda, and notice the references to the need for action on social inclusion (which can be contrasted with Sir Keith Joseph's remarks above about the problem of egalitarianism) (OECD 2013b, 4):

> Green growth will ultimately need to be achieved with the support of the international community and through bottom up local initiatives: this is the "vertical" challenge. It also needs to be supported by dovetailing policies that address both the environmental and the economic issues: this is the "horizontal" challenge. More broadly still, support for economic growth and development needs to balance economic interests, environmental concerns and social inclusion to ensure that growth is sustainable and benefit all citizens, including women and minorities.

Levi (2006) on Leadership and Government Effectiveness

Levi (2006) defines good government as those that were representative, accountable, and also effective. Although she says good government is representative, accountable, and effective, she is not only concerned with democratic governments and she takes what is probably a wide-scoped view of the nature of government effectiveness. According to her, government effectiveness includes being capable of providing citizens with protection from violence, guaranteeing property rights, and providing public goods that the population wanted and needed. She points out that not all democracies have effective governance and that there are responsive governments in non-democratic states. She is interested in the question of how do you build up and improve government. She is concerned with how do you get good government, whether it is democratic or not. It should also be noted that she tends to assume a government in which tax collection is important for funding the public services and activities of the state. So there may well be a question of just how applicable her thinking is to societies where there is a rentier state (as in the Arabian Peninsula).

In developing her analysis and point of view there were a number of points she either emphasized or accepted as assumptions. We note four of them here.

First, she suggests that governments are more likely to be effective if they develop consent or compliance. She calls these conditional consent or quasi-voluntary compliance. She says compliance is always conditional and will vary depending on government performance, honesty, reliability, and observation of due process. She defines quasi-voluntary compliance as compliance motivated by willingness to cooperate but backed by coercion.

Second, she thinks that societies are capable of learning and that learning is involved in the development of effective government. The development of effective government takes place over time, she says (Levi 2006, 7): "There is a long learning process during which publics and public officials discover what institutions and which people are reliable and in what settings."

A third point is that, unlike some variants of pluralist theory, she does not think governments are neutral or impartial in the rivalry and competition between interest groups. In fact, she is implying that government could be regarded as an interested party in its own right, with its own interests and its own agenda. This matters because government can affect the "rules of the game" and distributes and redistributes both political and economic resources.

A fourth point is to acknowledge that governments have to deal with the issue of violence and with the security dilemma. She may have been thinking of Thomas Hobbes when she remarks (Levi 2006, 9): "In virtually every state- or government-building project, it is necessary to "tame the violence" within the country's borders, to stop the "roving bandits," to halt ethnic violence and build a national identity, and to offer powerful constituents enough in the way of benefits to retain their loyalty and to desist from violent predation." She explains predatory behaviour by powerful constituents as being motivated by greed. The "security dilemmas" arise where fear develops and individuals form expectations of threats by others. If government is to tame the internal warring and violence, and prevent a spiraling of offensive and defensive action, then citizens have to cede to rulers the power to enforce laws. On the other hand, citizens may then worry that this government power will be used wrongly. We take this to be the essence of what she means by a security dilemma.

Crucially, for our purposes, she considers the quality of government is a function of both institutions and leadership, among other things (Levi 2006, 6):

> The quality of government depends on the quality of institutions and constitutional design *but also on the quality of leadership*, the accuracy of beliefs held by the population about the nature of the world in which they live, and the existence of preferences for a society that is just and fair for the minority as well as the majority. When a combination of individuals with the incentives and imagination to figure out how to operate better within or even to overcome the status quo, we observe institutional transformation and creation.
>
> (emphasis added)

One of the attractions of Levi's academic theorizing of the issues is her view that it is important to recognize the role of human agency. As we see, for her it is leadership that supplies a key element of human agency.

She lists as the essential ingredients of a new theory of government: institutional arrangements, leadership, realistic beliefs and expectations about what the government can do and wants to do, and preferences for outcomes such as "a clean government and a just society". She mentions the importance of institutions that, as she puts it, appropriately align incentives. She says, then, "The institutions are empty boxes without leaders and staff who have the capacity to produce the public goods the public demands and the facility to evoke popular confidence even among those who disagree with particular policies" (Levi 2006, 10). She backs up this assertion by pointing to the contrast between Pakistan and India, two countries she claims inherited very similar formal institutions as a result of colonialism, but which vary substantially in terms of the effectiveness of their governments. In other words, institutions cannot be a total explanation for government effectiveness.

So, what is the significance of leadership? She says (Levi 2006, 10): "Leadership aligns incentives, *helps design and redesign institutions*, provides the learning environment that enables individuals to transform or revise beliefs, and plays a major role in inducing preferences" (emphasis added). As suggested already, the insertion of leadership into the new theory of government is simultaneously an insertion of human agency (Levi 2006, 10): "Most importantly, leadership—both within government and within civil society—provides the human agency that coordinates the efforts of others."

Naturally, she is concerned with good leadership in a political context. She recognizes that leadership is in an interdependent relationship with both institutions and popular support. In other words, leaders may draw power from institutions and popular support but are also constrained by them.

She asserts that the quality of leadership is contextual. Leadership that serves one group may not serve another. Some of her discussion of good leadership puts us in mind of some research on chief executives in a small sample of US local governments by Gabris and his colleagues (2000). Whereas she talks about reliability, they operationalize the concept of leadership credibility, which includes keeping your promises. She talks about principles that compose the identity of the governmental organization and generate rules to guide behaviour in the case of the unexpected. She then links their reputation for reliability to the upholding of the principles (Levi 2006, 11):

> Governmental leaders establish reliability through reputations built on these principles. They sustain their reputation and that of the government by upholding these principles even when they are not the most organizationally efficient or in the personally best interests of the leaders. Indeed, some of our most revered public leaders have made great personal sacrifices.

They keep to the principles of their government and thus build reputations for reliability. They do not abandon the principles just for expedience or for reasons of self-interest. This sounds very much a parallel to the honest leaders studied by Gabris and colleagues, who were local government leaders who kept their word and practiced what they preached, and were seen as credible leaders.

She touches on the relationship between leaders and the people and, of course, on the matter of consent. Levi makes the point that leaders build consent by means of transparency, responsiveness, and by implementing policies. But they also do it, she implies, by educating people. She says (Levi 2006, 12): "leaders must provide leadership in the sense of clarifying what is possible and provide information that will enable constituents to form beliefs and preferences in keeping with the world in which they find themselves." She later suggests (Levi 2006, 12), "leaders have the power to misinform and to manipulate, but they also have the power to inspire change."

A very interesting part of her analysis is the role of leaders in changing institutions. She points out that institutions require adjustment from time to time and that leaders have the task of persuading relevant people that change is needed to maintain the institution. She tackles the link between leaders and institutional change from another point of view—leaders change institutions but are also constrained by them, and partly voluntarily so (Levi 2006, 12):

> Once in office, a leadership cadre has the power, within the limits of enforceable law and their bargaining clout, to write or revise the constitution and to establish or reinforce institutions. Leaders may supply institutions, but must also be restrained by them. This is only partially an effect of institutions and credible commitments. It may also be an effect of the moral obligations instilled in leaders.

The obvious question after all this is, what makes for a good leader? In the usual terms of this matter: is it nature or nurture? Levi implies it is both. She suggests that leaders may have a personality that suits them to the responsibility but she argues there is also a large "dose" of a learned skill.

Summary

This chapter has looked at the emergence of the idea that governments need to be strategic. The World Bank (1997) and writers such as Osborne and Gaebler (1992) either reflected or prompted (or both) a growing opinion in public policy circles that governments needed to be active and not supine in the face of economic and social problems. These new ideas quite clearly represented a very different perspective on government from that of neoliberalism that had dominated the thinking and policies of a number of politicians and governments. The financial and banking crisis originating in the United States and showing its symptoms in events in late 2007, before developing fully in 2008 and 2009, appeared not to weaken the belief in active and strategic governments, but, if anything, confirmed the need for more public governance reforms to deal with the aftermath of the crisis and the new pattern of global economic and competitive relations.

As we noted in this chapter, the OECD began conducting public governance reviews at the behest of various national governments. They championed, through these reviews, the reform and modernization of public governance on the basis of the development of a long-term strategic vision, the setting of national priorities for economic and social development, and a whole-of-government approach to government, involving both horizontal and vertical integration of governance machinery. They pressed for partnerships between government and societal actors (including the business community). They urged that governments consulted and engaged citizens, seeking to promote open, transparent, and responsive governments. In summary, they favoured government action that was selective, focused, and based on interactions and partnerships, both inside and outside the government's own structures.

In historical terms it can be seen as a hybrid of the focus on active and purposeful government as pursued by states with centralized economic top-down planning and the neo-liberalism of the 1980s. It sought the efficiency of the economic development process that neo-liberalism claimed to provide. It sought the long-term purposefulness of states with centralized economic planning. In addition, it espoused government transparency, accountability, and responsiveness, which were important for citizens; and strategic mobilization of business and citizens to create a holistic approach for the totality of a country.

In this chapter we have also underlined the need for a perspective that does not neglect the importance of human agency in the development of effective government. We relied on Levi's (2006) theoretical speculations to place on the table the idea that national leaders supply this human agency and that they have a role to play in enabling and encouraging learning needed for more effective government and in institutional change. We note here Levi's point that leaders can change institutions and are restrained by institutions, and that the restraint may be in part due to a voluntary and moral attitude on the part of leaders.

In conclusion, the last twenty-five years have seen the resurgence of optimism about the possibilities of active government that can address the development of the economy, the environment, and social life. In the next chapter we highlight the importance of variation and context. We explore different theories and models that might sensitize our consideration of public governance in the Gulf states.

Reference List

Cleveland, H. (1972) *The Future Executive: A Guide for Tomorrow's Managers.* New York: Harper and Row.

Cole, G. D. H. (1947) *The Intelligent Man's Guide to the Post-War World.* London: Victor Gollancz.

Dewey, J. (1927) *The Public and Its Problems.* Athens: Swallow Press, Ohio University Press.

Frederickson, H. G. (2004) Whatever Happened to Public Administration? Governance, Governance, Everywhere. *Working Paper QU/GOV/3/2004.* Belfast: Queen's University Belfast and Institute of Governance Public Policy and Social Research.

Gabris, G. T., Golembiewski, R. T. and Ihrke, D. M. (2000) Leadership Credibility, Board Relations, and Administrative Innovation at the Local Government Level, *Journal of Public Administration Research and Theory*, 11(1), 89–108.

Hayek, F. A. (1944) *The Road to Serfdom*. London and Henley: Routledge and Kegan Paul.

Hibbs, D. (1978) On the Political Economy of Long-Run Trends in Strike Activity, *British Journal of Political Science*, 8, 153–175.

Joseph, K. (1978) Proclaim the Message: Keynes Is Dead! In: Patrick Hutber (editor) *What's Wrong with Britain?* London: Sphere Books Ltd. Pages 99–106.

Kooiman, J. and van Vliet, M. (1993) Governance and Public Management. In: K. A. Eliassen and J. Kooiman (editors) *Managing Public Organizations*. London: Sage. Pages 58–72.

Kuhn, A. (2010) Managing the Crisis: An SGI Perspective. In: Bertelsmann Stiftung (editor) *Managing the Crisis: A Comparative Analysis of Economic Governance in 14 Countries*. Gütersloh: Verlag Bertelsmann Stiftung. Pages 27–41.

Levi, M. (2006) Why We Need a New Theory of Government, *Perspectives on Politics*, 4(1), 5–19.

OECD (2013a) *Poland: Implementing Strategic-State Capability*, OECD Public Governance Reviews. Paris: OECD.

OECD (2013b) *Strategic Insights from the Public Governance Reviews: Update*. GOV/PGC(2013)4, Public Governance and Territorial Development Directorate. Public Governance Committee. Paris: OECD.

Osborne, D. and Gaebler, T. (1992) *Reinventing Government: How the Entrepreneurial Spirit Is Transforming the Public Sector*. Reading, MA: Addison Wesley.

World Bank (1997) *World Development Report 1997: The State in a Changing World*. New York: Oxford University Press.

World Bank (2000) *Reforming Public Institutions and Strengthening Governance*. Washington, DC: World Bank.

3 Contingencies and Variations

Introduction

In the previous chapter we explored the concept of public governance and did this in part by emphasizing its antecedent philosophies of government, meaning those offered in justification of centralized state planning in some varieties of socialist and communist thinking and in justification of neo-liberalism in the free market doctrines of the West. These past ways of thinking about designs of the role of government corresponded to a state-dominated approach to national development and a minimalist state approach.

In the 1990s the concept of public governance emerged as an intellectual resolution of the challenge of transcending both centralized state planning and neo-liberalism, both of which were vulnerable to critiques of their shortcomings in terms of their consequences. Centralized state planning could for lengthy periods of time produce very rapid investment and increasing levels of output (Cole 1947; Kerr et al. 1973), but there were doubts about its efficacy in sustaining economic dynamism and its responsiveness to growing expectations of more consumption-minded times. The application of neo-liberalism had turned out to be either a lot more complicated than imagined or just plainly ineffective when attempts were made to apply it to very poor countries. The answer, for some commentators, was a turn to a call for better public governance in poor countries to allow them to gain more benefits from any foreign assistance provided by rich countries. And by better governance, bodies such as the World Bank (1997) meant more active government than envisaged by the advocates of neo-liberalism and more selective and enabling government than implied by centralized state planning of the economy. The importance of better governance was also underlined by concerns about the extreme problems experienced in some countries where government was almost completely absent. Back in the 1990s this would have included countries such as Liberia and Somalia.

In this chapter we look at what developments in thinking occur when the general idea of the need for good public governance is applied to the variable situations of individual countries in the world. In essence, this chapter draws attention to the need for awareness of situational contingencies and thus the design of variations in application of public governance for social and economic development. First, however, we introduce the possibility of contingency and variation in governance through a conceptual framework based on pluralism and industrialization, which emerged in the United States in the 1950s and early 1960s, and through a more recent study that was concerned with comparative analysis of public management (Pollitt and Bouckaert 2004).

Pluralist Theory and Conceptions of Industrialism

Distinctively, the liberal-pluralist political theorists saw society as composed of a multiplicity of interest groups and saw the existence of power struggles and conflict as normal (Kerr et al. 1973). It could also presume that the role of government was to facilitate constructive settlement of conflicts.

Back in the 1950s and 1960s, the theorists of liberal-pluralism assumed governments would be playing a larger role than did laissez-faire counterparts. They envisaged this would be the case because of the nature of industrial society, which they characterized as one having an advanced technological component. They also appreciated that governments would be expected to provide services and infrastructure such as health and education, transport (including roads), and cultural and sporting amenities. They thought government could play an effective role in society.

The liberal-pluralist approach was compatible with a comparative approach to the study of different societies. They did not necessarily diagnose the existence of a universal political or institutional model for each country. Kerr et al. (1973), for example, distinguished five "ideal" types, while accepting that mixtures of them might be found in reality. Their characterization of the "middle class" ideal type was as follows (1973, 61–63):

> The middle class ideology is economically individualistic and politically egalitarian. Each individual is held to be morally accountable to himself, within the limits of the law, which is supposed to apply equally to all members of the community . . . The system is based heavily on consent, and the appeal in politics and in economics is to self advantage . . . Relative emphasis is placed on many centres of decision-making power and on a system of checks and balances. The checks and balances in political life involve the separation of church and state and of the legislative, administrative, and judicial authorities. In economic life, economic units are typically separated into discrete and competitive entities . . . The worker may indeed be in organised opposition to the enterprise manager—some degree of conflict is built into and accepted by the system; and a whole series of economic and political institutions is in fact devised to channel and settle such conflicts . . . Progress is taken for granted in the belief that it flows naturally out of the day-to-day decisions of many people. It should not be retarded nor should it

be forced unduly by state action . . . economic advance is not centrally planned . . . Such a system will be intermediate in its record of economic growth.

This recognition by Kerr et al. of organized opposition (trade unions) shows that their middle-class system was not the same as a pure or simple type of neo-liberalism, which is characterized by hostility to trade unions as well as hostility to much action by government. The neo-liberal idea of a well-organized society is one organized so that competition between business units is as unconstrained as possible by government (and laws) and by trade unions. We should also note here the idea in a middle-class system that conflict may be institutionalized by creating institutions (political and economic) to channel and settle conflict. While this is very different from the neo-liberal perspective, the middle-class system described by Kerr et al. is a capitalist one in the sense that profits and competition are core to the mechanism for coordination of the economic activity of society and that innovation and change in the economy emerges from the competition processes.

A second ideal type of system offered by Kerr and his colleagues is labeled a dynastic elite. This is described as a system oriented to the preservation of tradition. The ruling elite is said to be normally a closed group and membership of it is based on family and class. It's a hierarchical system, formed of superiors and subordinates, and interactions within it are defined by interlocking duties and obligations. The paternalism of both the economy and politics are balanced by an expectation of loyalty from those who benefit from the paternalism. It can be inferred from the description offered that this type of system is not primarily motivated to make economic growth the top priority: the rulers in this system are interested in preserving tradition but may pursue industrial and economic progress in response to pressures placed on them.

They also incorporate societies with centralized state planning into their framework. These appear as a third type of elite. Initially, they say, the ruling class is drawn from revolutionary intellectuals. It is a centralized state and has an ideology about making a better future society. As this type of society matures, high-level political administrators and bureaucrats emerge as the rulers. They place a lot of importance on industrialization and on new technology. Kerr et al. consider that this type of society can achieve a high rate of state-directed industrialization and economic growth. (Arguably, examples of this ability to direct a fast pace of economic development might be the Soviet Union in the 1920s and 1930s and China from the late 1970s onwards.)

There were two further types of elites: colonial rulers and nationalist rulers. We will pass over the colonial elite and briefly mention industrialization under the last type of elite—a nationalist elite. Kerr and his colleagues portrayed nationalist elites as often characterized by charismatic, national heroes. The pattern of industrialization under nationalist elites was said to involve the following: an excessive level of public expectations in the immediate aftermath of independence; an over-reliance on big development projects; an episodic flow to industrialization efforts; and the mobilization of patriotic zeal. It is claimed that this nationalist model evolves into a mixed economy type of society that is positioned between one based on private initiative (the middle-class system) and one based on centralized state control (the revolutionary-intellectual system).

This framework seems to make assumptions (implicit or explicit) about societal integration. For example, some governments might provide benefits but expect loyalty in return (dynastic elite), or some government might expect a moral integration of the individual in which private interests should be subordinated to revolutionary zeal or patriotic zeal.

It might be imagined that Kerr and his colleagues would identify the middle-class elite as the most superior type of elite in terms of economic development and rates of economic growth. Not so. They suggest the revolutionary-intellectual elite can achieve the highest economic growth rates. In the case of the dynastic system, they consider that pursuit of economic growth is a response to pressure on the rulers. So, the middle-class elite might outperform the dynastic elite or lag behind it depending on the extent of pressure on the dynastic elite rulers. For simplicity's sake, we will assume that on average the amount of pressure on the dynastic elite rulers is insufficient for them to match economic growth rates achieved by societies with middle-class elites. On this basis, we can hypothesize that the middle-class elite may achieve a higher rate of economic growth than a dynastic elite but not as much as a revolutionary-intellectual elite. This hypothesis is depicted in Figure 3.1. However, this leaves out the qualifying judgments that maintaining economic dynamism may eventually be difficult for revolutionary-intellectual elites or that they may be vulnerable to catastrophic mistakes (Dreze and Sen 2013). It may also be false to assume that the pressure on dynastic elite rulers is generally not enough to place their societies in the category of high economic growth rates.

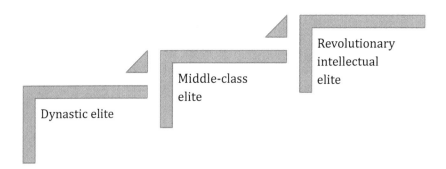

Figure 3.1 Hypothesis: Economic Growth Rates Vary by Type of Industrializing Elites

What might this framework mean for understanding government economic strategies? A government in a middle-class type of system will favour strategies supportive of profit making; they will have strategies that assume economic progress is best led by private initiative; and government strategies aim at piecemeal adaptation of the economy rather than strategic transformation. The governments with revolutionary-intellectual rulers will equate strategy with top-down long-term planning and public investment (for example, Lenin's plan for the electrification of the Soviet Union). The governments in dynastic systems will be reluctant strategists and tend to make decisions in a very hierarchical fashion. They will be trying to reconcile tradition and modernization of the economy, with the tensions between the two being dependent on the pressures placed on government. These tensions ought to lead to a focus on strategic issue management, but it is possible that a preference for conservation may lead to attitudes that see strategy and planning ahead as of little value. Nationalist elites might favour steering the economy by means of government strategic planning; they may like to focus government investments on big strategic development projects.

Using a liberal-pluralist perspective focused on industrialization scores well on recognizing the differentiation of societies in the world and thus the need to understand variations in government strategies and actions. One of its weaknesses, arguably, is that non-economic aspects of society can tend to be neglected. Why is this? It may be believed that everything needs to be aligned to the economy and its development, or even that everything is totally determined by the economy. For example, if other aspects of society are not aligned to the economy and its requirements, it may be assumed that this will cause problems for economic development and economic growth. Its strength is surely to draw attention to the importance of the public leadership of a society (which they approach in terms of the concept of an industrializing elite). And we think one virtue of them making use of the concept of elite types is probably to warn us that leadership of society probably has to be understood as multi-dimensional and rich in its meaning. In contrast, the management literature (especially for private business) often provides rather "thin" and individually focused conceptions of leadership (such as transformational leadership).

Variations Based on Political Institutions

Pollitt and Bouckaert (2004) were interested in public management reform, whereas this book is focused on public governance and social and economic development (including development on a sustainable basis). Nevertheless, their work does suggest that there might be some merit in considering the possibility that national development may be impacted by institutional factors. We selectively pick out some of their remarks on the institutional dimension, without trying to provide a complete summary of their thinking.

The remarks they make about institutions are fairly straightforward. They say that networks of institutions mediate the effects of forces on changes in public management. The specific characteristics of institutions, and of networks of institutions, it is argued, influence not only the changes in public management but also the final results and outcomes. They accept that networks of institutions (and presumably individual institutions) can change. They say that the fundamentals of political and administrative systems change but the change tends to be gradual and infrequent. But, of course, we can add to their judgments the point that calling any approach an institutionalist approach must be because institutions tend to be difficult to change or slow to change, and thus it makes some sense to spend time understanding how the institutions influence behaviour and events.

They were interested in classifying and evaluating the results of the public management reforms. Importantly, they assumed that public management is always part of public governance and they identified a number of "regime types." So, their work could inspire a concern for seeing how public governance connects to an institutionalist approach.

Pollitt and Bouckaert provided a comparative analysis of 12 countries with the aim of explaining programmes of public sector reform and modernization. Two of the governance variables considered by them as explanatory variables to categorize countries were: (1) centralized versus decentralized government, and (2) majoritarian styles of governance versus consensual styles of governance. Their categorization of the 12 countries using these two dimensions is shown in Table 3.1.

They then associate the type of public governance with the pattern of reforms. They link government that is centralized and has a majoritarian style of governance with a pattern of deep, wide, and rapid reforms. Government that is decentralized and majoritarian in style is less likely to have reforms that are deep and wide because of decentralized government. They suggest that reforms will be less severe and less speedy the more that a government is consensual in style.

Table 3.1 An Institutional Approach to the Comparison of Public Governance

		Nature of Executive Government At Central Level		
		Majoritarian	*Intermediate*	*Consensual*
Multi-level governance variable (vertical dispersion of authority)	Centralized	New Zealand United Kingdom	France	Italy The Netherlands
	Intermediate	Sweden		Finland
	Decentralized	Australia Canada United States	Belgium Germany	

(Source: Adapted from Pollitt and Bouckaert [2004, 47])

Their use of these two variables to explain public management reform patterns is very nuanced and they emphasize that some of the countries they are comparing are not clear-cut cases. So, we must be careful to acknowledge that their comparisons are far from simplistic. For example, they say that France has quite a majoritarian "tinge" when the President is of the same party as the major party in government. The governance system of the United States is affected by the very strong power of the legislature relative to that of the President. And Italy is described as hard to classify; it was highly centralized but regions, provinces and municipalities had become stronger.

Some of Pollitt and Bouckaert's further remarks in relation to the United Kingdom may suggest that their institutionalist approach is tempered or modified by an awareness of the importance of what we might call public leadership. They suggest that the two variables of the public governance system (vertical dispersion of authority and style of governance) work in combination with other factors. They write (Pollitt and Bouckaert 2004, 50):

> They permit, but do not, of themselves, 'drive'. That requires the intervention of some dynamic agency, such as a flow of new ideas allied to determined leadership.

They quote a review of the United Kingdom experience during the premiership of Margaret Thatcher to illustrate the dynamic agency at work. Prime Minister Thatcher was a determined leader and reform was justified using a clear ideological strategy (Rhodes 1997).

What can we take from this? First, while Pollitt and Bouckaert (2004) were clearly intent on using the comparisons to understand public management reforms, it is clear that there may be some sense in being sensitive to the effects of governance institutions on national development. Second, Pollitt and Bouckaert's remarks on the United Kingdom, and on Prime Minister Thatcher, prompt the idea that institutional factors need to be combined with public leadership factors to provide a more complete model of national development.

Capability-Based Modernization

In 1997 the World Bank published a *World Development Report* in which it took as its starting point not leadership nor the institutions of governance, but government capabilities. In a nutshell, the World Bank said government action had to be feasible in terms of resources and capabilities. Governments should not do too much since their resources and capabilities were always limited. And what they should do by way of action should evolve according to the extent of their resources and capabilities. This starting point led to emphasis on the need for governments to be focused and selective in what they did. It also logically matched the World Bank's advice that government's needed to work with other stakeholders in society, that is, not try to operate in a self-sufficient way. The logic was obvious: with limited resources governments needed to mobilize citizens and other stakeholders to achieve the long-term priorities for national social and economic development.

The World Bank, in this report, was not concerned only with economic growth and wealth creation. Firstly, it was keen to see poverty tackled as well as economic growth pursued. It took the view that the rich tended to be better looked after by government than were the poor (World Bank 1997, 110):

> In nearly all societies the needs and preferences of the wealthy and powerful are well reflected in official policy goals and priorities. But this is rarely true of the poor and the marginalized, who struggle to get their voices heard in the corridors of power. As a result, these and other less vocal groups tend to be ill served by public policies and services, even those that should benefit them most.

Second, like the pluralist theorists of the 1950s and 1960s, the World Bank was also aware of the presence and significance of interest groups, and it was particularly aware those working to create a more effective state to deliver sustainable development and to reduce poverty would come up against vested interests in the status quo. The World Bank acknowledged that handling such interests would cost political effort and take time. But even if progress in making government more effective was slow because of vested interests, it was worth the effort and time—any advances in the creation of an active and effective state would produce significant benefits in terms of economic progress and social welfare. We will now provide more detail of the capability-based approach suggested by the World Bank.

The context for the report was the demands of a globalizing world economy. The World Bank was unequivocal in its belief about the importance of the state but it also had a clear view of how the state should be active (World Bank 1997, 1): "the state is central to economic and social development, not as a direct provider of growth but as a partner, catalyst, and facilitator."

While this role description echoed some of the ideas of Osborne and Gaebler (1992) and their model of reinventing, or reforming, government, they seemed to be more concerned with (1) services, and (2) community and societal problem-solving generally. This World Bank report was proposing a move towards being a partner, catalyst and facilitator of social and economic development. So, overall the World Bank had a similar idea but probably was more focused on national development than was Osborne and Gaebler.

The World Bank did not consider that there was one best way for states to be effective. "What makes for an effective state differs enormously across countries at different stages of development" (World Bank 1997, 1). While the report accepted that there was an enormous range of differences between

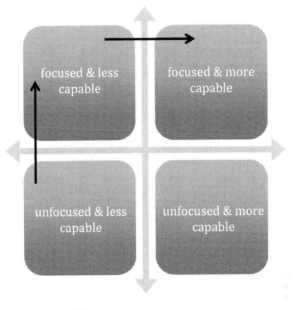

Figure 3.2 Paths to More Effective Government

states and that the states were in very different situations, the World Bank nevertheless tried to offer advice and it did this by having a simplified categorization for states, based on two dimensions: focus and capability.

The report, at one point, discussed a hypothetical country that had less state capability and is not focused. It is suggested that the first step (because building capability takes time) is for the country to become more focused in what it does so as to make the best use of its capability through partnerships with the business community and civil society. And then as a second phase countries could increase their capability over time.

More specific ideas about how to make the transitions were provided. For example (World Bank 1997, 40):

> States with weak institutional capabilities should focus on providing the pure public goods and services that markets cannot provide (and that voluntary collective initiatives underprovide), as well as goods and services with large positive externalities, such as property rights, safe water, roads, and basic education.

Credibility is vital for success. States with weak institutional capabilities should also focus on the tools for policy-making and implementation that give firms and citizens confidence that state officials and organizations will not act arbitrarily and will live within their fiscal means.

Matching role to capability is a dynamic process. As institutional capability develops, states can take on more difficult collective initiatives (initiatives to foster markets, for example), and use efficient but difficult-to-manage tools for collective action, such as sophisticated regulatory instruments.

States were advised to increase their capability by reinvigorating public institutions. This is addressed in various parts of the report but early on a thumbnail sketch of this capability building work was provided (World bank 1997, 3):

> This means designing effective rules and restraints, to check arbitrary state actions and combat entrenched corruption. It means subjecting state institutions to greater competition, to increase their efficiency. It means increasing the performance of state institutions, improving pay and incentives. And it means making the state more responsive to people's needs, bringing government closer to the people through broader participation and decentralization.

The report argued for strengthening central agencies for strategic policy formulation, which in recent years the OECD described as strengthening the "centre of government" for the purpose of providing more coordination and supervision of government strategies. And, as we saw in the quote above, it argued for more competition, which could be seen as implying a move away from bureaucratic service delivery. It also wanted more responsive government and suggested the state should be seeking more feedback from users about the delivery of public services. As well as the state engaging more with citizens (as service users), it also supported more working with labour unions. A summary of the World Bank thinking on making the public sector effective, including some of the points made in this paragraph, are summarized in Figure 3.3.

The report also picked up the idea that leadership matters if the state is to be made more effective. It can be usefully noted that they were meaning political leaders and not appointed officials (World Bank 1997, 14):

> Reform-oriented political leaders and elites can speed reform by making decisions that widen people's options, articulate the benefits clearly, and ensure that policies are more inclusive. In recent years farsighted political leaders have transformed the options for their people through decisive reform. They were successful because they made the benefits of change clear to all, and built coalitions that gave greater voice to often-silent beneficiaries. They also have succeeded—and this is crucial—because they spelled out a longer-term vision for their society, allowing people to see beyond the immediate pain of adjustment. Effective leaders give the people a sense of owning the reforms—a sense that reform is not something imposed from without.

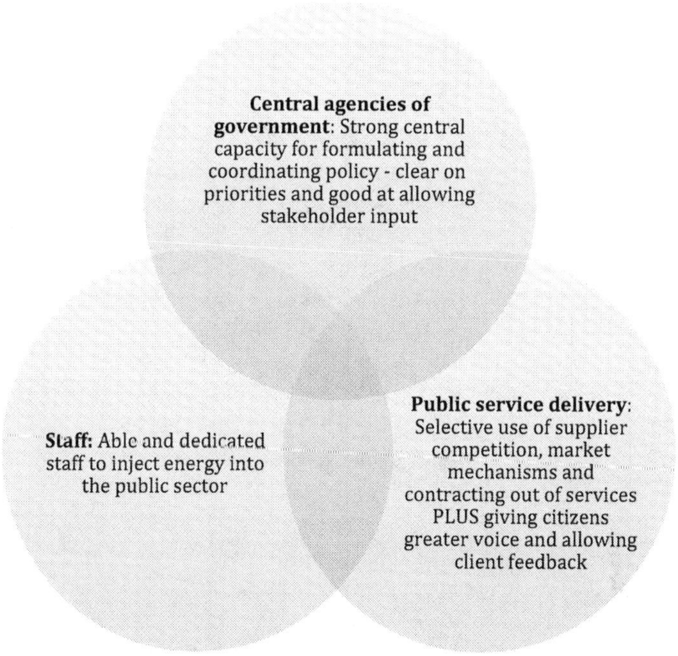

Central agencies of government: Strong central capacity for formulating and coordinating policy - clear on priorities and good at allowing stakeholder input

Staff: Able and dedicated staff to inject energy into the public sector

Public service delivery: Selective use of supplier competition, market mechanisms and contracting out of services PLUS giving citizens greater voice and allowing client feedback

Figure 3.3 The Three Building Blocks of an Effective Public Sector According to the World Bank (1997)

In this quote we get the ideas, first, that political leaders are important for reform to make government more effective and, second, that leaders offer long-term visions for their society, and, third, that this strategic leadership is not command and control leadership. In other words, the World Bank was advocating long-term change, strategic leadership, and a widespread sense of ownership of reform.

Some of the many things the report backed were familiar—such as descriptions of the institutional settings that best suited markets. The best settings included property rights, peace, law and order, and rules supporting long-term investment. However, the report also drew attention to a set of countries, the emergent economies of East Asia and praised them for several things. First, they mentioned active government policy on economic markets. More praise for East Asian countries was contained in remarks about partnership between the state and the private sector (World Bank 1997, 46): "The East Asian miracle shows how government and the private sector can cooperate to achieve rapid growth and shared development." The World Bank also highlighted the way in which governments in East Asia provided societal leadership (World Bank 1997, 117): "In East Asia, by institutionalizing public-private deliberation councils comprising representatives of labor unions, industry, and government, policy makers were able to get broad agreement on economic policy issues and the necessary commitment to intervene quickly and flexibly."

The report was clear that governments needed good policies. That is, governments needed to do the right things. The World Bank suggested many good policies: in relation to macroeconomic stability (avoid high inflation and fiscal deficits), price distortions (e.g., caused by taxes, high minimum wages, high reserve requirements), and liberalizing trade and investment (open markets, use of Value Added Tax). The report was also clear that economic growth was a function of good policies and institutional capability (to develop and deliver the policies effectively). See Figure 3.4.

The World Bank sought to provide evidence to support their conclusions that state capability and good policies both mattered. The report referred to a statistical analysis of a large number of countries and variations in income per capita (World Bank 1997, 32):

> In countries with weak state capability and poor policies, income per capita grew only about half a percent per year. In contrast, in countries with strong capability and good policies, income per capita grew at an average rate of about 3 percent per year. Over a thirty-year period, these differences in income growth have made a huge difference to the quality of people's lives.

The World Bank was therefore arguing that reforming public governance institutions to increase state capability mattered: national development was not simply a matter of government choosing the right social and economic policies. Of course, what follows on from this is the question of how institutional capability can be measured. In the report mention is made of the quality of the government bureaucracy, regulatory quality, and the degree of autonomy of the bureaucrats from political pressures.

It should be noted that the World Bank did not make any clear claims that democracy improved economic growth. The report indicated that an attempt to evaluate the evidence on this matter had been made but the

Figure 3.4 Doing the Right Things Effectively

overall judgment seemed to be that a link between democracy and economic growth was not proven (see page 149 of the World Bank report). Indeed, one motif of the report was the success of some of the emerging industrializing East Asian countries, which were in some respects the exemplars of the effective state (World Bank 1997, 163):

> In the newly industrializing countries of East Asia, the state is generally viewed as effective, engaged in a productive partnership with the private sector. With few exceptions, it has matched its role to its capability very well and thereby enhanced its effectiveness . . . many East Asian countries have experienced remarkable growth (with some improvement in equity) under authoritarian regimes . . . the link between authoritarianism and economic decline, so evident in Africa, has been inoperative in Asian countries, largely because of their powerful commitment to rapid economic development, strong administrative capability, and institutionalized links with stakeholders such as private firms, as well as their ability to deliver on the economic and social fundamentals: sound economic management, basic education and health care, and infrastructure.

The report ended as it had begun, on an upbeat note about the state. The World Bank (1997) was sure of the importance of an effective state (World Bank 1997, 157): "The state's potential to leverage, promote, and mediate change in pursuit of collective ends is unmatched. Where this capacity has been used well, economies have flourished. But where it has not, development has hit a brick wall."

The OECD and the Strategic State Framework

Over time, there has been some important rethinking of what institutional capability means in a government context, and the work of the OECD on public governance in the last decade deserves special mention in that respect (Joyce 2015). The reviews of public governance that the OECD carried out tended to suggest that effective states had the following set of institutional practices and characteristics, which they termed a strategic state framework (OECD 2013, 7–8):

> The Strategic States framework emphasizes leadership and stewardship from the centre, integrity and transparency, the importance of networks and institutions (both inside and outside government), the need to draw inspiration from sub national initiatives and citizens, and crucially the importance of effective implementation of strategies and policies in support of positive outcomes and impacts for a country's economy and society. [. . .]
> Public governance is ultimately tested on its ability to deliver on a strategy and vision of the future . . . the central State cannot directly

implement most or even any policies alone; these require the active engagement of other actor (for example, through co design). The views and opinions of a large range of actors beyond the central State, not least citizens, is equally essential to help shape and update strategies. [. . .]

Governments are not a monolithic structure but rather a network of organizations, including ministries, agencies, semi-autonomous bodies, sub national entities, and critically, institutions and entities beyond the executive, such as audit offices, and outside the State, such as civil society. Thus, to deliver on a strategy, a key challenge faced by government is to solve coordination and principal-agent problems. [. . .]

The network of public institutions is connected by some key systems and processes, such as budgeting, HRM, auditing, and ICT. The functioning of these systems and use of some (e.g. ICT) as part of the strategic thinking is fundamental to generating coordination and alignment; to formulate more integrated and relevant strategies; and to enable better implementation of actions. [. . .]

Effective governance is reflected in tangible (and perhaps measurable) outcomes and impacts . . . The long term management of so called "wicked" issues is also relevant, as is the ability of the State to manage crises. Together these represent critical tests of the merits of investing in public governance and whether public governance reforms are going in the right direction to achieve desired outcomes. Ultimately, public governance is a process that exists to serve citizens.

The continual stress in the OECD work on the need for engagement with citizens and with civil society might sound just like a matter of values or principles, but it can be noted above that the suggestion is that the central State requires the active engagement of other actor because it not able to implement policies alone. This is somewhat reminiscent of the World Bank view of government effectiveness, as set out in the World Development Report 1997 (World Bank 1997).

In fact, engaging with external actors may influence governments in a variety of ways. For example, a recent study of governance looked at three variables that are of interest to this chapter (Hertie School of Governance 2013). These variables were:

Civil society strength: this was a variable that measures the existence of a civil society with a high level of civic engagement, a strong organizational infrastructure, and an egalitarian recruitment.

Transparency: this was measured using a score of transparency in revenue management compiled by Revenue Watch and also measured using a survey compiled by the International Budget Partnership on the public availability of budget information and other accountability measures.

Effectiveness: this was an index based on a measure of the Weberian nature of government (impartial bureaucracy) and a measure of intellectual resources within state administration.

The study made country level comparisons and found that effectiveness and budget transparency were correlated, and that civil society strength was correlated with both revenue transparency and budget transparency. This was interpreted as follows (Hertie School of Governance 2013, 145): "More effective [public] administrations are also more transparent ones . . . more transparent public sectors are associated with vibrant civil societies." France, New Zealand, Norway, Sweden, and UK were included in the countries that were rated as having high scores on effectiveness. Sweden, UK, and the United States were some of the countries with high scores on civil society strength. All of these countries were also rated as high on budget transparency. Lebanon and Afghanistan were rated low on budget transparency and they were rated low on the other two variables as well.

We can obviously infer that these three variables are linked, but how are they linked? Visual inspection of the study's graph of effectiveness and budget transparency (see Hertie School of Governance 2013, 143) suggested that it was the strongest of the correlations, so it was tempting to suggest that civil society strength was a supplementary effect on budget transparency. The only relationship that is not mentioned among the three variables is that between civil society strength and effectiveness. So, a possible interpretation might be that effective governments cause more budget transparency by government and that civil society strength may also pressurize or encourage more budget transparency, as shown in Figure 3.5. But this is quite speculative.

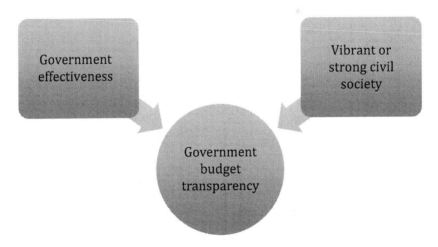

Figure 3.5 Causes of Government Budget Transparency

The OECD work on a strategic state framework has probably produced the simplest and clearest profile of an effective state with strategic-state capabilities.

Of course, the OECD model needs tailoring to individual countries and presumably this means taking account of their context. A delegate to an OECD meeting of the Public Governance Committee in 2012 was quoted as saying "The framework is a starting point from which each country can decide based on its specific context what should be elaborated" (OECD 2013, 9). This sounds like a suggestion that what is a good governance system varies according to context. The OECD officials thought the context also mattered in relation to how to reform public governance. OECD (2013, 11) advised taking the context into account:

> Public governance in countries is usually framed by very specific contextual factors, such as the size and openness of the economy, the resource base, legal framework, historical legacies, the political system, the size and nature of the state in the economy and society, the supranational context, and so on. Ignoring the effect of these contextual factors runs the risk of undermining efforts at effective reform of the public administration and structural reform.

Going back to the Hertie School of Governance (2013) study, it might be suggested that a significant variable in the context of governance reforms might be the strength of civil society. A government in a country with a very strong civil society might need to engage with it as a partner and as a co-designer of reforms in public governance—or such a government might find it relatively easy to engage it.

Summary and Comments

The pluralist theory of industrialism (Kerr et al. 1973), which we outlined in this chapter, could look like just a rehash of the political controversy that dominated the last century about the best social system—assuming a binary choice of the model provided by the socialist-communist experiment in the Soviet Union and the free enterprise system identified with the United States. However, it usefully extended our appreciation of national diversity in the world by emphasizing a framework consisting of five elite types (middle-class, revolutionary-intellectual, dynastic, colonial and nationalist). It suggested, furthermore, interesting issues about how the type of elite might be correlated with different approaches to governing and different strategic agendas, and also different consequences for the rates of economic growth.

One of the ideal type systems outlined by Kerr and his colleagues, the dynastic elite, may be seen as an obvious fit with the monarchies and emirates in the Arabian Peninsula. First, the rulers do seem sensitive to issues of preserving tradition in their communications with citizens, even when championing reform and modernization. Second, the royal families of the various Gulf states are families and moreover families that can trace their national leadership back a number of generations, even in some cases hundreds of years. Third, public governance has in the past had a strong reliance on hierarchy, including in the civil service where subordinates sometimes appeared (speaking impressionistically about earlier times) mostly responsive upwards to superiors, and only to a small extent outwards to citizens. Fourth, the communications of national leaders have at times emphasized the responsibility of citizens to work for a better future for the country and have emphasized that the youth should be well educated and aspire to work and have careers in the economy of the future. In return leaders have said that they want to provide good public services, high standards of living, and a good quality of life for the people. In the care and concern for the well-being of the citizens we can detect a form of paternalism, and maybe this has been coupled with a hope that citizens will reciprocate with loyalty. At the outset of writing this book, the biggest questions we have about this fit between dynastic elites and the monarchies and emirates in the Arabian Peninsula are about the impact of parliaments (for example, Kuwait) on public governance and just where and how the balance has been struck between economic modernization and the preservation of tradition.

The framework of Pollitt and Bouckaert was examined in a selective way. One key idea that emerged from this examination is the importance of understanding leadership in an institutional setting. In which case, when we apply this to the Gulf states, the institutional form to be considered is a monarchical institution combined with systems that vary from parliamentary systems (that have been quite challenging to government executives and may seek to constrain them) through to systems that are largely advisory in nature. On the whole, these appear to be very centralized systems of governance. Such systems might be seen to be prone to imposition of radical changes rather than piecemeal and evolutionary change. On the other hand, account has to be taken of the leadership operating within the institutional forms. Even brief acquaintance with the leaderships of the Gulf states suggest that they have operated, in recent years at least, a style of leadership that is very concerned to meet the aspirations of citizens and to provide high standards of living. So, the leadership style has had a service element to it: there have been communications that evoke images of national leaders as service-leaders. At the same time, there have been events in recent years that suggest the capability for determined governance in the face of political tension.

It might be expected, therefore, that the monarchical culture could lend itself to very decisive and speedy moves towards (or away) from programmes of economic and social reforms. Based on the style of leadership, with its preference for serving the aspirations of citizens and respecting their traditions and values, we can, however, speculate that the Gulf states will not want to adopt overtly aggressive or conflictual approaches to reform. This might, therefore, lead to much stress on reconciling strategic reforms with existing traditions and values when communicating the visions and plans of government.

Turning now to the World Bank's late 1990s pronouncements on effective government, it would seem that the most important factor in the variation of effective government action was the weakness or strength of institutional capabilities. They charged some governments with the mistake of trying to do too much when they had weak institutional abilities. Such governments were recommended to do less and act in a very focused way. What might this look like? Governments with weak institutional capabilities should provide basic public services (such as education, health, roads, safe water), they should provide for the rule of law and property rights, and they should concentrate on honest and sound policy-making and public finances.

More capable governments could be more ambitious. They could do more to promote economic progress through active intervention. These more capable governments would need strong central capacity for formulating and coordinating policy. They would be strategic in the sense of having long-term visions for national development and being selective in what they did, that is, clear on priorities. They would be enabling in the sense that they would be good at allowing stakeholder input. They would harness competitive forces, for example, by selective use of supplier competition and contracting out of services. They would work in partnership. And they would be responsive to citizens.

The obvious question is, where do the Gulf states fit into this World Bank framework? Are they governments with weak institutional capabilities or are they governments with strong capabilities? And do their actions fit, in a broad sense, the prescriptions of the World Bank—concentrate on the basics or active intervention to bring about economic and social development? The reputations of the Gulf states, in terms of government effectiveness and regulation, are taken up in Chapter 5, where it will be seen that the United Arab Emirates, Qatar, and Bahrain have good reputations for government effectiveness (including the quality of the civil service and public services) and for regulatory quality (meaning having sound policies and regulations in place). Other countries in the six have tended to have more middle-of-the-road reputations. Presumably, this indicates that we should expect to see some significant variations in the national visions and strategies of the six countries—but as we see in Chapter 6, there is much commonality in the long-term visions and strategic priorities of all six Gulf states.

The ideas of Kerr and colleagues, of Pollitt and Bouckaert, and of the World Bank are great for sensitizing us to issues and problems we might encounter in studying the public governance of the Gulf states. However, it has to be recognized that there is much of interest in the national development of countries—in terms of, for example, priorities, issues, and methods—that have not been incorporated into any of these three frameworks.

If we look at the last twenty years, one word commonly laced into statements about development is the word "sustainable", which may be a reference to a sustainable natural environment or to a sustainable economy, the latter of which may imply some strategic tensions in trying to deliver both a growing economy and a better natural environment, rather than economic sustainability. Perhaps in this case, the choice of priorities for national development might be understood as partly explicable as simply a response to current problems. For example, the concerns about the natural environment, including global warming and pollution, may gradually impose themselves on the agendas of national leaders, in one way or another

There are also words such "poverty", "social inclusiveness", and "fairness". Arguably, these words reflect a more perennial issue in relation to governance and development. To put this in a philosophical and academic context, we might note that Aristotle built his own understanding of public governance on the assumption that all societies have rich and poor people. In more modern times, Max Weber argued about one hundred years ago that public administration based on bureaucracy was crypto-plutocracy. He thought that there were at least two rival groupings that might be served by the government bureaucrats: the propertied classes (the bourgeois) and the "propertyless masses". The tension within a crypto-plutocracy consisted of the fact that the government bureaucrats were actually mainly serving the interests of the propertied classes and the propertyless masses saw in the state the means of compensating them for relatively disadvantaged economic and social life-opportunities. In effect, we might say the challenge for modern government is how to govern in a way that is seen by most people in society as fair and not partisan, even though there are inequalities of income and wealth.

In fact, there are signs that the extent of inequality has become more of an issue again for public governance in recent years, of concern, in part, because it might cause social resentment and political instability (OECD 2013, 5):

> Inequality has been on the rise since the 1980s, posing new challenges for governments. In the two decades prior to the onset of the crisis, real disposable household income increased across the OECD, but most OECD countries experienced a growth of income inequality, which appears to have accelerated since the crisis. The crisis also exacerbated pre-existing regional disparities, which combined with often significant differences in fiscal capacities, deepened inter regional differences in services for citizens and businesses. This has implications for public governance, in terms for example of dealing with reforms to address issues such as social resentment and political instability.

The final point we would like to make here concerns the relationship between elites (leadership) and governance institutions, which we suspect concerns the question of capability building. The idea of leadership as human agency in the development of government effectiveness was introduced in the last

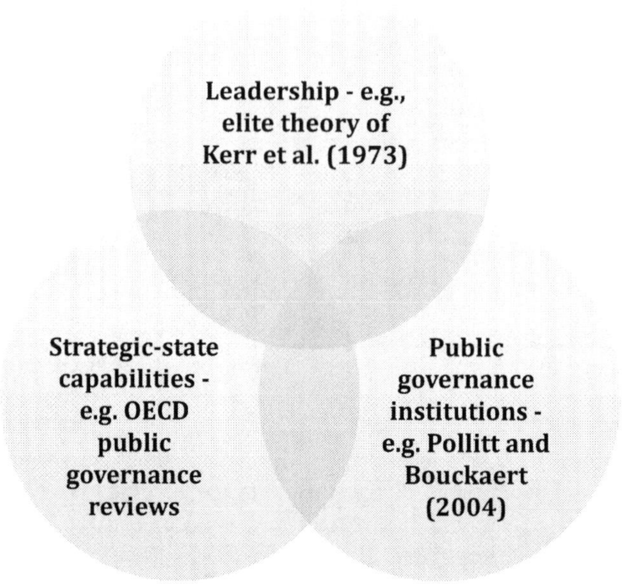

**Leadership - e.g.,
elite theory of
Kerr et al. (1973)**

**Strategic-state
capabilities -
e.g. OECD
public
governance
reviews**

**Public
governance
institutions -
e.g. Pollitt and
Bouckaert
(2004)**

Figure 3.6 A Synthesis of Theories and Models Important for the Effectiveness of
Public Governance

chapter (Levi 2006), in which was suggested that leaders can change constitutions and institutions, even while, for a variety of reasons, being constrained by them. If leaders also steer the process of capability building, then
we can suggest a comprehensive model of government effectiveness—and
thus the effectiveness of public governance—requires conceptual elements
drawn from: leadership theory, models of public governance institutions,
and models of strategic-state capabilities. See Figure 3.6.

Reference List

Cole, G. D. H. (1947) *The Intelligent Man's Guide to the Post-War World*. London:
Victor Gollancz.
Drezes, J. and Sen, A. (2013) *An Uncertain Glory: India and Its Contradictions*.
London: Allen Lane.
Hertie School of Governance (2013) *The Governance Report 2013*. Oxford: Oxford
University Press.
Joyce, P. (2015) *Strategic Management in the Public Sector*. London: Routledge.
Kerr, C., Dunlop, J. T., Harbison, F. and Myers, C. A. (1973) *Industrialism and
Industrial Man*. Harmondsworth: Penguin.
Levi, M. (2006) Why We Need a New Theory of Government, *Perspectives on Poli-
tics*. 4(1), 5–19.

OECD (2013) *Strategic Insights from the Public Governance Reviews: Update.
GOV/PGC(2013)4*. Paris: OECD.

Osborne, D. and Gaebler, T. (1992) *Reinventing Government: How the Entrepreneurial Spirit Is Transforming the Public Sector*. Reading, MA: Addison Wesley.

Pollitt, C. and Bouckaert, G. (2004) *Public Management Reform: A Comparative Analysis*. Oxford: Oxford University Press.

Rhodes, R.A.W. (1997) Un*derstanding Governance*. Buckingham: Open University Press.

World Bank (1997) *World Development Report 1997: The State in a Changing World*. New York: Oxford University Press.

4 Constitutions and Institutions

Introduction

This chapter is intended to provide a description of, and insights into, the constitutions and governance institutions and practices of the six countries. Whenever possible it also pays attention to the nature of the national leadership of the state in each country.

The assumption that we make at this point in the book is that the constitution of a country may affect the effectiveness of a country's government and may do this by influencing the strategic capabilities of the state (Joyce 2015).

Saudi Arabia

Saudi Arabia, which constitutionally speaking is an absolute monarchy, was founded in 1932. Its institutions for public governance during the first years of its existence were very simple. It was a system of personal rule. The person was the King, who made all the key decisions. There was little by way of a conventional civil service system. The King would be brought issues, he would decide on them, he would issue orders, and his employees carried out the orders. It was a minimalist state administering a pastoral society and an economy that was largely agricultural and artisanal (Ulrichsen 2011, 16):

> As late as the 1940s the political economy of the young state was still based upon rudimentary and subsistence-based techniques and traditional modes of production located within the boundaries of the village or the tribe. The major sources of economic livelihood remained pastoral agriculture and trade, alongside small-scale artisanal and commercial activities in the towns. A minimal state operated within strict financial constraints and considerable resource poverty, with little distinction between royal and state resources as the state initially appeared little more than an extension of the ruling family.

The next stage of development of public governance, in the late 1940s and early 1950s, coincided with the occurrence of new opportunities and new

Figure 4.1 Constitutions and Government Effectiveness

demands of an emergent oil industry. The state took responsibility for the exploitation of oil and for the redistribution of oil rents. (Oil rents may be approximately defined as related to the difference between world prices and the costs of production of oil, with the traditional economic sense of the concept of rent being the extra return derived from a natural advantage in an input into production). However well the Saudi oil industry did in the 1950s and 1960s, the biggest returns came in the 1970s, as a result of the actions of OPEC in 1973, and by the time the 1970s were over, in 1981, the oil industry dominated the economy. Looking back now, we can say that the process of institutional development from the late 1940s through to 1981 created a "rentier state" to take advantage of the opportunities for creating wealth from oil resources. (Ulrichsen 2011, 65):

> Classical rentier state theory was developed further in the 1970s and 1980s to examine the impact of external rents such as oil on the nature of states such as Saudi Arabia and their interaction with society . . . With its petroleum sector accounting for 89.29 per cent of budget revenue and 41.5 per cent of GDP at the end of the first oil-price boom in 1981, yet a mere 1.5 per cent of civilian employment (in 1980), Saudi Arabia came to represent an example of an oil state par excellence.

Whereas the state had been a minimalist one before, it now made a much bigger difference to the lives of Saudi people and the interactions and the nexus between the state and people had changed. The rentier state delivered benefits and services to the public without the citizens having to contribute significantly through taxes. Perhaps the rulers hoped that this would earn the gratitude and loyalty of Saudi people? Perhaps it was hoped that individuals would feel a sense of identity with the Saudi ruler and create social stability. We might guess that the substantial fall in the value of oil exports per capita in the 1980s and 1990s could have proved a concern to the Saudi state, on the basis that the rentier state model being operated would be delivering less and less to citizens.

What is the current set up in terms of the key institutions of public governance (executive, legislature, and judiciary)? The government executive within the state structure is the most powerful and active part. Members of the judiciary are appointed and dismissed by royal decree. Saudi Arabia's state has functioned without a legislative chamber of either a parliamentary type with elected members or a national assembly of appointed members. It did, in 1993, create a Consultative Assembly (Majlis al-Shura) to provide advice to the King and the ruling family. The members of the Assembly were appointed by the King and had four-year terms. There were sixty members originally, but the number was subsequently increased to 150 members. The members of the Assembly included merchants, technocrats, civil servants, religious clergy, academics, and retired military personnel. In the early days the Assembly met behind closed doors, but later on its debates were held in public.

One danger we see with succumbing to the plausibility of applying rentier state theory to Saudi Arabia is that it may unwittingly encourage a deterministic analysis of the actions and consequences of Saudi governments. One way to put agency and purposefulness back into the analysis is to look for evidence that governance institutions of the Saudi state interact with the national leadership of the state. So, while the Saudi state that evolved from the late 1940s to the early 1980s might be provisionally described as a rentier state, we still need to characterize the nature of the national leadership of the state. Our starting point in characterizing this national leadership is to note what we have noted already, that the Saudi kingdom was an absolute monarchy. A lot of official power was vested in the person of the king in this absolute monarchy; he headed up not only the state but also headed up the government, being the prime minister in the council of ministers.

To this might be added the judgment that the Saudi state's leadership looked to be a dynastic elite—at least in the sense that there had been a ruling family and the hereditary principle had been applied to the selection of a succession of rulers. As a result of the Basic Law of 1992 succession was narrowed to male descendants of Abdulaziz bin Saud, who had been the first ruler and who had died in 1953. It might also be mentioned that succession has not just been a matter of the eldest son of the king automatically being the heir to the throne and then automatically becoming king on the death of his father. In the past the heir to the throne, known as the crown prince, had been decided by an informal consensus within the ruling family. However, King Abdullah, who came to the throne in 2005 and died in early 2015, changed that. He institutionalized the process by establishing new rules for succession and a committee was made responsible for making the key decisions on succession. As of 2015, the committee decided on succession by secret ballot, with the decision of the committee requiring a majority. The committee also had to be quorate, and there was a requirement for a quorum of two-thirds. Some details of this succession mechanism were published recently in the Khaleej Times (Saturday, January 24 2015):

> The committee is formally charged with the "preservation of the state and the unity and cohesion of the ruling family, as well as the unity of

the nation in the interests of the people". Upon the death of a King, the committee meets in an emergency session to formally declare the crown prince as the new ruler. The new monarch must then propose to the Council within 10 days his candidates for the post of crown prince. It chooses a crown prince from up to three candidates put forward by the king, but it has the authority to reject them all and put forward its own name. The king can reject its nominee and the committee will then have a month to hold a vote to choose between the king's candidate and its own. Members of the committee have a four-year term each, non-renewable without the consensus of their brothers and the king's approval.

In fact, we are not convinced that the dynastic elite concept, discussed in the previous chapter, fits exactly the case of contemporary Saudi Arabia. Specifically, we think the dynastic elite concept may need to be redefined to recognize that Saudi's type of state leadership is focused on both respect for tradition and the need for reform and modernization. This combination is suggested in a media assessment of King Salman Bin Abdulaziz Al Saud, who became Saudi Arabia's new ruler in early 2015 (Reuters 2016):

A reputed moderate with a deft understanding of the competing demands of conservative clerics, powerful tribes and an increasingly youthful population, King Salman is expected to juggle those social reforms well.

"It appeared to me he had a good handle on the delicate balancing act he had to do to move society forward while being respectful of its traditions and conservative ways," says Robert Jordan who was US ambassador in Riyadh from 2001 to 2003.

As governor of Riyadh Province, Salman worked closely with both conservative traditionalists and liberal technocrats as he oversaw the development of the Saudi capital from a small desert town to a major metropolis.

As it says in the quote above, the King has to manage competing demands. The head of the Saudi state may be an absolute monarch but this does not mean that he has all the power or that there is an absence of rivalry and conflicting ambitions. The King needs to manage any rivalry and any potential conflicts that might emerge (Ulrichsen 2011, 73): "both political structures and policy-making are intertwined around the need to construct consensual coalitions and balance princely factions that can coalesce around a particular policy." It would seem that a pluralist perspective still seems to have relevance to public governance, even within a kingdom with an absolute monarch backed up by a ruling family.

The personality and personal agenda of the state leader may also matter a great deal within the Saudi system of public governance. One sign of this is that the King may be seen to initiate and lead a reform initiative, and not just sanction or approve it. For example, King Abdullah (2005–15) was seen as a reformer, a supporter of a dynamic private sector, and a supporter of human resource development policies that would better prepare young people for employment in a successful and diversifying economy. He was also seen to be personally championing the advancement of women in Saudi society, including their participation in local elections to municipal councils. This could be regarded as him taking a personal leadership risk, challenging cultural assumptions, and upsetting other types of leaders. According to a media report published after his death (Reuters 2015):

> Under King Abdullah, who died in January and who announced in 2011 that women would be able to vote in this election, steps were taken for women to have a bigger public role, sending more of them to university and encouraging female employment. However, while women's suffrage has in many other countries been a transformative moment in the quest for gender equality, its impact in Saudi Arabia is likely to be more limited due to a wider lack of democracy and continued social conservatism. Before Abdullah announced women would take part in this year's elections, the country's Grand Mufti, its most senior religious figure, described women's involvement in politics as "opening the door to evil".

A new possibility for interaction between rulers and governed within Saudi Arabia was added in early 2005 when the first municipal elections were held. In 2005 and 2011 only men were allowed to vote in municipal elections. (The second round of municipal elections were scheduled for four years after the first ones, in 2009, but were delayed until 2011.) The response to this opportunity was a little disappointing—voter turnout was low in many municipal precincts, in the order of 30 percent. In 2015 Saudi women were allowed to vote and stand as elected representatives in the third round of municipal elections. On this occasion, it was reported that over 700,000 people voted in the municipal elections, including 130,000 women. Twenty-one women were elected as councilors in various parts of Saudi Arabia.

But if this was opening up a new interface for interaction between the state and the citizens, there was a wish by a Saudi official to constrain how the successful men and women councilors would interact within the municipal bodies. The official was the director-general of Municipal Council Affairs, Judai Al Qahtani, who apparently warned that the new women councillors were not allowed to have face-to-face interactions with male councilors (Staff Writer 2015):

> [He said], "We are making a lot of new adjustments with the participation of women in the council. However, we will not compromise the

religious boundaries." [He also said:] "Female members have equal rights as male members of the council but they will not have mixed meetings." According to Al Qahtani, women councillors should have separate meetings and offices from men.

So, to sum up the Saudi history of public governance (Figure 4.2), the rulers of Saudi Arabia have, arguably, successfully maintained their power base within the evolving institutions of governance for nearly ninety years. The King is still the central figure in national decision-making and he is still supported by a ruling family, from which he selects members of his core leadership coalition. In terms of institutional forms, the Saudi state first added a capacity for more systematic public administration to administer a state that came to resemble what is known as a rentier state, and more recently there have been attempts to add strategic-state characteristics. The implications for the citizens of these changing institutional forms were (and will be) enormous.

It could be argued that public governance in Saudi Arabia has so far had three stages. First, from 1932 when the Kingdom of Saudi Arabia was established, until the late 1940s or early 1950s there was a minimal state in which the decision-making power was almost entirely concentrated in the hands of the Saudi King and there was no systematic institution for public administration. The second period, until, let us say, 2000, was the development and maintenance of a rentier state which was equipped with bureaucratic administration structures, and which provided public services and welfare

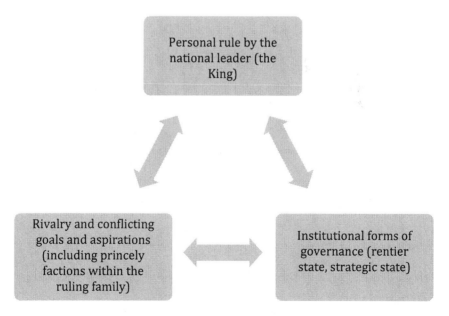

Figure 4.2 Public Governance in Saudi Arabia

support. From 2000 onwards a strategic state started to emerge from within what was still a rentier state. We can point to three indications of a transition to a strategic state. These are, first, the preparation of a long-term strategic vision for Saudi Arabia's national economic and social development. Second, there is the evolution of five-year plans into strategic plans, with the express intent of using national strategic plans to move the country towards a long-term vision. Third, we think the development of a representative interface at the municipal level of governance is a sign of an emergent strategic state, because this representation (of women as well as men) should produce more engagement of citizens with public governance processes.

Qatar

Qatar signed a treaty of protection with Britain in 1960 and became a fully independent state in September 1971. A provisional constitution was set out in the Basic Law, which was enacted in 1970 and revised in 1972. This constitution provided for succession to be based on the hereditary rule of the Al-Thani family, with the actual decision of who was to succeed and become the new ruler requiring a consensus among members of the ruling family.

The provisional constitution established a Council of Ministers and an Advisory Council (Majlis al-Shura). The Advisory Council was to consist of 20 regular members as well as the Council of Ministers. The Emir of Qatar was given the power of choosing the members of the Advisory Council. In 1975 the Advisory Council was expanded. While elections were required, terms of office could be extended by emiri decree.

It was only in 2003 that the provisional constitution was replaced by a permanent constitution. Sheikh Hamad bin Khalifa Al-Thani became the ruler in 1995 and he appointed a national committee (in 1999) to draft a permanent constitution. The new constitution set up a procedure to govern the succession of new rulers of Qatar. The new constitution also created the Ruling Family Council, with the Emir as the head of it, with the heir as a member and with the remaining places filled by Al-Thani family members. The Ruling Family Council was intended to provide stability in times of succession. The 2003 constitution expanded the size of the Advisory Council once again, so that it comprised 30 members directly elected by the people and another 15 appointed by the Emir, with the latter group being appointed from ministers and officials.

Both the government executive and the Advisory Council can propose laws and decrees; however, proposals coming from the Advisory Council have to get the approval of the Council of Ministers.

There is an element of multi-level governance in Qatar. At the local level, there is the Municipal Council. It appears to have been set up in the early 1950s. Sheikh Hamad bin Khalifa Al-Thani made a decree in 1998 that required the Municipal Council to have a system of direct elections to council seats. In 1999 elections were held for an electorate of over 20,000 Qatari citizens and voter turnout was 55 percent.

Bahrain

Bahrain has a dynastic ruling family, which is called Al-Khalifa. This dynasty has a long history. It came to power in the late eighteenth century. They came from the mainland Arabian Peninsula, took control of the Bahrain archipelago, and then negotiated Britain's protection for their role under a series of treaties from 1830 onwards.

Oil was discovered in the early 1930s, creating a new source of income for Bahrain's rulers. Kinninmont (2011, 35) offers an interesting observation on one consequence of the development of the oil industry in Bahrain:

> Oil gradually altered the relationship between the merchants and the royal family, which now had an independent source of income. Officially, oil revenues were split three ways between the ruler, the administration run by Belgrave [who was an adviser to the rulers from 1926 to 1957], and an oil reserve fund.

Bahrain became independent in 1971 when Britain withdrew from the Middle East region. When Britain left the region in 1971, military facilities in Bahrain, which Britain had formerly used, were leased to the US Navy, and in effect the United States took the protection role that the UK had previously carried out.

The newly independent Bahrain had a constitution that included a fully elected parliament, with the electorate being defined as male citizens aged over 20 years. The new parliament began to sit in late 1973 but did not last very long, being dissolved by the ruler in 1975. There were a number of reasons why the ruler dissolved the Parliament (Kinninmont 2011, 38):

> The parliament quickly fell out with the ruler over the state budget, the US presence in Bahrain, internal security legislation, and its member's desire for land reform. Public finances had become particularly contentious because oil revenues had swollen after the 1973 oil crisis. In 1975 the ruler dissolved parliament the country was without parliament until 2002, with a fully elected parliament never being reinstated.

In 2001 there was a referendum on the National Action Charter (NAC). This suggested that Bahrain had always been a direct democracy with customs of dialogue and consultation. But the Charter talked about creating a bicameral parliament with an elected and an appointed chamber. The elected chamber was going to be enacting laws and the appointed chamber would be providing advice. The ideas contained in the referendum proved to be very popular and over 98 percent of voters supported them. (The voter turnout was very high—an impressive 90 percent.).

A new constitution followed in 2002. But the new institutions were not exactly as considered in the referendum of the previous year. Instead of two chambers having quite distinct functions—with the elected chamber enacting new laws and the appointed chamber being advisory—the new constitution set up parliament so that both chambers had a role in passing new laws.

According to Bahrain's 2002 constitution, the government executive is the dominant institution (Kinninmont 2011). The legislature and the judiciary were much less important within the constitution. The reinstated parliament comprised elected members but their powers were judged to be significantly less than their predecessors in the parliament of 1973 to 1975.

Within this system of governance the ruling family has had a strong power base. The core leadership group comprises the ruler, the prime minister, and the crown prince. In fact, the ruler, the King of Bahrain, appointed his uncle as the prime minister and the crown prince, who was the eldest of the King's sons. As can be seen, the three members of the ruling family occupy the top three positions in the state. No wonder that Kinninmont (2011, 40) arrives at the following judgement: "the lines between the state, government and ruling family are very blurred." The 2002 constitution defines a very powerful role for the King and enables the concentration of power in the hands of the ruler and the ruler's family. Remarkably, it should be noted that the prime minister in 2011 had been prime minister for 40 years.

However, just because the ruler of a kingdom has much personal power and the ruling family occupies key government executive positions, this does not mean that governance is totally harmonious and cohesive. Conflicts and tensions can occur within families. In the case of Bahrain there are reports that there was a long-term power struggle between the prime minister and the crown prince, which might be summed up by saying that the prime minister represented a faction within government that was conservative in its agenda whereas the crown prince faction was very interested in modernizing the economy (and politics). Such factionalism and rivalry, whatever the constitution provides, is affected by changing circumstances. After a period of ascendancy, the crown prince fraction lost some influence in 2011, presumably as a direct result of the Arab Spring making national development less important and national security more important.

Finally, Bahrain does not have a party political system in the fullest sense, even though it does license political societies since 2006. These political societies have included the Al-Wefaq National Islamic Society, which has been described as championing the interest of the Shia population (which is in a majority and coexists with a Sunni state leadership). It won seats in the parliamentary elections in 2006 and 2010, but all Al-Wefaq members of parliament resigned in 2011 as a protest at the suppression of protests that were taking place. So, the political process in 2011 did register the Arab Spring protests in Bahrain—but this mainly took the form of the protest resignations and attempts by opposition groupings to get concessions from the government before discussing political reforms.

To sum up, Bahrain has a king, and, since 2002 it has a parliament and that parliament includes an elected chamber. It has a quasi-party politics organized through licensed political societies. The factionalism within the state (focused around the prime minister and the crown prince) suggested that some receptivity to modernization and reform of public governance might exist.

Oman

The current ruler (2016) of Oman is Sultan Qaboos. He is the fourteenth in a family dynasty that has been ruling Oman since the mid-eighteenth century. He came to power in 1970 when his father, Sultan Sa'id, was pressured into abdicating in favour of Sultan Qaboos.

The public finances of Oman were transformed by its oil era, which commenced in 1967 when Petroleum Development Oman (mostly owned by Shell) began its operations to exploit the country's oil resources. According to Valeri (2011, 145), this immediately benefitted the public finances: "In 1969 oil rent already represented forty times the total annual revenue of the Sultanate in the early 1960s." The Omani state took a 60 percent stake in the company's capital and its revenue from oil rose steeply in the 1970s.

Although Oman has had its family dynasty, Oman has not been ruled by a family—at least not since 1970. It has been ruled by Sultan Qaboos.

The Oman case exhibits a form of personal rule that is at the extreme end of personalization of governance. A royal decree in 1975 proclaimed the Sultan to be the source of all laws. This is a very obvious definition of a personalization of governance. But the personalization went beyond this. According to the constitution, the Sultan of Oman dominates all the major parts of the state. He chairs the central bank; he is Chief of Staff of the Armed Forces; he is Minister of Defence and Minister of Foreign Affairs. He has had the power to appoint and dismiss judges. He has had the power to grant pardons and commute sentences. The extremeness of this personalization of governance is perhaps suggested by article 41 of the Basic Law of the State, which says that respecting the Sultan is a duty and that his orders must be obeyed.

This situation may have been partly created by the personal preferences of Sultan Qaboos (Peterson 2005, 7–8):

> Qabus's personality in this context include his clear determination to retain all ultimate authority in his own hands. This conviction surfaced early in his reign during his struggle over conflicting goals with his uncle and Prime Minister Tariq b. Taymur: the Sultan saw himself as a benevolent monarch, retaining all authority, while Sayyid Tariq pushed for implementation of his conception of a constitutional monarchy. Tariq lasted little more than a year in the office before he felt himself forced to resign and there has never been another prime minister (apart from the Sultan declaring himself as holder of the office).

The Basic Law of the State (1996), mentioned in the preceding paragraph, did not follow a referendum or pass through a parliamentary process—it was authorized by a royal decree, again reflecting a personalization of governance.

The Sultan has had ministers and a Council of Ministers whose function is to implement policies of the state. And there are government departments. But, in addition to ministers and departments, there is a Diwan of the Royal Court which functions as a centre of government, operating above both cabinets and departments. Valeri (2011, 139) described the Diwan of the Royal Court as follows:

> The structure that best symbolizes the extreme personalization of authority in Oman is the Diwan of the Royal Court. Qaboos soon showed his determination to keep control of all matters in the country, while giving the image of a ruler close to his subjects' problems. The Diwan has the role of filtering all cases coming before the ruler, while managing those national and private affairs which do not concern any other department but do not require the Sultan's personal intervention. As such, the Diwan has slowly become a super-ministry above all the other Cabinet departments.

If we compare the development of governance in Oman with that in Saudi Arabia, it is striking that Saudi Arabia moved away from a personal-centred governance in which decision-making was concentrated in the hands of the King to a more bureaucratic system of government as a result of the exploitation of oil resources; in the case of Oman the governance has taken an extreme form of personalization since 1970 even though there was a large quantity of public revenue derived from the oil industry.

Oman has a Consultative Council (Majlis al-Shura), which was set up in 1990, and which was preceded by a State Consultative Council. The president of the Council is appointed by royal decree and there are 84 members. The method of election of members of the Consultative Council (and selection) was as follows: each administrative area proposed three candidates, and then Sultan Qaboos chose one of the three. The process for electing the members of the Consultative Council has evolved over time. In 1993 the number of representatives from an administrative area was related to the population size. In 1997 women were enfranchised—meaning they could vote and they could stand for election. In 2000 the electorate was increased to 175,000 people, which was 25 percent of adults. In 2003 universal suffrage was introduced and the term of members of the Consultative Council was increased from three to four years.

The Consultative Council has a role of preparing legislation. If the Council of Ministers chooses to do so, it can send proposed legislation to the Consultative Council where it is discussed, amendments suggested, and a vote taken before sending it back to the relevant government ministry. The ruler has the option of listening to, or ignoring, the changes suggested by the Consultative Council. The Consultative Council can be involved in other government processes—it can make proposals to the Council of Ministers for legislation and it can contribute to national development plans and budgets.

The Basic Law created the Council of Oman, comprising the Consultative Council and the State Council, the latter being an appointed body. In 2011, Sultan Qaboos used a royal decree to signal his intent to give the Council of Oman more powers—a possible indication of a shift away from the personalization of governance, maybe?

United Arab Emirates

The United Arab Emirates was established in 1971 with Abu Dhabi's ruler, Sheikh Zayed bin Sultan Al Nahyan, becoming its first President. It was formed from a number of sheikhdoms that had in the nineteenth century signed truces with Britain and had come under its umbrella of protection and support. The ruling families from that period have continued to be the ruling families of the modern-day United Arab Emirates.

The relationship between the ruling families and the merchants of the lower Persian Gulf sheikhdoms appears to have been an important dimension of the context of governance in the sheikhdoms in the 1930s. Tensions between rulers and merchants built up at that time, which was a time when, economically speaking, things were about to change significantly because of oil. The tension existed because the merchant community was feeling dissatisfied with their rulers (Davidson 2011, 7–8):

> [the] merchant community . . . was suffering a severe recession in the 1930s in the wake of global economic depression and declining interest in the region's principal industry, the export of pearls. Leading merchants were frustrated with their ruler's close relations with Britain, as the latter effectively restricted access to foreign markets and foreign technologies in an effort to maintain the Gulf as a 'British lake'. Resentment was exacerbated by the ruler's personal enrichment from rents being paid directly to them by British companies in return for approving oil exploration concession agreements and air landing rights. In 1938 matters came to a head in Dubai . . . Dubai's merchants had taken control of half the city and were pressing the ruler to limit his personal income and distribute rents in the name of the state . . . Britain intervened in favour of the ruler by flying aircraft low over Dubai and distributing pamphlets that encouraged residents to respect the status quo.

It appears that an important factor in the formation of the United Arab Emirates was the decision by Britain to withdraw from the region both militarily and politically. This decision seems to have evoked concerns about the

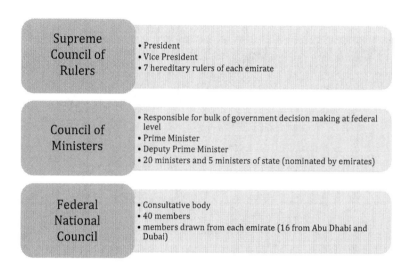

Figure 4.3 Governance Institutions at Federal Level in the United Arab Emirates

security of the sheikhdoms and the risks of aggression by neighbours. Such concerns must have been intensified when Iran grabbed some islands that it had been claiming (including Abu Musa) the day before the British officially left the region in late 1971. A decade later, the formation of the Gulf Cooperation Council (in 1981) appears to have also have been motivated by fears of aggression by other countries in the region.

A new constitution was designed in 1971 and this created a loose confederation, a supreme body for governance comprising rulers from the seven emirates, and a fairly decentralized system of governance, with the lower (emirate) level of governance retaining responsibility for defence and oil. The capital was made Abu Dhabi.

The 1971 constitution provided for several key institutions at the federal level (see Figure 4.3):

(i) At the top was a supreme council with seven rulers from each of the emirates but with Abu Dhabi and Dubai clearly being the dominant voices. The President has been the ruler of Abu Dhabi, the ruler of Dubai has been the Vice-President, and both the Abu Dhabi and the Dubai rulers have had the additional power of being able to exercise a veto. Abu Dhabi's influence may be underpinned to some extent by its financial strength based on its oil.

(ii) There is a Council of Ministers at the federal level. This body was responsible for most of federal level government decision-making. Abu Dhabi and Dubai have been influential within the Council of Ministers.

The Prime Minister has been the ruler of Dubai and the deputy Prime Minister came from Abu Dhabi. The largest share of ministerial positions was held by Abu Dhabi.

(iii) The constitution provided for a consultative body called the Federal National Council. It comprised 40 members, with members being sent from each emirate. As with the other key institutions, the Federal National Council tended to be dominated by people from Abu Dhabi and Dubai. Each of these two emirates supplied eight members. That is, a total of 16 out of the 40 members of the Federal National Council came from Abu Dhabi and Dubai.

Half the membership of the Federal National Council was to be filled by election in 2006. The electorate comprised a few thousand United Arab Emirates nationals. The next round of elections was scheduled for 2010 (but was put off).

There is some decision-making at the emirate level. The rulers and crown princes have private offices and courts, but actually in recent years "emiri decrees" by rulers were only to be found in Abu Dhabi and Dubai. There have been executive councils in Abu Dhabi, Dubai, and Sharjah, and there have been national consultative councils operating in Abu Dhabi and Sharjah. The consultative council in Abu Dhabi had been operating for nearly 40 years in 2011, all its members were appointed, and most of the members had been serving on the Council for more than 18 years. None of the members were women back in 2011, but Sharjah's national consultative council did have some female members (less than a fifth).

It would appear from much of the preceding description that responsibility for governance in the United Arab Emirates has tended to be lodged with the rulers of Abu Dhabi and Dubai, their crown princes, and members of the ruling families. According to Davidson (2011, 15): "Beyond Abu Dhabi and Dubai, few of the other emirates rulers now have significant influence in UAE politics." To this conclusion can be added some observations about the perceived levels of transparency and accountability achieved by governance in the United Arab Emirates (Davidson 2011, 28): "most government departments and authorities remain opaque and secretive . . . most male members of the ruling family occupy key positions in government . . . there is a growing feeling that these individuals and institutions must submit to more domestic scrutiny."

Kuwait

Kuwait has a ruling family—the Al-Sabah, a family which has been ruling since 1752. But Kuwait is also sometimes described as having the most advanced democratic culture in the Arabian Peninsula. Roberts (2011, 110) is among those making claims of a relatively high degree of democratic cultural development in Kuwait:

The ruler is however unlikely to be able to revert to a more typically
Gulf-style parliament (where the parliament has essentially no power)
as the notion of Kuwait as the region's most advanced democracy is
now thoroughly embedded in Kuwaiti culture.

Kuwait has not only a reputation for a democratic culture, but it is also one
of the Gulf states with a very strong position in terms of oil revenues. In
2014, it was the only one of the six Gulf states that had oil rents constitut-
ing more than 50 percent of its GDP. The oil revenues have been converted
into big sovereign wealth funds. Presumably, these economic facts may have
a big bearing on how governance works in Kuwait and how the people who
live in Kuwait think of the state.

Roberts (2011) makes an interesting point about the style of the very
first ruler from the Al-Sabah family; it seems that the style was consultative. It might be important to consider the possibility of intergenerational
inheritance in governing, and whether the style adopted back in the mid-
eighteenth century created a cultural legacy that eventually explained the
current institutions of governance, and in particular created an inheritance
that enabled democratic values to flourish.

Certainly, it can be argued that Kuwaiti governments have long tended
to have a soft and at times an accommodating approach. As with the case
of the sheikhdoms that preceded the United Arab Emirates, the relationship
between rulers and the merchant class was an important one for public
governance. It has been suggested that the Al-Sabah family arrived at an
accommodation with the merchant class in Kuwait. In 1921 the Consultative Council was formed in respect of the merchant class. It is claimed that
the ruler of the day, Sheikh Ahmed, was responsive to the merchants' desire
to be more consulted. Roberts (2011, 93) notes that: "The Council was
however soon crippled by bickering and dissolved by the ruler."

It is also an interesting part of Kuwait's history that in 1920 it was about
to be invaded by Saudi forces. The invading forces were met by Kuwaiti
forces, and then, with British soldiers joining in with the attempt to halt
the invasion, Saudi forces gave up the attempt. Roberts (2011, 90) attaches
great significance to this military action, suggesting it played a critical role in
crystallizing a Kuwaiti national identity. Thus, he notes the choice of 1920
as the "cut off" date for deciding on claims of Kuwaiti citizenship. In other
words, the year in which the Kuwaiti military defended the country from
invasion was the year in which Kuwait came of age in terms of national
sentiments.

Kuwait entered the oil age with its export of oil in 1946. The revenue
from the oil industry from 1950 onwards funded national developments
such as the building of hospitals and schools to serve the population. Also in
the 1950s, Sheikh Abdullah III, set up Kuwait's government on the basis of
ministries and development committees. Selecting members of the family to
be the heads of these ministries and committees protected the grip on state

power of the Al-Sabah family. So, it might be argued that the Al-Sabah rulers created the rentier state during the 1950s, meaning both the systematic form of government machinery and the state provision of health and education. By the time Kuwait became independent from Britain, in 1961, it was judged to have a relatively well-developed state compared to other countries in the Arabian Peninsula.

With independence came a new constitution, which was drawn up in 1961. The new constitution institutionalized the hereditary rule of the Al-Sabah: only male descendants of Sheikh Mubarak, who ruled from 1986 to 1915, could rule. This new constitution also provided for a National Assembly comprising 50 members. This National Assembly, sometimes referred to as a parliament, was filled through an electoral process. The election in 1963 produced about 210 candidates for the 50 seats in the National Assembly. Only literate male Kuwaiti nationals were eligible to take part in the election and compete for a place in the National Assembly.

The ruler was formally quite powerful. The ruler of Kuwait would make the decision on who would be the crown prince—and the crown prince then was also prime minister. The crown prince (and at the same time prime minister) then appointed cabinet members in the executive government. Only one of the cabinet members had to have been elected to the National Assembly. This constitutional framework meant that the ruler, the Emir, had control over the make-up of the government. The ruler could also, constitutionally, dissolve parliament at any time—but the Emir had to then call an election. So, the constitution was requiring that the ruler had to have a parliament, they could not rule without one for a lengthy period of time. But, presumably, the constitution was trying to make it possible for the ruler to have a cooperative Parliament because the ruler could dissolve it. And the ruler could legislate on urgent matters when Parliament was not in session.

But the Kuwait Parliament also had a significant constitutional power base. Parliament was given power over setting the Emir's salary. The members of the Parliament were able to vote on the ruler's choice of crown prince. And members of parliament could have votes of no confidence in the executive.

Also with profound significance for the nature of politics in Kuwait, the system of governance provided no role for political parties. It might be thought that the ability of members of Parliament to call for votes of confidence in response to the cabinet proposals gave it quite a lot of moral authority. On the other hand, it could be argued that the constitution was designed to deliver a parliament that was really just a rubber stamp for the decisions made by the Al-Sabah family.

In the 1970s Parliament developed a combative character and became more oppositional to executive government. The work of government became bogged down in debate and setting the budget became delayed. In 1976 the ruler of Kuwait dissolved the Parliament; it was restarted a few years later, but this time with many more districts (25 as opposed to 10). Apparently, people who were recently nationalized populated many new districts, they had been stateless, and as a consequence of being recently nationalized, such people were perceived to be supporters of government.

It is reported that Kuwait was prominent in the setting up of the Gulf Cooperation Council in 1981. Given some of the claims and actions of other countries such as Iraq and Iran, perhaps it was understandable that the Kuwait Al-Sabahs were keen to build stronger bonds of cooperation and mutual support among the states of the Gulf area.

Telling us much about the relationship between ruler and Parliament, and the power balance between them, the ruler decided to dissolve the parliament again in 1986. This was in the wake of an attempt to assassinate the ruler in 1985 and a series of bombings.

Parliament was restarted after the Iraq invasion and after the 1990–91 war to free Kuwait. The parliaments of the 1990s contained a vigorous opposition to the government, although there was a loyalist group in Parliament. Some of the complaints of the opposition in Parliament concerned government corruption.

It has also been reported that the ruler of Kuwait, during one of the periods between governments, promoted the idea of enfranchising women. But when Parliament sat again the idea of enfranchising women was rejected. It appears that there were a variety of reasons why Parliament rejected the idea of enfranchising women. For some, who were Islamists, votes for women were rejected on the grounds of principle. For others, the rejection of including women in politics was based on constitutional reasoning. It was reported that there were even some who were concerned about who would look after children if women were enfranchised. On the face of it, the rulers were a progressive voice in relation to women and voting and Parliament appears to have been a conservative voice. We can note that women were enfranchised in 2005 and were able to run for election in 2006 and 2008. And, in 2009, four women were actually elected to Parliament.

The working relationship between the executive and Parliament appears to have been a bumpy one in the 2000s. Kuwait's parliament was dissolved in 2006, 2008, and 2009. It appeared that there was also a difficult relationship between the Prime Minister, Sheikh Nasser Al-Sabah and Parliament. In late 2008 a motion was filed to question the Prime Minister. This triggered the resignation of the cabinet, which was followed by another set of elections and the reappointment of Sheikh Nasser Al-Sabah as the Prime Minister. Following the elections in 2009, support for the government (executive) slightly improved and as a result it was possible for new legislation to be passed relating to an economic stimulus and to privatization. It had taken many years to see this legislation become law. In late 2010 the Prime Minister endured a marathon session and survived a vote of no confidence. And in early 2011 the cabinet resigned again over the number of interpellations filed by members of Parliament against ministers. So, all in all, it seemed that Parliament was not a rubber stamp, was quite prepared to be oppositional, and prepared to give government ministers a hard time.

Summary

Some of the governance systems in the Gulf states seem to have evolved over many years in ways that left intact much of the personal power of the ruler to govern—for example, Oman and Saudi Arabia. There does seem to have been a trend towards creating consultative bodies and then changing the way in which members of these bodies take up their seats, with the shift being away from appointment towards elections (for example, Qatar). Perhaps it might even be argued that there have been some signs that consultative bodies are gaining or will gain in powers (for example, Oman). All that being said, the general perception of some commentators (for example, Roberts 2011) is that the consultative bodies tend to be without power. In this chapter, we have seen that Kuwait has had a fairly vigorous national assembly and we might argue that in Bahrain the 2001 referendum and the 2002 constitution were indications that the nature of the public governance system could evolve further in the future.

The massive oil resources still held in Gulf states may well be a factor in how the various parties and stakeholders interact within the institutions of public governance. For example, with the rulers and the government executive on one hand concerned about the transition to a post-oil economy and post-oil society, members of national consultative bodies or parliaments may find themselves, on the other hand, more concerned with redistribution of existing oil revenues because they want to maintain public support.

The evidence of this chapter is that parliamentary bodies do not always end up in totally harmonious and cohesive relationships with government executives. The parliamentary bodies may find themselves "bickering" with government executives and seeking to block government executive proposals. The members of such bodies may use, at times, the constitutional powers of their chamber to put the government executive under pressure. For example, they may use votes of no confidence and "grilling" government executives in marathon sessions (Roberts 2011, 97–98). The Kuwait story could be seen as disappointing to anyone believing that democracy can assist a modern state in being effective and that a lively parliamentary chamber is a constructive aspect of democratic dialogue and problem-solving. As Roberts (2011) seems to show, Kuwait had a parliament that acted as a brake on economic modernization, was resistant to enfranchising women, and might have been mainly interested in representing certain sections of the Kuwait community in terms of the redistribution of state benefits of oil revenues.

So, perhaps we should stress that parliamentary mechanisms, when used in the Gulf region, may work differently and have different effects from Western theoretical models of good governance. In any case, parliamentary democracy without political parties, combined with a restricted electorate, could be seen as emphasizing sectional interest groups in society rather than society as a whole. Parliament cannot be assumed to represent all the people—and for a long time this might have been, and might still be true, in respect of women.

In fact, it is possible that a parliament based on a restricted electorate might serve to entrench a rentier state model in a country. And we might be wrong to assume that a dynastic elite will focus only on maintaining tradition rather than modernizing and adapting. The dynastic elite, in fact, may want to take the step of enfranchising women, a very non-traditional agenda. Conversely, parliamentary bodies may oppose the enfranchising of women, and it could be seen that they are trying to maintain the traditional status quo rather than being an instrument of change and progress. If parliament opposes every move to dismantle the rentier state, for example, in whose interest will they be acting? Roberts (2011) makes the following interesting suggestion as part of his analysis of Kuwait (2011, 109):

> If members of parliament want to be elected, it takes a strong willed and highly principled position not resort to the low but effective politics of a service platform, promising greater subsidies, industry protection and resolutely no taxes. Such policies meet an electorate safe in the knowledge that Kuwait has 'loads of oil' and thus understandably feeling it has the right to receive some part of this wealth.

What might be expected of oil-rich countries trying to prepare and move towards a post-oil economy? Pessimistically, it might be expected that it will prove too difficult to really advance national development along the lines of a modernizing agenda in relation to the economy. We might predict an inability to break out of a dependence on revenue from the oil industry.

However, if we look at a system of governance that is based on very personal power lodged in a ruler, we might expect, given the pluralist theory of industrializing elites that we considered in an earlier chapter, that this would be a system of leadership and governance that was uninterested in modernizing, and only concerned to hang onto traditions. According to this theory, only if there is pressure from the public to modernize the economy might it be expected that the dynastic elite, one that is oriented to tradition, will pursue reform and change to achieve economic dynamism.

Actually, what we will see in a later chapter is that countries that have rulers with a lot of personal power do actually seem to care about and pursue economic modernization. A strong dynastic elite (Oman, Saudi Arabia) manages to be concerned about both tradition and pursuit of modernization and change.

We began this chapter presuming that constitutions might be important because of their effect on the strategic capabilities of states, and that in turn these capabilities matter for the effectiveness of government. It is difficult to argue that this chapter has made this causal link clear—except in one case.

Roberts (2011, 92) did suggest a direct link between constitutional defects and (failures in terms of) strategic capabilities of government in the case of Kuwait: "The late 2000s saw continued bickering in Kuwait's Parliament, to the detriment of long-term planning and development." The different parts of a system of public governance (for example, an executive and a parliament) may be abdicating responsibility if they are too acquiescent and accommodating, but the opposite problem of a lack of integration and coherence may also be dysfunctional for strategic national development. If this judgment is correct, then constitutional design and the execution of that design do matter for government effectiveness in achieving national development.

Reference List

Davidson, C. M. (2011) United Arab Emirates. In: C. Davidson (editor) *Power and Politics in the Persian Gulf Monarchies*. London: Hurst & Co. Pages 7–29.

Joyce, P. (2015) Case Studies in Public Governance, Strategic Management and Economic Performance. In: R. Jucevicius, J. Bruneckiene and Gerd-Bodo von Carlsburg (editors) *International Practices of Smart Development*. Frankfurt am Main: Peter Lang. Pages 241–254.

Kinninmont, J. (2011) Bahrain. In: C. Davidson (editor) *Power and Politics in the Persian Gulf Monarchies*. London: Hurst & Co. Pages 31–62.

Peterson, J. E. (2005) The Emergence of Post-Traditional Oman *Working Paper*. Durham: University of Durham, Centre for Middle Eastern and Islamic Studies.

Reuters (2015) Saudis Elect 17 Women in Landmark Election. [online] [15 December 2015]. Available from: Missing http: http://www.arabianbusiness.com/saudis-elect-17-women-in-landmark-election-615193.html

Reuters (2016) Saudi Arabia: Smooth Succession but a Bumpy Road Ahead. [online]. [7 February 2016]. Available from: http://www.arabianbusiness.com/saudi-arabia-smooth-succession-but-bumpy-road-ahead-580375.html

Roberts, D. (2011) Kuwait. In: C. Davidson (editor) *Power and Politics in the Persian Gulf Monarchies*. London: Hurst & Co. Pages 89–112.

Staff Writer (2015) Saudi Official Warns against 'Interaction' between Male and Female Counterparts. [online] [17 December 2015]. Available from: http://www.arabianbusiness.com/saudi-official-warns-against-interaction-between-male-female-councillors-615745.html

Ulrichsen, K. C. (2011) Saudi Arabia. In: C. Davidson (editor) *Power and Politics in the Persian Gulf Monarchies*. London: Hurst & Co. Pages 63–88.

Valeri, M. (2011) Oman. In: C. Davidson (editor) *Power and Politics in the Persian Gulf Monarchies*. London: Hurst & Co. Pages 135–160.

Wright, S. (2011) Qatar. In: C. Davidson (editor) *Power and Politics in the Persian Gulf Monarchies*. London: Hurst & Co. Pages 113–133.

Other Sources

Anonymous (2015) Abdullah Laid Down Rules of Succession. In: *Khaleej Times Saturday*, January 24 2015. Page 10.

5 Reputations for Governance and Competitiveness

Introduction

The World Governance Indicators published by the World Bank are one of the best-known options for sourcing secondary data for cross-societal comparisons to explain economic development and economic growth. The World Economic Forum's Global Competitiveness Reports provide a similar function in terms of benchmarking and comparing economies. Both aggregate a lot of data to form indicators and aspects of the whole phenomena they address. Together they provide a convenient source of data about governance and economies. Moreover, there is some evidence that governments who rank highly on the indicator of government effectiveness tend to do better in terms of competitiveness ranking. Both the World Governance Indicators and the Global Competitiveness rankings are no doubt vulnerable to critique in terms of their construction and use. There are additional problems when the World Governance Indicators are aggregated using an equal weighting to provide a measure of the institutions of public governance (Pinar 2015). But there is no doubting that both sets of data meet an increasing need for more data to do national benchmarking.

When Bahrain published its vision statement, Our Vision (2008), it expressed interest in the public sector becoming more productive and accountable for delivering better quality services. The vision statement identified the World Bank ranking for government effectiveness as a potential measure of success for action in this area.

When Saudi Arabia identified increasing the competitiveness of the national economy as being of great importance in its Ninth Development Plan (2010–14), it referred to the Global Competitiveness Report issued by the World Economic Forum. The Ninth Development Plan noted that Saudi Arabia's competitiveness had improved to twenty-eighth in 2008 and that there were three areas of excellence or improvement: macroeconomic stability, health and primary education, and efficient market for goods. While it was not the only international report it used for benchmarking, it was one of a small number.

Rather than see these sets of data as objective measures, we see them as both very important influences on the reputations of countries. In fact, it should be noted that the World Bank data is reliant on perceptions and while we assume that perceptions do to some extent reflect reality, we take a pragmatic view that perceptions matter. Hence, we are discussing this data in a chapter headed reputations for governance and competitiveness.

International Comparisons of Perceptions of Public Governance

The World Bank publishes world governance indicators (WGI) for countries. In the Table 5.1 below we have provided data on three of the indicators for a purposeful selection of 41 countries. Our purpose was to display data on a diverse sample of countries from a variety of continents. We wanted to include the so-called "BRIC" countries as well, in recognition of the changing global economic context. The data is displayed as percentile rank, with 0 being the lowest rank, and 100 the highest rank.

Table 5.1 Public Governance—Key Dimensions in 2000 and 2014 (Percentile Rank Scores)

Countries	Government effectiveness		Regulatory quality		Voice and accountability	
	2000	2014	2000	2014	2000	2014
Argentina	58.5	45.7	61.8	13.0	57.2	58.6
Australia	91.7	91.8	94.6	98.1	95.7	93.6
Bahrain	71.7	72.6	74.0	74.0	18.2	11.3
Belgium	92.2	92.8	86.8	85.1	92.3	94.6
Brazil	58.1	47.1	64.2	50.5	52.4	60.6
Cambodia	18.5	25.5	43.1	35.9	23.6	17.7
Chile	84.9	84.1	91.2	91.8	74.5	80.3
China	53.7	66.4	36.3	45.2	11.5	5.4
Denmark	97.6	96.2	96.1	94.7	97.6	97.0
Egypt	49.8	20.2	35.8	25.0	24.5	14.8
France	91.2	88.9	80.3	82.2	86.1	89.2
Germany	94.1	94.7	91.7	94.2	89.9	96.1
Ghana	57.6	44.2	49.0	51.0	49.5	64.5
Iceland	98.1	90.9	96.6	94.1	96.6	94.1
India	51.2	45.2	42.6	34.6	56.3	61.1
Ireland	90.2	92.3	97.1	95.2	93.3	92.3
Italy	78.5	66.8	78.9	72.6	79.3	75.9
Jamaica	56.6	60.1	57.8	56.7	67.8	65.5
Japan	87.3	97.1	79.4	84.1	75.5	79.3
Kazakhstan	25.9	54.3	27.0	44.7	20.7	15.3
Kuwait	52.2	47.6	44.6	55.5	43.8	29.1
Lebanon	50.7	40.9	34.8	46.6	42.3	34.0

(*Continued*)

Table 5.1 (Continued)

Countries	Government effectiveness		Regulatory quality		Voice and accountability	
	2000	2014	2000	2014	2000	2014
Lithuania	60.0	78.9	77.9	87.0	73.1	74.9
New Zealand	89.8	98.6	95.1	99.0	100.0	97.5
Nigeria	14.6	11.5	20.6	23.6	30.3	29.6
Norway	94.6	96.6	84.3	92.3	97.1	100.0
Oman	65.9	63.9	54.4	73.6	29.8	19.7
Poland	73.2	74.5	76.5	81.7	80.8	81.8
Qatar	69.3	78.4	51.0	70.7	37.5	22.2
Russian Federation	23.4	51.4	27.9	36.5	37.0	20.2
Saudi Arabia	46.3	62.0	51.5	53.4	8.2	3.5
Singapore	100.0	100.0	100.0	100.0	54.3	45.3
South Africa	75.6	65.4	64.7	63.9	70.2	68.5
Spain	92.7	84.6	89.7	75.5	88.5	77.3
Sweden	97.1	95.7	90.7	96.2	99.0	99.5
Tunisia	71.2	48.6	52.0	40.9	28.4	49.8
Turkey	57.1	67.3	63.7	66.3	34.6	37.9
UAE	78.1	90.4	75.0	80.3	31.7	19.2
UK	93.7	92.8	98.0	97.1	90.9	92.1
US	93.2	89.9	95.6	88.5	91.3	79.8
Vietnam	38.5	52.4	22.1	30.3	12.0	9.9

Source: World Bank (data accessed 10 November 2015)

Government Effectiveness is a measure based on perceptions of (1) the quality of public services, (2) the quality of the civil service and its independence from political pressures, (3) the quality of policy formulation and implementation, and (4) the credibility of the government's commitment to policies.

Regulatory Quality refers to the ability of the government to formulate and implement sound policies and regulations that permit and promote private sector development.

Voice and Accountability is a combined measure based on perceptions of the extent to which citizens of a country are able to participate in selecting their government, and perceptions of freedom of expression, freedom of association, and a free media.

We have used the data to produce a tabular analysis to bring out more clearly some of the variations between governments in 2014. This is Table 5.2.

We have been slightly arbitrary in our classification decisions because we have made them so that the 41 countries might be to some extent dispersed

Table 5.2 Public Governance Indicators in 2014 (World Bank Data)

Government effectiveness	Regulatory quality	Voice and accountability		Countries
High (Above 90%)	High (Above 90%)	High (Above 90%)	1	Australia, Denmark, Germany, Iceland, Ireland, New Zealand, Norway, Sweden, UK (n=9)
		Medium (50–90%)	2	
		Low (Below 50%)	3	Singapore
	Medium (50–90%)	High (Above 90%)	4	Belgium
		Medium (50–90%)	5	Japan
		Low (Below 50%)	6	UAE
	Low (Below 50%)	High (Above 90%)	7	
		Medium (50–90%)	8	
		Low (Below 50%)	9	
Medium (50–90%)	High (Above 90%)	High (Above 90%)	10	
		Medium (50–90%)	11	Chile
		Low (Below 50%)	12	
	Medium (50–90%)	High (Above 90%)	13	
		Medium (50–90%)	14	France, Italy, Jamaica, Lithuania, Poland, South Africa, Spain, USA (n=8)
		Low (Below 50%)	15	Bahrain, Oman, Qatar, Saudi Arabia, Turkey (n=5)
	Low (Below 50%)	High (Above 90%)	16	
		Medium (50–90%)	17	
		Low (Below 50%)	18	China, Kazakhstan, Russian Federation, Vietnam (n=4)

(*Continued*)

Table 5.2 (Continued)

Government effectiveness	Regulatory quality	Voice and accountability		Countries
Low (Below 50%)	High (Above 90%)	High (Above 90%)	19	
		Medium (50–90%)	20	
		Low (Below 50%)	21	
	Medium (50–90%)	High (Above 90%)	22	
		Medium (50–90%)	23	Brazil, Ghana
		Low (Below 50%)	24	Kuwait
	Low (Below 50%)	High (Above 90%)	25	
		Medium (50–90%)	26	Argentina, India
		Low (Below 50%)	27	Cambodia, Egypt, Lebanon, Nigeria, Tunisia (n=5)

between different categories. In fact, that said, over three-quarters of the 41 cases are to be found in just five of the categories. We think there are some interesting patterns to be discovered in the table and some intriguing individual cases.

A visual inspection of the table suggests that the three public governance indicators may not be independent of each other: there is a clear clustering with three-quarters of the countries in just five categories:

Group 1—highly ranked on all three governance indicators—Australia, Denmark, Germany, Iceland, Ireland, New Zealand, Norway, Sweden, and UK (n=9).

Group 2—medium ranked on all three governance indicators—France, Italy, Jamaica, Lithuania, Poland, South Africa, Spain, United States (n=8).

Group 3—low ranked on all three governance indicators—Cambodia, Egypt, Lebanon, Nigeria, Tunisia (n=5).

Group 4—medium ranked on two governance indicators but ranked as low on 'voice and accountability'—Bahrain, Oman, Qatar, Saudi Arabia, and Turkey (n=5).

Group 5—medium ranked on 'government effectiveness' but ranked as low on the other two governance indicators—China, Kazakhstan, Russian Federation, and Vietnam (n=4).

We can observe that half of the countries were in groups 1–3. It is possible, therefore, that the three governance indicators are not independent of each other. In other words, a country that scored a high rank on one of the three indicators often scored a high rank on the other two indicators; a country ranking low on one often ranks low on the other two, and so on.

Furthermore, referring back to the study that we briefly covered in Chapter 3, which included data on effectiveness, budgetary transparency, and civil society strength (Hertie School of Governance 2013), it is clear that there was some overlap in terms of the countries mentioned there. We noted the countries with high scores on effectiveness and budgetary transparency included New Zealand, Norway, Sweden, and UK. We also noted that Lebanon was rated low on government effectiveness and budget. This is not a scientific corroboration of the categorization in Table 5.2 by any means, but it lends some credence to the groupings.

If the three indicators are not independent of each other, it could be that one dimension of public governance causes or influences another one. Or perhaps there is some other governance variable that influences all three of the indicators so they appear to be interdependent? For example, it may be that the power of citizens and civil society (as indicated by 'voice and accountability') puts pressure on to government to be effective and that, in turn, effective governments are better at managing policies? Of course, this is all speculation based on the tabular analysis.

There are some countries that appear to be all by themselves in the table. The case of Singapore is very interesting. It appears relatively unusual because it is ranked as high on 'government effectiveness' and 'regulatory quality' but is ranked low on 'voice and accountability.' Referring back to a speculation above, this would suggest that the power of citizens and civil society had not been the cause of government effectiveness and regulatory quality—unless Singapore is an exception to the rule. However we make sense of the table, we can note that Singapore is very different in its public governance profile from the Nordic and other countries we have put into group 1.

The Gulf States

It is interesting that group 4 in Table 5.2 is comprised mainly of four Gulf states—Bahrain, Oman, Qatar, and Saudi Arabia. This group appears to have reputations for "middling" government effectiveness and regulatory quality and a reputation for a poor performance on voice and accountability. The other two Gulf states—the United Arab Emirates and Kuwait—were also ranked low on 'voice and accountability'.

Arguably, based on World Bank ideas in the World Development Report 1997 and the OECD strategic state framework, the Gulf states, with the exception of the United Arab Emirates, should be working at capability building in terms of the effectiveness of their governance and should be seeking to develop appropriate ways to engage with their citizens and civil society (including business). Since they are all rated as middling in terms of regulatory quality, they should all be capability building in terms of their regulation of the private sector.

From the point of view of explaining government performance, the key thing to note from Table 5.2 is that, based on reputation, the most effective government is considered to be the United Arab Emirates; then comes Bahrain, Oman, Qatar, and Saudi Arabia; and Kuwait is perceived as the worst of the Gulf states for government effectiveness (Figure 5.1). Of course, this takes no account of either circumstances or of the assistance and support governments may get by working in partnerships and engaging citizens and civil society in national development efforts.

While the year-to-year changes in the World Governance Indicators tend to be small, looking at the changes over a 10 or more year period might suggest that the six Gulf states cannot be lumped together easily. For example, taking the period 2000 to 2014, the public governance reputation of Bahrain changed very little in terms of government effectiveness, regulatory quality, and voice and accountability. Saudi Arabia's reputation changed in only one dimension: there was a big increase in government effectiveness. Its percentile ranking went from 46.2 percentile in 2000 to 62.0 percentile in 2014 (see Table 5.1). The United Arab Emirates percentile ranking changed a lot in respect of voice and accountability—down from a low 31.7 percentile ranking in 2000 to an even lower 19.2 percentile ranking in 2014. Two countries—Kuwait and Oman—can be lumped together, with them having a big increase in regulatory quality and a decrease in voice and accountability. Kuwait had a biggish increase in government effectiveness and regulatory

Government Effectiveness - World Governance Indicator (2014)

1: United Arab Emirates

2: Bahrain, Oman, Qatar, and Saudi Arabia

3: Kuwait

Figure 5.1 The Gulf States' League Table of Government Effectiveness (Perceptions)

quality (as measured by percentile ranking) and a decrease in voice and accountability. These negative changes in voice and accountability for four of the countries may in part explain why all six countries in 2014 were very definitely in the low category for voice and accountability (that is, below the 50th percentile).

The substantial improvement in the perceptions of Saudi Arabia and Qatar's government effectiveness between 2000 and 2014 is of great interest given the themes of this book. Table 5.3 presents the government effectiveness indicators for the six countries, on an annual basis, between 1996 and 2014. The table displays the perception data in the form of units of a standard normal distribution varying from –2.5 to 2.5. In looking at the fluctuations from year to year, we are assuming a difference in estimates of 0.5 to 0.7 from one year to the next is not very much.

Looking at Table 5.3, it is tempting to suggest that three of the countries had estimates that changed very little over the period 2000 to 2014. These were Bahrain, Kuwait, and Oman. But the estimates for Qatar and the United Arab Emirates appeared a little higher in the period after 2008 than in the period between 2000 and 2008. On a much smaller scale, perceptions of Saudi Arabia's government effectiveness appeared to change after 2009, with negative estimates dominating the period before and zero or positive estimates dominating the period afterwards.

At first sight, all of these governments—all six of them—were engaged in serious experiments with long-term strategic thinking and strategic planning

Table 5.3 Government Effectiveness Estimate—World Governance Indicator

Year	Bahrain	Kuwait	Oman	Qatar	Saudi Arabia	United Arab Emirates
1996	0.6	0.1	0.6	0.5	–0.3	0.6
1998	0.6	–0.1	0.5	0.4	–0.2	0.8
2000	0.6	–0.1	0.3	0.4	–0.2	0.8
2002	0.5	0.1	0.4	0.5	–0.3	0.8
2003	0.5	0.1	0.5	0.5	–0.3	0.6
2004	0.6	0.1	0.5	0.5	–0.4	0.8
2005	0.4	0.2	0.3	0.4	–0.4	0.8
2006	0.4	0.2	0.3	0.6	–0.2	0.9
2007	0.4	0.1	0.4	0.4	–0.1	0.9
2008	0.4	0.0	0.4	0.6	–0.1	0.9
2009	0.5	0.2	0.4	1.0	–0.1	1.0
2010	0.5	0.2	0.4	0.9	0.0	0.9
2011	0.5	0.0	0.3	0.8	–0.3	1.1
2012	0.5	–0.1	0.3	0.9	0.0	1.1
2013	0.6	–0.1	0.2	1.1	0.1	1.2
2014	0.6	–0.1	0.3	1.0	0.2	1.5

Source: World Bank (data accessed 10 November 2015)

over the years between 1995 and 2010. Could this explain the changes in estimates of government effectiveness? For example, Qatar launched a long-term vision statement in 2008. The United Arab Emirates introduced its first government strategic plan in 2007 and a vision statement and its second government strategic plan in 2010. Saudi Arabia developed a long-term vision and long-term strategy in 2004 after a strategy event in 2002. Its Ninth Development Plan was launched in 2010, which was the second of the five-year Development Plans to be launched on the basis that their function was to deliver the country's long-term vision and long-term strategy. Assuming that these strategic management developments might be linked to changes in the reputations of government effectiveness, the specific timings of changes in estimates in Table 5.3 might need to be seen as affected by time lags in the real effects of the initiatives or time lags in awareness of these initiatives which affected reputational effects. There still would need to be explanations for why similar changes were not occurring in the estimates of Oman (which had a long-term vision launched in 1995, Bahrain (long-term vision launched in 2008) and Kuwait (long-term vision launched in 2010). It would be speculative to suggest that Oman had already begun its experiment with long-term visions and their use to steer five-year developments back in 1995, which might explain the steady but positive value of the estimate between 2000 and 2014. Perhaps Kuwait's difficulties in implementation of its long-term vision in the period 2010 to 2012 explained the lack of change in its estimates of government effectiveness? Perhaps, likewise, Bahrain may have launched a long-term vision in 2008, but perhaps it was not executed to have enough impact? These are, of course, speculations. More detail of these initiatives will be provided in the next chapter.

Global Competitiveness Rankings

The Global Competitiveness rankings are fairly well-known and seem an obvious tool for governments when benchmarking economic development (Schwab 2015). They are based on the aggregation of a lot of evaluations covering various aspects that are thought to be important for productivity and competitiveness in global markets. Inevitably, there could be all sorts of questions raised about construct validity and the reliability of the process of making judgments. That said, many of the countries did well in these rankings during recent years. This was explicitly recognized in the following remarks (Schwab 2015, 22):

> There are stark differences in competitiveness across the Middle East and North Africa region. Led by Qatar (14th), the United Arab Emirates (17th), Saudi Arabia (25th), and Bahrain (39th), many Gulf Cooperation Council (GCC) countries are already fairly competitive and can build on past progress to improve further.

Table 5.4 shows that the Global Competitiveness ranking can fluctuate a lot from year to year.

The 2014–15 rankings placed United Arab Emirates and Qatar in the highest positions, which was more or less the same in the 2015–16 rankings, but the positions of the remaining four looked significantly different. Saudi Arabia was in the middle whereas Kuwait, Bahrain, and Oman seemed to form a lower ranked grouping together. With improvements in the rankings of Kuwait and Bahrain, and with a very big drop in the ranking of Oman, the league table groupings for 2015–16 can be plausibly presented shown as in Figure 5.2.

Table 5.4 Government Effectiveness (World Bank) and the Global Competitiveness Rankings 2015–16

Country	Government Effectiveness (Category based on percentile rank)	Global Competiveness Index (Score) 2015–16 (N = 140)	Global Competitiveness Ranking 2015–16 (N = 140)	Global Competitiveness Ranking 2014–15 (N = 144)
United Arab Emirates	High	5.24	17	12
Bahrain	Medium	4.52	39	44
Oman	Medium	4.25	62	46
Qatar	Medium	5.30	14	16
Saudi Arabia	Medium	5.07	25	24
Kuwait	Low	4.59	34	40

Source: Schwab (2015, xv).

The Global Competitiveness Rankings 2015–16 (World Economic Forum, Geneva)

1: Qatar, United Arab Emirates

2: Bahrain, Kuwait, and Saudi Arabia

3: Oman

Figure 5.2 The Gulf States' League Table of Global Competitiveness Rankings 2015–16

As we remarked above, there is some evidence to suggest the World Governance Indicator for Government Effectiveness correlates with competitiveness using a large sample of countries. At face value, the grouping of the Gulf states by government effectiveness (Figure 5.1) has some correspondence to their grouping based on global competitiveness ranking. But it is far from perfect correspondence. This is perhaps predictable. The World Bank data of (perceptions of) government effectiveness for many different countries seems to suggest little change or change only slowly over a period of ten to fifteen years. But we can see from Table 5.3 that there can be substantial movements in the global competitiveness rankings comparing one year with the previous year. In some cases, the volatility is caused by data availability. For example, the United Arab Emirate dropped in rank because an indicator on tertiary education became available and caused the assessment of higher education and training to be less satisfactory. Assuming that not all of the volatility is down to data availability changes, global competitiveness must require explanation using causal variables that include at least some volatile independent variables. If government effectiveness changes only slowly, and, as we have just noted, this seems to be the implication of the World Bank perception data on government effectiveness, then it is unlikely that it will explain all or nearly all the variation in the global competitiveness of an economy.

Why did Oman come so low in the 2015–16 rankings? Why do Qatar and the United Arab Emirates do so well in these rankings?

Oman did not score well on a component of the index known as "innovation and sophistication factors" even though it did quite well on "basic requirements." Its score on innovation was very poor, and Oman was ranked 103rd out of 140. For the components of basic requirements it scored well on most things (its institutions, infrastructure, and macroeconomic environment) but very poorly on "health and primary education." There were also some weak scores on an efficiency component of the ranking, especially its 89th ranking on labour market efficiency and its 88th ranking on higher education and training. If there was a theme in these areas of weakness, it was probably human resource-related (investment in people through health provision and schooling and through higher education and training) and human resource allocation (through poor labour market efficiency). Presumably, innovation depends on investment in people as well as R&D investment.

Qatar was rated very positively on basic requirements for competitiveness (especially its institutions and its macroeconomic environment) and its business sophistication and innovation. The few blemishes on its profile were for domestic market size and (less so) for its technological readiness (for example, low rate of fixed broadband internet subscriptions). Some of the positive rating of Qatar was due to its oil resources (Schwab 2015, 12):

Qatar leads the Middle East and North Africa region at 14th position. The country's main strength is its stable macroeconomic environment

(2nd), which is driven by public budget surpluses and low government debt—the result of high windfall revenues from energy exports. However, the recent decline in the price of oil and gas, which is not captured in this year's edition because of the time lag in the data, may undermine the country's performance in future.

In fact, as we note in the next chapter, Qatar experienced a 50 percent drop in its foreign trade surplus in the year to September 2015. While there were predictions that there would be a small government deficit, the Qatar government still wanted to carry on investing in economic development projects and did not want to cut its provision of subsidies (Staff Writer 2015).

United Arab Emirates, like the case of Qatar, was very positively rated in respect of the basic requirements for competitiveness, with the exception of health and primary education, where it was ranked 38th. It was also relatively poor in terms of higher education and training (37th out of 140), market size, and technological readiness. And it was only 26th on innovation (even though it is classified as an innovation-driven economy in the rankings publication). So, again it might be said that investment in human resources via health provision, schooling, and universities and training was a relative weakness that it shared with Oman, even though overall it did well in these judgments about global competitiveness.

In terms of governance of national development these findings about how the Gulf states are perceived in terms on global competitiveness, we can make a couple of comments based on the World Bank ideas about government strategy. First, if we assume that several of the Gulf states are middling in terms of their institutional capabilities, then they should still be focusing on providing basic public services well, such as health, primary education, transports and roads, and ensuring the rule of law is well administered to provide a basic framework for economic activity. But if they are middling in terms of their institutional capabilities, they may well be appropriately intervening more actively in markets to foster economic growth and developing more sophistication in regulating business activity.

In which case, relatively poor ratings of health and primary education need attention, as does the possible need for more active intervention to encourage innovation in the business sector.

Summary

The Gulf states appear to vary substantially in their government effectiveness and the global competitiveness of their economies. For example, the United Arab Emirates and Kuwait are perceived quite differently from each other in terms of government effectiveness, with United Arab Emirates ranked very high, and Kuwait ranked very low. The league table positions change quite a bit when we turn to global competitiveness. The United Arab Emirates remains very highly ranked for competitiveness, but so is Qatar. The United Arab Emirates is also seen as an innovation-driven economy. In contrast, in the 2015–16 rankings, Oman was much lower ranked than the other countries of the Gulf Cooperation Council. At least in terms of these two things—public governance and global competitiveness, Saudi Arabia and Bahrain feature as middle of the road in the comparisons with the other Gulf Cooperation Council countries.

What we also learn in this chapter is that the reputation of the Gulf states tended to worsen over the period 2000 to 2014 in relation to a World Governance Indicator known as "voice and accountability." This is based on deteriorating scores for the United Arab Emirates, Qatar, Kuwait, and Oman. In 2014 all six were in the low category for voice and accountability, which means below the 50th percentile.

The government effectiveness of three of the Gulf states appears to be perceived more favourably over time. The estimates for Qatar and for the United Arab Emirates appeared a little higher in the period after 2008 than in the period between 2000 and 2008. Maybe less noticeably, Saudi Arabia's government effectiveness appeared to change around 2009, with negative estimates of government effectiveness dominating the period before and zero or positive estimates dominating the period afterwards. In this chapter we raised the possibility that changes in perceived government effectiveness might be linked to government initiatives involving long-term strategic thinking and strategic planning over the years between 1995 and 2010. We asked: Could this explain the changes in estimates of government effectiveness? The following chapter explores in greater detail the nature, context, and some results of the shift to strategic thinking and planning.

Reference List

Hertie School of Governance (2013) *The Governance Report 2013*. Oxford: Oxford University Press.

Pinar, M. (2015) Measuring World Governance: Revisiting the Institutions Hypothesis, *Empirical Economics*, 48, 747–778.

Schwab, K. (editor) (2015) *The Global Competitiveness Report 2015–2016*. Geneva: World Economic Forum.

Staff Writer (2015) Qatar's Foreign Trade Surplus Halves to $3.3bn from Year Earlier. [online] [21 December 2015]. Available from: http://www.arabianbusiness. com/qatar-s-foreign-trade-surplus-halves—3-3bn-from-year-earlier-611059. html#.Vne_MYSWHQM

6 Becoming Visionary and Strategic

Introduction

The Omani government held a conference in Muscat in 1995 to create a long-term vision called "Oman 2020," and which was labeled the Vision for Oman's Economy. Saudi Arabia's Ministry of Economy and Planning organized a "Symposium on the Future Vision" in Riyadh in 2002, which produced conclusions that became the basis for the Long-Term Strategy 2025 and the Vision for the Saudi economy. In 2008 Qatar created its "National Vision for 2030" and Bahrain published its "Economic Vision for 2030". The United Arab Emirates had a cabinet meeting in February 2010 at the end of which was released "Vision 2021". Also in 2010, the Kuwait Supreme Council for Planning and Development (SCPD) launched the Kuwait Vision 2035 and the 2010–14 mid-term development plan. So all six countries had prepared and publicized long-term vision statements within the period 1995 to 2010. The Saudi Government launch of Saudi Vision 2030 in April 2016 confirmed the previous vision statements' strategic intent of diversifying economic activity, and thus moving the country away from being an oil-based economy to non-oil-based economy.

In this chapter we look at the vision statements and how they were to be delivered. We will also consider some preliminary evidence of the impact of planning. The summary at the end of the chapter offers a composite picture of the visionary and strategic pattern emerging mainly between 1995 and 2010 in the Gulf states.

Oman

Ahmed Macki, Oman's Minister of National Economy, claimed in 2008 that the Sultanate of Oman "has been transformed into a modern state with a stable and strongly growing economy" and that the "process of comprehensive all-embracing reforms and modernization is continuing apace" (Ministry of National Economy 2008, 11). He described the Oman economy as having been "a liberal and open economy for years . . . and integrated with the world economy" (Ministry of National Economy 2008, 11).

Peterson (2005) described Sultan of Oman Said b. Taymur Al Said (ruler from 1932 to 1970) as a neo-traditionalist. He (2005, 4) defines such a leader as trying "to preserve traditional society, values and goals, by enhancing or enlarging the capability to control the state." But his son, Sultan Qaboos bin Said, who became Sultan in 1970, is said by Peterson (2005) to have had an intention to modernize Oman. Early in his rule Qaboos promised that he would create a modern government and better lives for the people he ruled (Peterson 2005, 7):

> I promise you to dedicate myself to the speedy establishment of a modern government in no time . . My people, I shall work as promptly as possible to ensure a better life in a better future . . . My people and brothers, yesterday we were completely in the dark, but with the aid of God, tomorrow a new dawn will arise for Muscat and Oman and its people.

The central challenge for economic development was identified as reliance on oil (Ministry of National Economy 2008, 13–14):

> Through consecutive Five-Year development plans, Oman has achieved remarkable progress on both the economic and social fronts in a relatively short period of time. Nevertheless, after three decades of intensive development efforts, Oman still faces a host of challenges stemming mainly from the fact that the economy is reliance on oil which is a non-renewable dwindling resource subject to a high degree of price volatility. Recognizing this challenge, the Government has initiated a structural adjustment process aimed at laying down a solid foundation for a diversified economic base led by the private sector.

At this time, Oman was very new to being an oil-rich economy—oil had been discovered and exported only in 1967. A development strategy was established early in Qaboos's rule. This was the Socio-economic Strategy of 1975. It provided the framework for Five-Year Development Plans, which were implemented by the Development Council (which was created in 1975). The First Five-Year Development Plan (1976–80) was implemented against a background of a booming oil sector. It was, in part, focused on developing Oman's infrastructure (for example, power stations). The Second Five-Year Plan (1981–85) aimed at more development of the infrastructure and better living standards. The targets of the Third Five-Year Plan (1986–90) included maintaining living standards and improving basic public services (for example, health and education). But this plan was implemented against a serious fall in oil prices. The Fourth Five-Year Plan (1991–95) included targets in respect of investment, diversification of the economy, human resource development, and increasing Omani labour force participation,

In the summer of 1995 a conference was held in Muscat to consider the economy and look ahead 25 years—this was the "Vision Conference: Oman 2020". It was a planning event. The desired outcomes were higher growth and prosperity based on structural transformation—Oman would no longer depend on the oil sector and non-oil sources of national income (industry and services) would become more important than oil income. It was projected that crude oil would be 9 percent of GDP in 2020, as against just over 37 percent in 1995. At the same time, the non-oil sector of industry would deliver 29 percent of GDP in 2020 and the service sector would be nearly 50 percent of GDP in 2020. The planning involved looking at what had been achieved, identifying development challenges, and proposing policies and actions.

One of the notable proposals related to process. The Vision articulated a partnership model. It not only wanted an effective and competitive business sector, it also envisaged (Ministry of National Economy 2008, 18) "the consolidation of the mechanisms and institutions that will foster shared visions, strategies and policies between the private sector and the Government."

Oman adopted the Vision for Oman's Economy 2020 in 1995. It imagined a future of economic growth, led by the private sector, an economy successfully exporting to other countries, and a diversified economic structure in place of the oil-dominated economy of the last couple of decades. It was this Vision that guided the Fifth Five-Plan and subsequent ones.

A 2008 statement of its economic agenda was presented by the Government to the World Trade Organization as part of its trade policy review report (Oman 2008, 5):

> In the wise words of His Majesty, the economy is the main concern of the Sultanate of Oman, with the aim of improving the standard of living of the people, ensuring that they benefit from the fruits of development.

Successive Five Year Development Plans have been pursued towards self-sustained growth in a private sector-led, export-oriented economy with diversified sources of national income.

The long-term goals of Oman are laid down in "Oman Economic Vision 2020," where main policy areas are as follows:

- Development of human resources and upgrading Omani skills and competencies to keep abreast with the technological progress.
- Creation of a stable macroeconomic framework aimed at development of a private sector capable of the optimal use of human and natural resources of Oman.
- Encouraging the establishment of an effective and competitive private sector.
- Providing appropriate conditions for the realization of economic diversification.

- Enhancing the standard of living of the people, reduction of inequality among regions and among various income groups, and ensuring that the fruits of development are shared by all citizens.
- Preserving the past achievements and safeguarding and developing them.

The Fifth Five-Year Plan was considered to break new ground (Ministry of National Economy 2008, 19):

> The Fifth Five-Year Plan (1996–2000) was regarded as the beginning of a new era in development planning in the Sultanate. This Plan differs from the previous plans in many ways as it entailed a wider public and private sector participation, the use of sophisticated computerized macroeconomic modeling techniques, and planning Oman's development process within a regional and a global context.

Arguably, any five-year planning system by the state that achieves significant levels of engagement by non-governmental stakeholders is moving towards strategic planning and away from centralized state planning of a command and control variety. This argument rests on the ideas that the use of strategic planning by government can be defined as involving (i) selectivity and focus, and (ii) greater interaction with citizens and non-government stakeholders during a process of formulation of the plans. Since the remarks by the Ministry of National Economy included a suggestion that there had been wider public and private participation, this does hint at the new era in development planning being in part a turn to strategic planning by the state. The planning of the development process within a regional and global context also suggests changes to the planning that made it more like strategic planning: strategic planning tends to be very concerned with an examination of the situation in which strategic decisions are being made.

The intentions of the Fifth Five-Year Plan included: supporting a competitive private sector, economic diversification (to lessen dependence on oil), human resource development, increasing skills, and improving living standards of people in Oman. At the end of this plan period, Oman joined the World Trade Organization (in 2000).

During the Sixth Five-Year Plan (2001–05) a key development was the formation of the GCC Customs Union in 2003. The Sixth Five-Year Plan was the second for the period 1995 to 2020. It was meant to pursue higher per capita income, economic diversification, private sector development, and human resource development. All these themes were in keeping with the Vision for Oman's Economy 2020.

Naturally, investments in infrastructure do not provide an immediate return if it takes some time to make the investment, for example, the building of new modern docks and roads. But even 10 years after the adoption of the Vision for Oman's Economy 2020 in 1995, the Five-Year Plans were having no dramatic impact on the economy's dependence on oil. Two indicators seemed to go in the wrong direction: the oil sector as a percentage of GDP had risen from 38 to 48 percent and oil revenue as a percentage of total government revenue had gone up from 77 percent to 79 percent. There was a drop in oil export earnings as a percentage of total exports—down from 78.5 percent to 71.8 percent. So, in respect of the intention to diversify the economy away from the oil sector, the early evidence, part way through the period to 2020, was that most of the transformations would have to occur in the latter period. See Table 6.1 for data on these matters published by Oman's Ministry of National Economy.

The explanation for these adverse trends could partly involve oil price movements. If oil prices go up a lot and the costs of producing the oil rise more slowly, then oil rent, as measured by the World Bank, rises. Because a large proportion of government revenue was oil revenue, a sharp rise in oil prices (assuming no matching rise in cost of production) can generate a budget surplus for the government. And oil price movements can also explain substantial developments in the economy, as is shown by these comments to the World Trade Organization in 2008 (Oman 2008, 6):

> The share of industry has increased from 11.5% of GDP in 2002 to 14.2% in 2006. The share of services sector, however, declined from 46.8% in 2002 to 37.7% in 2006. It is worth noting that the share of industry and services would have been higher but for the steep rise in oil prices between 2002 and 2006.

In 2008, it appears that the Oman government felt that the main evidence of success in diversification was to be found in export figures (Oman 2008, 6): "The progress and success of diversification is borne by the fact that the share of non-oil and non-gas exports to total exports of Oman increased from 6.8% in 2003 to 9.8% in 2006."

Table 6.1 Oman and its Diversification Strategy

Year	GDP per capita (US$)	Oil sector (% of GDP)	Oil Export Earnings (% of Total Exports)	Oil Revenue as % of Government Revenue
1970	460	68	Not available	Not available
1975	2,539	67	99.8	96%
1980	5,956	61	96.1	92%
1985	7,327	50	93.2	85%
1990	7,191	48	91.7	85%
1995	6,477	38	78.5	77%
2000	8,271	49	78.7	78%
2005	12,325	48	71.8	79%

Source: Ministry of National Economy, Oman (2008) pages 117, 119, and 120.

Obviously, the selection of the time period is quite crucial in judging the success of the diversification efforts. As Table 6.1 shows the oil sector share (as measured by percentage of GDP) fell a lot between 1975 and 1995, and this included periods of rising prices and periods in which prices fell sharply. From 1995 to the year 2000 the oil sector share of GDP increased substantially (up from 38 percent of GDP to 49 percent of GDP), and then it barely changed comparing 2005 to 2000. So, if we take 1995 as the baseline year, the size of oil sector looked bigger in both 2000 and 2005—arguably a very disappointing result for the Government of Oman. Likewise, if we look at government revenue and take 1995 as the baseline year, the government's dependence on oil revenue showed no sign of improvement whether we take 2000 or 2005. However, the diversification story does look different if we consider the trajectory of oil export earnings (as a percentage of total exports). In 1995 oil export earnings were 78.5 percent of total exports; after rising to 78.7 percent in 2000, this statistic fell to 71.8 percent in 2005. So, in terms of all three indicators shown in Table 6.1, the one really positive change was the share of oil exports in total exports between 2000 and 2005. Was this enough to say that diversification was progressing and planned action had been successful? Probably not, although it might be seen as hopeful in terms of further progress in the remaining years of the period to 2020.

In 2008 there was explicit recognition by Oman's government of continuing dependence on oil. Oil was seen as still the mainstay of Oman's economy. Despite the efforts at diversification, this continuing dependence explains the perceived need to invest in oil and gas production to counter a decline in production (Oman 2008, 12): "To shore up production, plans are being implemented to invest about US$13 billion in oil and gas over the next five years to achieve a 50% ultimate recovery of oil in place, tapping heavy oil fields (with higher costs of extraction), new discoveries etc."

In 2008, the Oman government was also conscious of the dangers to the economy of a drop in oil prices—and it knew it could not discount this risk completely. It remarked (Oman 2008, 12):

> The other risk is a sharp fall in oil prices, however improbable it may look now. A big drop in oil prices would be a serious setback, slowing down growth, generation of employment etc. With the rapid development of gas and the gas based industries and other diversification projects in the last decade, Oman is now expected to be far better prepared and resilient to withstand such oil shocks in future and surge ahead on her growth path.

The identification of a threat to the Oman economy if oil prices dropped proved to be right—we know this with hindsight.

The Ninth Five-Year Development Plan (2016–20) was the last in the series of development plans linked to "Oman Economic Vision 2020". Workshops for its preparation began in November 2014, just as volatility in oil prices had become a concern. According to reports at the time, it was aiming to deliver goals contained in Vision 2020, continue economic diversification, provide job opportunities for nationals, and provide a focus on the social dimension and on youth. The decline in the price of oil in late 2014 and early 2015 must have underlined the importance of economic diversification in the Ninth Five-Year Plan. This Ninth Five-Year Plan was also seen as a "gateway" to the new future vision of the Omani economy—which was "Oman 2040" (Oman Observer 2015b).

We noted above that the Fifth Five-Year Plan (1996–2000) was seen as an advance on previous ones because there was wider public and private sector participation in its preparation. There was also a claim that the Ninth Five-Year Plan (2016–20) was going to be special because of the involvement of citizens in its preparation, and this was presumably seen as important for what we might call the ownership of the Plan beyond government circles (Shaalan 2015):

> The quantum leap in this context is the involvement of citizens in the development of the ninth five-year plan, which will enable it to embody the aspirations and hopes of the Omani society through open meetings in all governorates to measure their aspirations and involving them in making the development plan of their areas, workshops for actor members and specialists who have the required expertise to contribute to the drafting of the plan, and through communicate via mail by investing energy and aspirations of the Omani young people through brainstorming on social networking sites which is data that gives confidence and vitality for government moves in the future.

Another interesting feature of the Ninth Five-Year Development Plan was the attention given by the work team preparing it to experience elsewhere in the world (Shaalan 2015):

> Sultanate aspires to have a leadership role in the region through the work team's dependence on studying leading development experiences in different countries and investing their expertise to build an Omani model that focuses on citizen and is consistent with the aspirations of the Sultanate to be one of the leading regional and global states. The work team of the plan studies several regional and international models to summarize the lessons learned and challenges they faced during the development of economic plans including the Economic Transformation Programme 2020 of Malaysia, the strategy of economic diversification of Singapore, development plans in the GCC states, plan for economic diversification in Chile, and the strategy of economic and social development of Brazil in 2025.

The starting point for Oman 2040 appears to have been in 2013. In early 2015 the main committee for Oman Vision 2040 met and discussed the first steps needed and the methodology required for preparing the strategy. Apparently, the committee believed that the Vision 2040 required a realistic and objective forecast. It also believed the Vision "should also receive consensus from all sectors of the society" (Oman Observer 2015a).

Work on Oman Vision 2040 involved learning about how other countries had pursued national development. For example, an event was held in 2015 that focused on how the Singapore Government had approached national development planning. This was organized by the General Secretariat at Oman's Supreme Council for Planning and was attended by "technical committee members of Oman vision 2040, and a number of decision makers, economists, businessmen and investors" (Al Nasseri 2015). Peter Ho, an adviser to the Singaporean Centre for Strategic Futures, told those attending the event about strategic planning in Singapore. It appears from his remarks that futures thinking had begun in the 1980s and that the Singapore Government had recently created an Office for Strategic Policies (2008) and an Office for Strategic Planning (2009).

Talal al Rahbi, Deputy Secretary General of the Oman Supreme Council for Planning, was quoted as passing the following comment on the same event (Al Nasseri 2015): "The world is changing continuously and many scenario plans emerge. We need to focus on implementing plans and learn from them." Presumably, he was implying that when the world is very dynamic then strategic planning for national development has to contend with a lot of novelty, which in turn presumably implies that governments cannot assume planned changes can be easily programmed—instead governments need to pay a lot of attention to implementation and need to be ready to learn from the experiences of implementation.

By the summer of 2015—specifically, at the end of July and beginning of August—the international oil price slumped to $50 a barrel, which can be compared with $115 a barrel in June 2014. Both the public and private sectors were reported to be operating hiring freezes. By November of 2015 the Omani finance ministry was releasing figures showing a budget deficit of 2.93 billion rials ($7.62 billion) for the first nine months of the year (Reuters 2015). By the last few months of 2015, the Omani government was raising a sovereign Islamic bond worth 250 million rials and seeking bank participation in a $1 billion sovereign loan. At the beginning of 2016 the Omani government planned to cut its budget deficit to 3.3 billion rials ($8.6 billion) through spending cuts and other means (Reuters 2016b). All this seemed to indicate that it is one thing to wish for economic diversification to reduce dependence on oil, but delivering this diversification is hard to do. As the financial problems increased in 2015 and 2016, the case for economic diversification in the national development strategy was being made abundantly clear. The urgency of spurring the non-oil sectors of industry was also abundantly clear. In February 2016 it was announced that the Oman government was hoping to develop an industrial strategy with the help of the United Nations Industrial Development Organization (Townsend 2016).

Saudi Arabia

National development planning began slightly earlier in Saudi Arabia than in Oman. The first of a series of five-year plans began in 1970. But a significant step in strategic planning terms was the creation of the Long-Term Strategy 2025. The Long-Term Strategy 2025 might be said to have its origins in Royal Consent, in July 1998, to the Ministry of Economy and Planning organizing a Symposium on the "Future Vision for the Saudi Economy." The Symposium took place in Riyadh in late 2002. The Long-Term Strategy 2025 followed on from that.

At the time, some of the key points in understanding the Long-Term Strategy 2025 concerned the changing thinking on the priorities of development and on the planning processes. First, there was a perception that earlier rounds of five-year plans had concentrated on government-led development of the infrastructure and projects such as ones in in health, education, and transport. Now the focus was to be on economic growth led by the private sector: the private sector was now to be "the main engine of growth". So, government would be encouraging and enabling the private sector. Second, in terms of planning processes, the thinking was now that government required a long-term perspective. Hence, the government had created the Long-Term Strategy 2025. The four five-year plans from 2005 to 2025 would be guided by the Long-Term Strategy; each five-year plan would be just one in the sequence of four aimed at delivering the aspirations of the Long-Term Strategy. These aspirations were encapsulated in a long-term vision statement:

> By the will of Allah, the Saudi economy in 2025 will be a more diversified, prosperous, private-sector driven economy, providing rewarding job opportunities, quality education, excellent health care and necessary skills to ensure the well-being of all citizens while safeguarding Islamic values and the Kingdom's cultural heritage.

As can be seen, the modernizing elements of the Vision were balanced by respect for tradition—as represented by Saudi Arabia's Islamic values and cultural heritage.

The third key point of new thinking in the Saudi approach to national development was the strong emphasis placed on effective implementation through following up and monitoring mechanisms. As it was explained in the Long-Term Strategy 2025:

> The third pillar [of the Strategy] consists of follow-up and implementation mechanisms to ensure that aspirations articulated in Vision 2025 are converted into reality on the ground. This pillar operationalizes the old adage: what gets measured gets done.

The Long-Term Strategy was supporting the use of clear targets and success indicators so that the five-year plans could be monitored effectively and also arguing for progress in the implementation of the Strategy to be reported to the Saudi cabinet by the Ministry of Economy and Planning and then, after approval was obtained, to be reported to the public.

The shift to long-termism plus the emphasis on implementation and follow-up appears to have been regarded as a change to a strategic planning methodology, as will be seen below when we consider some comments on the Eighth Development Plan by a government Minister.

From a pragmatic perspective, it is difficult to provide an a priori evaluation of the "rightness" of the thinking contained in any long-term strategy— since a pragmatist believes the "proof of the pudding is in the eating"—but we can note some of the thinking and arguments at the core of the Saudi Long-Term Strategy 2025.

First, what was the thinking about the challenges (that is, strategic issues) that might get in the way of Saudi Arabia realizing the long-term vision statement? The Strategy identified five challenges: employment generation; reduction of poverty; improvements in quality of life; sustainable development; and improvement in implementation and execution of public policies. The challenge of sustainable development was seen as requiring economic diversification, rationalization of use of water, balanced regional development, and better public finance management.

Second, what was the thinking about its situation? The authors of the Long-Term Strategy reported that a SWOT analysis of the Saudi economy had been undertaken. Among the strengths identified were the God-given resources of oil and gas—Saudi Arabia was described as having the largest oil reserves in the world and the fourth largest gas reserves. Other notable features of the Saudi situation were: Saudi citizens revering and nurturing Islamic and Arab traditions; political stability; available and plentiful Saudi investment funds; its location—Saudi Arabia can be seen as a bridge between east and west; and the youthful population (60 percent of people less than 18 years old).

Third, what was the strategic thinking on how sustainable development by means of economic diversification might be done? After all, it was said that diversification of the economy had been a key objective ever since the system of five-year planning had begun in 1970. What new moves could be made to deliver diversification? Furthermore, it should be noted that it was considered feasible even while growing average per capita income. The Strategy's target for average per capita income was for it to double in the period 2005–24. This was seen as a challenging but achievable target. It was assumed that this would be achieved while at the same time diversifying the economic base of Saudi Arabia (away from dependence on oil). This was to be made possible by means of public and private investments. The Strategy assumed that many Saudi investors were more interested than they had been in investment opportunities in Saudi Arabia. It was also assumed that there were some very good private businesses in Saudi Arabia and the private sector was capable of providing the leadership of economic development. Private investment was projected to sustain an annual growth rate of 10.3 percent over the 20-year period of the Long-Term Strategy. This was two and a half times higher than the projected growth rate of public investment. So, it was definitely imagined that the growth of the economy would be private sector-led. Arguably this was a plausible linking of an opportunity (availability and quantity of Saudi investment) and a challenge (economic diversification to bring about sustainable development).

The diversification strategy was expected to result in the oil sector growing at 4.4 percent per year over the period 2005–24, whereas industry would grow at more than double this annual rate (9.4 percent) and services would grow at 11.4 percent per year. In terms of exports, oil and gas exports were projected to grow at 2.5 percent a year, service exports at 7.3 percent and other exports (manufacturing, petrochemicals, oil refining, etc.) at 11.1 percent. These were average annual growth rates for the 20 years. The investment mentioned above was expected to be helping the growth rate of exports. So, oil would continue to grow but the rest of the economy would grow faster, and oil exports would grow but the services exports and other exports would grow faster. It was projected that other exports would constitute more than half of exports by the end of 2024, compared to only a fifth in 2004.

The explanation for the presence of poverty reduction in the list of challenges was explained as follows in the Long-Term Strategy:

> On November 20, 2002, HRH Crown Prince Abdullah, Deputy Premier, Commander of the National Guard and Chairman of the Supreme Economic Council, declared a war on poverty in the Kingdom. His visit to poor citizens' homes in Riyadh highlighted an aspect of Saudi development which no amount of statistics could have captured. In one swift move, dealing with poverty has become a high priority for Kingdom's development strategy. A country cannot enjoy prosperity till all its citizens are taken care of. This is not only consistent with our great Islamic traditions, but taking care of the needy is indeed a way of life for people in the Kingdom. Thus, the war on poverty strikes a chord with all Saudis and the Kingdom is determined to win this war."

The Eighth Development Plan, published by the Saudi Ministry of Economy and Planning (2004), was based on objectives and strategic bases approved by the Council of Ministers in 2004. It was intended to steer national development during the period 2005 to 2009. This plan was interesting in its implementation of what was seen by the Saudi planners as a strategic planning approach.

The preface to the Eighth Development Plan, written by Khalid Al Gosaibi, the Minister of Economy and Planning, claimed that the success of the state role in development could be seen in a range of areas: national welfare, provision of infrastructure, provision of public services, enhancement of living standards, and quality of life. He also claimed that joint government-private sector efforts were the source of achievements. "Indeed, public-private partnership has led to outstanding increases in output end expansion of production capacities in all economic sectors." We might comment here that the suggestion that the state had been successful in managing development and that national development achievements could be attributed to public-private cooperation would have been appreciated by the World Bank, based on their arguments and conclusions in the World Development Report 1997.

Khalid Al Gosaibi also suggested that the five-year planning system in Saudi Arabia was entering a new evolutionary stage, which was an evolution to a strategic planning approach:

> Indeed, the plan ushers in a new phase in the development process initiated over three decades ago. It constitutes the first link in a strategic path for the national economy, extending well into the next two decades and involved in four successive five-year development plans. This approach marks a step forward for the strategic planning methodology adopted by the kingdom.

While it might be regarded as largely symbolic, it is interesting that the Long-Term Strategy 2025 said that agencies that had been asked to produce operational plans as part of the five-year development system should be asked to rename these operational plans as strategic plans. However, perhaps the more substantial point was that there was a desire to see these plans aligned with the strategic long-term objectives for national development.

What the Saudis were doing was similar in some respects to the Omani approach adopted in 1995 of having a long-term vision and then using the five-year development plans to deliver it. In other words, the Saudi's Eighth Development Plan (and the next three) was conceived as a way of delivering the Long-Term Strategy 2025. The Minister stressed that the Eighth Development Plan had been prepared so that it was coherent with a number of other key documents and statements. The objectives and strategic principles approved by the Council of Ministers Resolution 175 in 2004 were the basis for the development planning. In addition, the Eighth Development Plan was influenced by a speech made by the Saudi King in a session of the Shourah Council and also by a concept paper on higher education written by the King. The conclusions and recommendations of the 2002 Symposium on the Future Vision, which was organized by the Ministry of Economy and Planning, were taken into account in preparing the development plan, as were the resolutions of the Shourah Council on development plans and plan implementation. Finally, it was suggested that the Eighth Development Plan was aligned to various other strategies, including the Strategy on Improved Living Conditions of All Citizens, the Privatization Strategy, the National Spatial Strategy, and the Manpower Development Strategy.

The key priorities of the Eighth Development Plan included: (i) improving living standards, (ii) improving quality of life, (iii) providing job opportunities to all Saudi citizens, (iv) expansion of education, training, health and social services, (v) expansion of science, (vi) and fostering initiative and creativity generally. In relation to the economy, the plan identified the following important priorities: (i) diversification of the economic base, (ii) improving productivity, and (iii) increasing the competitiveness of the national economy. Priorities for industrial development were: strategic manufacturing industries; the natural gas industry; mining; tourism; and information technology.

To all these priorities we can note the attention the development plan gave to the importance of increased participation of women in the economy, including employment opportunities.

Khalid Al Gosaibi, the Minister of Economy and Planning Saudi Arabia from 2003 until 2011 framed what Saudi Arabia was doing as modernization. Saudi Arabia was seeking to increase economic transformation and modernization at the same time that it wished to pursue economic growth, diversification of the economy, and balanced development across all the regions of the country.

The Minister of Economy and Planning acknowledged that it was results that mattered, and that good intentions were not enough. He offered the view that the impact of the Eighth Development Plan would depend on the "determination and resolve with which implementation is pursued."

The Eighth Development Plan was a huge document, running to 34 chapters and nearly 700 pages. It had 12 Objectives and 21 strategic bases, all of which had been approved by the Council of Ministers, as communicated in Decree 175 (in 2004). Table 6.2 provides five examples each of the objectives and strategic bases approved by the Council of Ministers in 2004 for the Eighth Development Plan.

Table 6.2 Objectives and Strategic Bases of the Eighth Development Plan

	Number	*Wording*
Objectives	5	To diversify the economic base with due emphasis on promising areas such as manufacturing industries, particularly industries that make intensive use of energy, and its derivatives, as well as mining, tourism and information technology industries.
	7	To increase private sector's participation in economic and social development.
	10	To conserve and develop water resources and ensure their rational utilization.
	11	To protect the environment and develop suitable systems in the context of sustainable development.
	3	To raise the standard of living, improve the quality of life and provide job opportunities to citizens, by accelerating the development process, increasing the rates of economic growth, and ensuring enhancement of the quantity and quality of education, health and social services.

(Continued)

Table 6.2 (Continued)

	Number	Wording
Strategic Bases	Ninth	Continue efforts to maintain a climate conducive to enhancing private sector participation in economic and social development, while intensifying government initiatives to encourage private domestic and foreign investments and bolster competitiveness of domestic products.
	First	Increase the share of Saudi manpower in total employment in various sectors, pay attention to upgrading their efficiency and productivity through training and re-training, and continue to substitute Saudi manpower for non-Saudis.
	Twentieth	Sustain care for environmental protection, promote environmental regulations, protect and develop wildlife, and conserve natural resources and rationalize their utilization.
	Fourth	Take care of the needy groups of citizens and pay attention to management and reduction of poverty by concentrating on the economic policies and programmes that lead to higher economic growth, along with achieving balanced development of all regions in the Kingdom.
	Second	Place emphasis on the welfare of women, upgrade their capabilities and remove the constraints that impede their participation in development activities, in line with the Islamic values and teachings.

The Ministry of Economy and Planning (2004) suggested that the Eighth Development Plan was innovative in its methodology, as compared to previous five-year plans. In essence, the methodology changed, it can be argued, to improve implementation and monitoring and evaluation. The Ministry had drafted more precise targets, which should have made monitoring and evaluation more effective. The implementation was planned: implementation schedules and responsibilities of implementation agencies were determined.

A Ninth Development Plan (2010–14) followed the Eighth. A new Minister of Planning and Economy Mohammad Al Jasser was appointed in December 2011, and who stayed in that role until April 2015, after the period of the Ninth Development Plan.

The Ninth Development Plan (2010–14) had five key themes (Ministry of Economy and Planning 2009). The first was improving the citizens' standard of living and quality of life; and this was linked to the real income of citizens, the services offered to them, eliminating poverty, and price stability. The second theme was concerned with the national labour force, which in the plan was connected to the national labour force participation rates, developing skills and capabilities, job opportunities, and increasing the share of nationals in the labour market. The third theme was balanced regional development. The fourth theme was concerned with (i) diversification to bring about a bigger contribution of non-oil sectors to GDP and to exports, (ii) increasing the participation of the private sector in the economy, and (iii) developing the knowledge economy. The fifth theme was concerned with the competitiveness of the national economy. This set of themes was largely similar to the key priorities of the Eighth Development Plan.

In terms of what were called "major implementation mechanisms," the Ninth Development Plan emphasized partnership between the public and private sectors, and speeding up privatization processes. It also affirmed the importance of implementation mechanisms and the evaluation of implementation policies in the Plan. A lot more implementation mechanisms were listed, including the following one on women (Ministry of Economy and Planning 2009 20): "To promote the effective participation of Saudi women in the Kingdom's development."

Towards the end of the Ninth Development Plan (2010–14), the Ministry of Economy and Planning published its assessment of evidence on the progress made in relation to the Development Plans. It is important here to note that the Ninth Development Plan continued to prioritize economic diversification and support for the private sector spearheading economic development.

Clear success was claimed in respect of diversification (Ministry of Economy and Labour 2014, 37–38):

> For a long time, economic development in the Kingdom was marked by the major role played by the oil sector in generating GDP and financing government investments geared at establishing the infrastructure and providing public services. Therefore, the successive development plans have persistently focused on diversification of economic base and boosting the private sector's role in the economy. Significant accomplishments were made in this area reflected in the high growth rates of non-oil sectors to which the private sector contributes a large share. Non-oil GDP, at 1999 constant prices, increased at an average annual rate of 6% over the period 1389/90–1434/35H (1969–2013G), a thirteen-fold increase, which demonstrates the success of the diversification policy.

In fact, the Ministry presented data on the non-oil private sector GDP at 1999 constant prices and this indicated a strong growth of contribution by the non-oil private sector to the national GDP figure during the Seventh, Eighth, and Ninth Development Plans. This sector went from about a half of the real GDP in 1999 to approximately two-thirds of GDP in 2013. The non-oil private sector's proportional share of approximately two-thirds for 2013 was confirmed by the Ministry's reported change in the share of the non-oil sector in real GDP at constant prices (Ministry of Economy and Planning 2014, 38): "its share increased from 34.7% in 1389/90H (1969G) to 65.9% in 1434/35H (2013G)." So it took 30 years for the share to go from a third to a half and only half that time to go from a half to two-thirds—the contribution to the economy of the non-oil private sector was expanding more quickly under the Seventh, Eighth, and Ninth Development Plans.

The Ministry's evidence suggested substantial progress in growing the private sector share of GDP between 1994 and 2004, and even faster progress between 2004 and 2009 (which was the period of the Eighth Development Plan). During the four-year period 2010–13 (most of the Ninth Development Plan period) the private sector share of GDP barely changed, and the slight change that did occur was downwards in 2011 and then upwards in 2013. The trend in the value of private sector gross fixed capital formation (that is, private investment) at current prices showed a steep rise in the 2004–09 period, which was during the Eighth Development Plan. The rise in private investment after these years also at first sight appeared to be at a fast rate. See Table 6.3.

One difficulty in making sense of the meaning of Table 6.3 is the fact that the private investment figures shown in column 4 are at current prices and it is known that both the GDP at current prices and the population were increasing. So, does this table give a correct impression of the relative of importance private investment? Our answer is maybe not if the importance is judged in relative terms and is based on a comparison to the quantity of public sector investment. In 2013 private investment was 53.2 percent of gross fixed capital formation. But the ratio of government investment to private investment seemed much higher in the years 2009 to 2013 than it

Table 6.3 Private Sector Share of Real GDP and Private Investments in Saudi Arabia

Year	(1) GDP at 1999 Constant Prices (Billion Saudi Riyals)	(2) GDP per capita at current prices (Saudi Riyals Thousand)	(3) Private Sector Share of Real GDP (%)	(4) Private sector gross fixed capital formation at current prices (Billion Saudi Riyals)
1994	547.8	28.4	46.9	60.9
1999	594.0	30.2	50.4	92.1
2004	741.3	43.0	53.9	138.6
2009	983.2	60.4	63.8	247.3
2010	1056.6	71.7	65.2	264.0
2011	1147.5	88.5	64.7	284.7
2012	1214.1	91.3	64.8	317.0
2013	1262.8	93.6	65.9	342.7

Source: Ministry of Economy and Planning (2014) Achievements of the Development Plans (Facts and Figures). Thirty-First Issue.

Note: Data taken from Figure 1.1, page 24; Figure 1.3, page 37; Figure 2.1, page 72 and Figure 2.2, page 75.

did in the years 1994 to 2004—government investment had become more important as a share of investment. This relative decline of private investment occurred after it had become a key target of the new Saudi Long-Term Strategy 2025 to achieve more private sector contribution to economic development.

The Ministry's 2014 assessment was less clear on other matters than it was on economic diversification and the increased importance of the non-oil private sector contribution to GDP. For example, the aspiration to high living standards is mentioned but no tables of data are provided on it. Another example is the scarcity of reference to environmental protection, conservation, or improvement. There is reference to environmental conservation and the General Environmental Law, which was passed following a Resolution by the Council of Ministers in 2001, and adherence to international environmental standards. There is also mention of spending on environmental projects for the development of water resources, oil and gas, and acceptance of the need to raise awareness in civil society and also to guard against negative effects of environmental pollution. But the assessment does not present data on environmental performance indicators and there are no conclusions on whether environmental problems are getting worse or better.

We turn to a specific aspiration of recent Development Plans, which is to see greater participation of women in Saudi's national development. This was articulated in both the Eighth and Ninth Development Plans. It was referred to in the 2014 assessment by the Ministry of Economy and Planning. However, its assessment did not provide useful data on the Development Plans' outcomes. For example, the assessment noted that there had been a Royal Decree and a Council of Ministers' Resolution on increasing women work opportunities, and it was noted that the Ministry had begun an initiative on women and work in the private sector. The Ministry provided some information on female participation in the Saudi labour force—it is reported that participation is up from 5.4 percent in 1969 to 12.9 percent in 2012. But how had the participation rate changed since, say, 2004, or 2009, and how much of the change could be attributed to the Development Plans? This is not clear. So, while the Ministry reported on the action taken to increase the participation of women in development, there appeared to be no monitoring and evaluation of the consequences of the Ninth Development Plan as such.

Saudi Arabia in 2016—Designing Governance Based on Strategic-State Capabilities

In 2016 Saudi Arabia produced a new vision statement for the development of Saudi Arabia, Vision 2030. This was under a new monarch, King Salman bin Abdulaziz Al Saud, and a new Chairman of the Council of Economic and Development Affairs, Mohammad bin Salman bin Abdulaziz Al Saud. Adel Fakeih had been appointed the Minister of Economy and Planning in April 2015.

In key respects the Saudi vision remained the same: to pursue economic diversification, to move away from dependence on oil (which made the country vulnerable to price volatility in external markets), to see the private sector grow in terms of its contribution to the economy, and to create a future of opportunity for the young men and women of the country. (One fact disclosed in the vision statement—which was that the private sector currently contributed less than 40 percent of GDP—suggested either that a lot of the earlier progress between 1994 and 2013 had been abruptly reversed, or that there was some problem with the monitoring data.) The Chairman of the Council of Economic and Development Affairs summed up a lot of this as follows (Kingdom of Saudi Arabia 2016, 7):

> We commit ourselves to providing world-class government services which effectively and efficiently meet the needs of our citizens. Together we will continue building a better country, fulfilling our dream of prosperity and unlocking the talent, potential, and dedication of our young men and women. We will not allow our country ever to be at the mercy of a commodity price volatility or external markets.

The vision statement also had social and environmental dimensions. It affirmed that the happiness and fulfillment of citizens was important to the national Saudi leaders. It expressed a desire to promote culture and entertainment to meet the aspirations of citizens and to promote sport in the interests of healthy and balanced lifestyles. The desire for greater participation of women was made clear (Kingdom of Saudi Arabia 2016, 37): "With over 50 percent of our university graduates being female, we will continue to develop their talents, invest in their productive capabilities and enable them to strengthen their future and contribute to the development of our society and economy." In relation to the environment, the vision said that Saudi Arabia would seek to reduce pollution, counter desertification, manage and recycle waste, and manage consumption of water.

The Chairman outlined an approach to the process of development that we think suggested continuity with the Long-Term Strategy of 2004: development to be guided by a vision, to be long-term thinkers in regards to national development, partnerships with the private sector, seeking active cooperation and responsibility from Saudi nationals, and paying attention to what we would categorize as the qualities and capabilities of modern governance, including capabilities focused on implementation and monitoring and accountability. There was even a hint of government receptivity to learning in the Chairman's statement that the government would welcome ideas on how to improve (Kingdom of Saudi Arabia 2016, 7):

> We will immediately adopt wide-ranging transparency and accountability reforms and, through the body set up to measure the performance of government agencies, hold them accountable for any shortcomings. We

will be transparent and open about our failures as well as our successes, and will welcome ideas on how to improve.

It seems that the Saudi government was trying to institutionalize its capabilities for performance management by setting up a Centre for Performance Management of Government Agencies. The message was that there would be a long-term effort to make sure all government activities and initiatives were accountable for their performance and transparent. And at the same time, the emphasis on strategic management capability and evidence-based decision-making were both being reinforced (which we mentioned in Chapter 1). The strategic capability of the centre of government was to be increased by setting up a strategic management office, with responsibility for coordinating government programmes and ensuring their alignment with the national Vision. It also had responsibility for seeing that the Vision was translated into sectoral strategies. The clout of this new strategic management office was being taken care of by placing it under the Council of Economic and Development Affairs. This institutional innovation suggests that the Saudi thinking in 2004 of developing the national development planning by absorbing strategic planning methodology had matured into an interest in building and reforming public governance based on strategic-state capabilities (OECD 2013).

The vision statement emphasized "engaging everyone". It is worth quoting this aspect of the vision in detail because it clarified the public governance system that was being designed or intended (Kingdom of Saudi Arabia 2016, 65):

> We will deepen communication channels between government agencies on one hand and citizens and the private sector on the other. We shall facilitate interactive, online and smart engagement methods and ways to listen to citizens' views, and to hear all insights and perspectives. We will encourage government agencies to improve the quality of their services, and to meet the needs of every citizen. We want to give everyone the opportunity to have their say so that the government can serve them better and meet their aspirations.

This was a design intending both responsiveness and engagement between government and governed. In saying there was a desire to serve better and meet the aspiration of citizens, the vision was also a vision for a strategic and enabling state. This made one of catchphrases offered by the vision statement very appropriate; the catchphrase was: "an ambitious nation . . . responsibly enabled."

Qatar

Qatar's General Secretariat for Development Planning published the Qatar National Vision 2030 in 2008. According to this statement, the National

Vision defined national long-term outcomes that were in line with Qatari people's aspirations and culture. Like the Long-term Strategy 2025 of the Saudis, this Qatar vision statement identified five challenges:

1 Modernization and preservation of traditions
2 The needs of this generation and the needs of future generations
3 Managed growth and uncontrolled expansion
4 The size and the quality of the expatriate labour force and the selected path of development
5 Economic growth, social development, and environmental management

The vision statement suggested that it would be possible for Qatar to combine the old (family life, culture, values) and the new (modern work patterns, pressures of competitiveness) in a balanced way.

The vision statement envisaged development occurring along four dimensions: human (resource), social, economic, and environmental. The importance of the development of Qatari people was connected to the limits to hydrocarbon resources (General Secretariat for Development Planning 2008, 6):

> Hitherto, Qatar's progress has depended primarily on the exploitation of its oil and gas resources. But the country's hydrocarbon resource will eventually run out. Future economic success will increasingly depend on the ability of the Qatari people to deal with a new international order that is knowledge-based and extremely competitive. To meet the challenge, Qatar is establishing advanced educational and health systems, as well as increasing the effective participation of Qataris in the labor force.

The statement included a number of outcomes under the heading of social development, which was said to include maintaining strong cohesive families that in turn maintained moral and religious values. One of the social outcomes concerned women: "Enhance women's capacities and empower them to participate fully in the political and economic spheres, especially in decision-making roles".

The discussion of the economic development of Qatar included the proposition that development would need to balance the diversification of the economy and depletion of non-renewable hydrocarbon resources. Like Saudi Arabia, Qatar identified an important role for the private sector in achieving sustainable development. More was needed, according to the vision statement, to increase economic competitiveness and attract investment. The economic outcomes of development were spelled out as suitable economic diversification that reduced dependence on hydrocarbon industries and increased the role of the private sector. One of the ways in which competitiveness was to be maintained was through the pursuit of a knowledge-based economy, which was itself based on innovation, entrepreneurship, a world-class infrastructure, efficient public services, and government that is accountable. The essence of environmental development was formulated as managing things "such that there is harmony between economic growth, social development and environmental protection."

The General Secretariat for Development Planning was responsible for following up the vision statement with the production of a National Strategy, which would provide a framework for sector and enterprise strategies. It was intended that this strategy development be carried out using consultation and partnership with civil society, the private sector, ministries, and government agencies. The importance of public-private cooperation and partnerships was stressed. The aim of this engagement of stakeholders was to secure commitment to the vision.

Qatar's National Development Strategy (2011–16) was published in early 2011. It was based on Qatar's National Vision. The document noted how it had been produced (General Secretariat for Development Planning 2011, 3): "The Strategy builds on situational analyses, diagnostics, regional and international benchmarking and detailed strategies for each of 14 sectors." It was aligned to the Qatar National Vision 2030 goals and included in its intentions the development of a diversified economy. Tamim Bin Hamad Al-Thani, Heir Apparent and Head of the Supreme Oversight Committee for implementing the Qatar National Vision 2030, highlighted the consultation process that had been followed that had involved consultation of all segments of Qatari society in the preparation of the strategy (General Secretariat for Development Planning 2011, iii): "A product of consultations with all segments of Qatari society, including the private sector and civil society, the Strategy takes into account Qatar's cultural and religious values, as well as the needs of future generations, covering all aspects of social, economic and environmental activity." The Heir Apparent became the new Emir in 2013 with the abdication of the previous Emir. The strategy for national development remained unchanged.

In the years that followed Qatar achieved high rates of GDP growth and the GDP per capita was among the highest in the world. The diversification of the economy was pursued through investments in infrastructure needed for a knowledge-based economy.

The extent of economic diversification, as shown by the make-up of exports, has been extremely modest. If we compare exports pre and post the publication of the Qatar National Vision 2030 in 2008, there has been a small change in the right direction: in 2006 non-energy product exports were 10 percent; six years later, in 2012, the non-energy product exports were 12 percent (World Trade Organization 2014, 13). By this it might be expected that the National Vision needed to be translated into a National Strategy and action taken before much diversification occurred.

Bahrain

A UNDP country programme document prepared in 2011 commented on the situation in Bahrain as follows (UNDP 2011, 2): "Strengthening governance and capacities in strategic planning and oversight are considered key challenges." By that time, Bahrain had already embarked on a more strategic style of governance. Bahrain, like Qatar, published a vision statement in 2008. Bahrain's statement was called Our Vision: The Economic Vision 2030 for Bahrain. This was to be delivered by means of the National Economic Strategy.

It was reported that Bharainis had helped develop the vision statement. According to the Bahraini Economic Development Board, consultation during preparation had been extensive (Bahrain Economic Development Board 2013):

> The launch of the Vision followed four years of extensive discussions with a range of opinion leaders in the public and private sectors, including governmental institutions and specialised organisations, as well as international consultancies and bodies.

The three principles mentioned in the next quote—sustainability, competitiveness, and fairness—were said to have emerged through the process of preparing the statement. However, many of the features of Bahrain's vision and strategy in relation to the economy were quite similar to other Gulf states. First and foremost, the Government wanted to reduce its dependence on oil resources as a source of revenue. It therefore was interested in economic diversification. It also considered that the private sector had a vital part to play in economic development: the private sector was expected to be in the driving seat of economic growth by 2030. It, too, favoured public-private partnerships. The economic vision for 2030 was summed up as follows (Bahrain 2008, 3):

> We aspire to shift from an economy built on oil wealth to a productive, globally competitive economy, shaped by the government and driven by a pioneering private sector—an economy that raises a broad middle class of Bahrainis who enjoy good living standards through increased productivity and high-wage jobs. Our society and government will embrace the principles of sustainability, competitiveness and fairness to ensure that every Bahraini has the means to live a secure life and reach their full potential.

The 2008 vision statement promised that the Bahraini government would develop strategic and operational plans to make the vision a reality. The Economic Development Board led the work of preparing the first National

Economic Strategy, which contained proposals for a wide range of actions, including,

1   encouraging innovation,
2   developing growth opportunities,
3   improving skills,
4   social entrepreneurship programmes,
5   empowering women and youth, and
6   increasing capacity for environmental sustainability.

It is interesting to note again the concern for women. It seemed that Bahrain had a long way to go in terms of the empowerment of women: the UNDP reported statistics in 2011 suggesting that women's participation in political and business leadership was modest. There were only two women cabinet ministers; only 12 percent of members of parliament were women; and women held few decision-making posts in either the public or private sector.

Sheikh Mohammad bin Essa Al-Khalifa, Bahrain's Economic Development Board chief executive, described the Board's role as being a catalyst for reform. When asked about the execution of Bahrain's Our Vision, he expressed concerns (McKinsey & Company 2008, 26):

> Execution is one of our biggest challenges. It's all well and good, and probably easy, to come up with a vision and strategy for executing that vision. But actually getting this done—having enough people with the appropriate abilities, experience and skills—is difficult. We realize that this is a continuous challenge, and we are addressing it. We are taking steps to build capabilities and, more important, to institutionalize knowledge management and capability building within the civil service.

He reported that the Bahraini Civil Service Bureau was rolling out training across the civil service, and argued that culturally the civil service should change to greater accountability and service to the customer. He also stressed the specificities of the public sector: the need for leaders sensitive to a greater variety of stakeholders than found in the private sector and the need to be flexible to cope with the complications created by politics.

Some impressions of the influence of the Our Vision statement and the National Economic Strategy were contained in a Trade Policy Review written by the secretariat of the World Trade Organization in early 2014. The view taken was that the diversification strategy was working (Secretariat 2014, 2):

> Since 2008, Bahrain has been implementing a development strategy, Economic Vision 2030 aimed at, inter alia, reducing its high dependence on oil and gas. The strategy has helped diversification efforts: the

services sector, led by financial services, contributed 58% of Bahrain's real GDP in 2012, and the manufacturing sector based on Bahrain's comparative advantages in energy-intensive industries (mainly aluminium and petrochemicals) contributed 15.2% of real GDP.

Assuming that the oil sector's contribution to real GDP was shrinking over time, there is still a question about the causes of that shrinking. The coexistence of a strategy to diversify the economy and a reduction in the importance of the oil sector could be spurious. According to the Secretariat, the Bahraini economy was still dominated by oil even though it was acknowledged that the country's oil and natural gas reserves were small. In 2012, the crude petroleum and natural gas sector accounted for nearly a quarter of GDP and three-quarters of government income.

In the same year as the Trade Policy Review, Bahrain's economy was badly hit by low oil prices. From the middle of 2014 onwards, low oil prices caused drops in government revenue and this in turn resulted in a budget deficit. In response, in November 2015, the government began planning cuts to subsidies for goods and services and the introduction of charges for government services (Staff Writer 2015). Fitch (the rating agency) reported a forecast 12.5 percent of GDP budget deficit for Bahrain in 2015 and a 10.7 percent deficit in 2016. (It should be noted that there had been fiscal deficits every year since 2008.) The problem for the government was that it had previously planned its budget based on $60 per barrel but was being faced by a reality of a price around $40; therefore, it either needed to cut spending or borrow more. In the previous year the government had relaxed borrowing limits to allow it to maintain spending. In December 2015 it was keen to invest in infrastructure to support long-term economic growth, but it was not clear what constraints on government spending would arise as a result of a vote in Parliament.

Two of the factors that may have slowed down or hurt successful implementation of Our Vision might be identified as the drop in oil prices and the political tensions that emerged in 2011. According to Trenwith (2015): "The government released its Economic Vision 2030 document in 2008, outlining various clearly defined and laudable targets and reforms, but progress has been slower than expected, due to the ongoing economic and political hurdles."

United Arab Emirates

The United Arab Emirates was formed in 1971. Initially, six emirates united and a year later Ras Al Khaimah joined as the seventh of the emirates.

It is claimed by Elbanna (2013) that the first show of strategic planning in the United Arab Emirates occurred in the centre of the Emirate of Dubai at the beginning of the 2000s. Then, in 2007, the Prime Minister of the United Arab Emirates, who was Dubai's ruler, introduced the federal organizations to strategic planning. And, during 2007–08, strategic planning spread to the local institutions in the Emirate of Abu Dhabi.

Elbanna (2013) also suggests that public sector organizations at both the federal and the local level produced their first strategic plan between 2007 and 2011. In which case, the production of "Vision 2021" by the federal government in 2010 occurred when strategic planning had only just taken root in the United Arab Emirates.

Thanks to Elbanna we also have some idea of the characteristics of the first wave of public sector strategic planning in the United Arab Emirates. A 2011 survey carried out of public sector organizations in Abu Dabhi and Dubai by Elbanna found the following:

1 All the surveyed organizations had written strategic plans.
2 Most had departments or sections responsible for strategic planning.
3 The strategic plans tended to be for either 3 years or 5 years.
4 The most frequently used tools for strategic planning included SWOT analysis, benchmarking, stakeholder analysis, and the balanced scorecard.
5 The surveyed public sector organizations were supportive of involving the private sector and using public sector partnerships with others.
6 The strategic plans were concerned with service improvement, new service users, and new services.
7 The strategic plans were backed up by budgetary decisions, management systems, and human resource systems.
8 Strategic planning had positive effects on achieving organizational objectives, service quality, and efficiency.

Based on the survey findings, Elbanna commented (2013, 435): "These results show that the impacts of strategic planning in the UAE federal and local organizations are largely beneficial."

UAE Vision 2021 was launched by H.H. Sheikh Mohammed bin Rashid Al Maktoum, Vice-President and Prime Minister of the UAE and Ruler of Dubai in 2010. The launch coincided with UAE's 50th National Day.

The Vision aimed to make the United Arab Emirates among the best countries in the world. There were four themes: United in Ambition and Responsibility, United in Destiny, United in Knowledge, and United in Prosperity. In order to translate the vision into reality, its pillars were mapped into six national priorities which were Cohesive Society and Preserved Identity, Safe Public and Fair Judiciary, Competitive Knowledge Economy, First-Rate Education System, World-Class Healthcare, and Sustainable Environment and Infrastructure.

The "Vision 2021" document contained, at the front end, pictures of both the President of the United Arab Emirates, His Highness Sheikh Khalifa bin Zayed Al Nahyan of Abu Dhabi, and the Prime Minister, His Highness Sheikh Mohammed Bin Rashid Al Maktoum of Dubai. One of the Prime

Minister's comments in the preface suggested the frequently voiced idea in the Gulf states that for these countries modernization involves rising to the challenge of change while hanging on to important features of the old way of life and its cultural values, getting the benefits of progress while preserving what is worthwhile in tradition (United Arab Emirates 2010b, Preface):

> The UAE can count many impressive accomplishments since its inception and now stands among the most advanced nations in the world. Emiratis have reaped many benefits from this remarkable pace of development while also preserving the fabric of their society the essence of their way of life and the strength of their culture.

One example of balancing of old ways and new ways was to be found in the remarks about women and their empowerment "in all spheres". The vision statement contained the idea of an emerging role for women and their greater active participation and empowerment in the future of the United Arab Emirates. It was coupled with a reference to respect for Emirati traditions. It was stated (United Arab Emirates 2010b, 5):

> Women will also gain greater opportunity to combine full participation in active life with the joy and fulfillment of motherhood. In pursuit of these noble goals, women will be protected against all forms of discrimination at work and in society.

The vision summary contained a number of elements, including economic ones (competitive success, knowledgeable, and innovative), social ones (high standard of living, socially cohesive) and an environmental one (sustainable environment):

> Vision 2021 Summary: "In a strong and safe union, knowledgeable and innovative Emiratis will confidently build a competitive and resilient economy. They will thrive as a cohesive society bonded to its identity, and enjoy the highest standard of living within a nurturing and sustainable environment."
>
> (United Arab Emirates 2010b, 1)

The point about a resilient economy must have had some resonance for the Emiratis living in Dubai given the economic problems they had experienced in the preceding two years before Vision 2021 was launched. In common with other Gulf states, the United Arab Emirates embraced the idea of economic diversification and becoming less reliant on oil (United Arab Emirates 2010b, 4): "A diversified and flexible knowledge-based economy will be powered by skilled Emiratis and strengthened by world-class talent to ensure long-term prosperity for the UAE."

We can note the reference to skilled Emiratis and world-class talent. Like other Gulf states, the United Arab Emirates was keen to project a future vision with a human resource dimension. Emiratis would be educated, their abilities and talents then harnessed as part of the National human capital, with Emiratis participating in national development through employment and as captains of industry and as entrepreneurs. The vision statement emphasized the importance of education for economic development and for social cohesion.

Finally, we can note the willingness expressed in the vision statement for the United Arab Emirates to play its part protecting and sustaining the environment (United Arab Emirates 2010b, 25): "The government will act decisively to reduce the national's ecological deficit, promoting environmental awareness and responsible behavior among Emiratis." Specifically, government action would be taken on climate change, carbon dioxide emissions, and fragile ecosystems. Government would ensure clean air and water for future generations and protect citizens from environmental health hazards.

Vision 2021 was clear and straightforward on what was to be the target in terms of a better future. But nothing was said about how the vision would be delivered.

The vision was followed up in 2014 by the UAE National Agenda, which comprised a set of national indicators in the sectors of education, healthcare, economy, police and security, housing, infrastructure, and government services. These indicators were long-term, were to be used to measure performance outcomes in each of the national priorities, and were to be used to compare the UAE against global benchmarks. The national indicators were to be periodically monitored by the Government with the aim of ensuring that the targets are achieved by 2021.

The first United Arab Emirates Government Strategy appeared in 2007 and a second one, UAE Government Strategy 2011–13, was launched in February 2010. The second one was the means of delivering Vision 2021. The first Government Strategy seemed to have as a focus improving government machinery. It contained principles regarding cooperation between the federal and local authorities; the regulatory work of ministries; policy-making work of the ministries; efficiency of governmental bodies; focusing on customer needs; civil service regulations; competence; Emiratization; leadership development, and so on. It also clarified goals in policy sectors (for example, economic development, rural areas, and infrastructure). Later, in 2010, the Prime Minister expressed satisfaction with the first government strategy, saying (United Arab Emirates 2010a): "It is without doubt, that this strategy has realized many accomplishments despite the challenges that it faced." He suggested that planning, together with execution and excellence, was proven to be of key importance for "the well-being of the country and its citizens."

The second strategy, UAE Government Strategy 2011–13, was introduced with the Prime Minister's ringing endorsement of strategic planning (United Arab Emirates 2010a):

> It gives me great pleasure to see that the concept of strategic planning in the UAE Government has become one of the main and deep-rooted pillars in all government entities. Unified efforts and resources are used to achieve specific goals and objectives inspired by the vision of the country's wise leadership, within a clear time frame and with accurate measures.

The government's strategy for 2011–13 contained seven priorities for the three-year period (United Arab Emirates 10a 8):

1   Cohesive society and preserved identity;
2   First-rate education system;
3   World-class healthcare;
4   Competitive knowledge economy;
5   Safe public and fair judiciary;
6   Sustainable environment and infrastructure; and
7   Strong global standing.

As ever, the big question in strategic planning is not the intentions behind a vision statement or behind the words of a government strategy, but the consequences. The strategy promised to align financial resources to strategic priorities and to enhance the governance framework within the Federal Government (in part) by "fostering a culture of accountability". It also promised more evidence-based decisions, joined-up government policy-making, and more consultation of stakeholders. The Government said it would (United Arab Emirates 2010a, 24):

> Develop and implement an integrated policy development mechanism by ensuring alignment of cross-sectoral policies developed by various Federal Entities, assessing the cross-sectoral impact of policy proposals, encouraging a culture of statistical analysis and evidence-based policy-making, and encouraging consultation of relevant stakeholders in policy making.

Finally, in terms of strategic effectiveness, there were promises of improved inter-government integration and coordination mechanisms and the use of strategic partnerships within adequate regulatory frameworks. All this would be in keeping with the concept of governance based on a strategic state framework promoted by the OECD (2013), a framework that included ideas of evidence-based decision-making and the importance of networks and institutions inside and outside government to deliver integration and coordination.

Even with the best approach possible to delivering strategic government, implementation is bound to be challenging, because of difficult and even threatening circumstances. One media comment in 2015 suggested not only doubts about the realization of the environmental aspirations of the

Government but also raised the possibility of tensions—contradiction—between different strategic targets (Townsend 2015):

> With the UAE on a bigger push than ever to diversify its economy and attract 20 million tourists by 2021, sceptics have dismissed its relatively recent focus on sustainability as a 'talking shop'. There is an apparent contradiction, they say, between the UAE's ambitious environmental targets and plans for eye-catching yet unnatural schemes such as Damac's Dubai Rainforest, intended to be the first tropical rainforest in the Middle East.

Kuwait

There is a long history of planning in Kuwait. For example, an Amiri decree in 1970 made the Planning Council a body under the Council of Ministers. In 1986 a law was passed leading to Supreme Councils for Planning for different periods. In 2007, the work of the Ministry of Planning was moved to the General Secretariat of the Supreme Council for Planning and Development.

In 2010, the Kuwait Supreme Council for Planning and Development (SCPD) launched the Kuwait vision statement and strategic objectives (2035), and a mid-term development plan (2010–14).

The Emir made the first development plan official by ratifying a law in February 2010. The development plan covered the period from 2010/11 until 2013/14 and featured performance targets on key priorities. For example, there were targets for diversification (share of fiscal revenue from non-oil sectors) and growth (real GDP growth). Medium-term development plans were the intended means of delivering the vision for 2035.

In 2014 an online statement about the vision of the Amir of Kuwait, Sheikh Sabah Al-Ahmad, also expressed a commitment to work through the use of strategic planning (Sabah Al-Ahmad 2014): "Through this plan, the Kuwaiti government aims at establishing a new ideology for strategic planning and visions to transform into a true reality, and will act as the first move towards attaining the desired vision for 2035."

The four-year plan was focused on Kuwait being a financial and commercial hub attracting investment, and with the private sector leading the economic activity. It emphasized a spirit of competition and efficiency.

Kuwait's development plan encountered implementation difficulties, which became very public. Some observers suggested these were partly caused by the relationship of the parliament with the planning system. In particular, that there had been disagreements between the parliament and the government. Issues were said to concern value for money and private sector financing, and led to delays in capital spending planned in the development plan. It was considered unlikely that performance targets would be met as a result of the delays. In December 2012 a new parliament was elected and faster progress in implementing the development plan was considered possible.

The budget approved for 2015–16, which was approved in July 2015, projected a deficit of nearly half of total spending. By early 2016, the government was attempting to deal with the problems of budget deficit caused by the fall in oil prices. In January 2016, "Kuwait's emir, Sheikh Sabah al-Ahmed al-Sabah, . . . called for budget cuts and better management of spending to cope with declining revenues due to lower oil prices" (Reuters 2016a).

Summary

The narrative around five-year plans and the strategic planning of national development was often the need for modernization of the economy and of society. This was usually combined with a commitment to maintaining traditional values and culture. Economically, modernization aspirations led to goals being approved in relation to themes such as economic growth, better living standards for nationals, more human resource development, more job opportunities for nationals, greater participation by the business sector in the drive to advance national economic development, and economic diversification to reduce dependence on oil.

In Saudi Arabia's case there was also an explicit desire to reduce poverty and pay attention to needy groups. Socially oriented goals included increasing the quality of life and the enhancement of participation of women in employment and development activities. On the environment, the goals might include protection of the environment, concern for sustainable development going forward, and responsibility in the conservation and utilization of natural resources such as water.

At the levels of design and intention, the national development planning system has seemed to be changing, especially in the last 20 years. First, there seems to have been a self-conscious attempt to reform development planning to make it more like strategic planning. As shown in Table 6.4, this move towards strategic planning would appear to have been associated with: (i) taking a long-term perspective (for example, 20 years), (ii) the preparation of long-term vision statements, (iii) the steering of five-year (and/or shorter term) development plans by long-term visions and long-term strategy, (iv) engaging citizens and other interested parties in the planning process, (v) promoting public-private partnerships, (vi) and paying much more attention to implementation, monitoring, and evaluation. In respect of the growth of attention to implementation and follow-up of monitoring, there was even a hint of the need to build in more learning to the national development process. This was evident from a statement we noted earlier in the chapter, made by Talal al Rahbi, Deputy Secretary General of the Oman Supreme Council for Planning, who argued that there was not only a need

Table 6.4 A Composite Picture of the Visionary and Strategic Pattern

	Examples	*Comments*
Modernization rhetoric for planning national development	Oman: Early in his rule Sultan Qaboos bin Said promised a modern government for the people he ruled. Kuwait: The vision for 2035 included the following call: "We cannot afford to stagnate, we must move forward. We have a duty to transform Kuwait into a centre of hard work and innovation, a testament to progress and modernity."	One issue for rulers embarking on modernization must be that of deciding if modernization is to be pursued in all institutions in society or whether modernization would be restricted to the economy.
Commitment to modernize and maintain traditional values and culture	Qatar: Qatar's 2008 vision statement suggested that it would be possible for the country to combine the old (family life, culture, values) and the new (modern work patterns, pressures of competitiveness) in a balanced way. Saudi Arabia: The Long-Term Vision statement suggested a balancing of economic development and traditional aspects of Saudi society: "By the will of Allah, the Saudi economy in 2025 will be a more diversified, prosperous, private-sector driven economy, providing rewarding job opportunities, quality education, excellent health care and necessary skills to ensure the well-being of all citizens while safeguarding Islamic values and the Kingdom's cultural heritage."	The combining of innovation and reform with maintenance of tradition is one of the most important perceived sources of tension and conflict within a strategic planning process.
Self-conscious move towards strategic planning	Kuwait: Online statement about amir's vision included following comment in 2014—"Through this plan, the Kuwaiti government aims at establishing a new ideology for strategic planning and visions to transform into	Whatever definition of strategic planning was in the mind of the Gulf state leaders, their statements can be seen as hinting at the conclusion that national development planning

(*Continued*)

Table 6.4 (Continued)

	Examples	Comments
	a true reality, and will act as the first move towards attaining the desired vision for 2035." Saudi Arabia: Khalid Al Gosaibi, the Minister of Economy and Planning, suggested, in respect of the Eighth Development Plan, that the planning system was in an evolution to a strategic planning approach: "This approach marks a step forward for the strategic planning methodology adopted by the kingdom." United Arab Emirates: The Prime Minister said in 2010: "It gives me great pleasure to see that the concept of strategic planning in the UAE Government has become one of the main and deep-rooted pillars in all government entities."	needed reforming and that strategic planning was perceived to possess special characteristics that were needed for greater government effectiveness.
Publication of a long-term vision	Oman: Socio-economic Strategy (1975) & Oman 2020—Vision for Oman's Economy (1995). Saudi Arabia: Vision for the Saudi Economy (2004). Qatar: National Vision for 2030 (2008). Bahrain: Economic Vision for 2030 (2008). United Arab Emirates: Vision 2021 (2010). Kuwait: Vision 2035 (2010).	All six countries prepared and publicized long-term vision statements within the period 1995 to 2010.
Preparation of a long-term strategy	Saudi Arabia:—Long-Term Strategy (2004) Bahrain: The National Economic Strategy was prepared to deliver Our Vision statement published in 2008.	Some countries developed strategies to deliver visions. Others, including Oman and Saudi Arabia, used their five-year development planning systems to implement long-term strategic visions and plans.

	Examples	*Comments*
Involvement of citizens and/or other interested parties in preparation of plans	Oman: "quantum leap" in involvement of citizens in the development of the ninth five-year plan (2016–20) Qatar: It was intended that the National Strategy would be prepared using consultation and partnership with civil society, the private sector, ministries and government agencies. Saudi Arabia: 2016 vision—"engage everybody"	In the case of Qatar it was made explicit that engagement of stakeholders was intended to secure wide commitment to the vision.
Partnership of private sector sought; public-private partnerships for delivery	Oman: The 2020 Vision articulated a partnership model. It not only wanted an effective and competitive business sector, it also envisaged (Ministry of National Income 2008 18) "the consolidation of the mechanisms and institutions that will foster shared visions, strategies and policies between the private sector and the Government." Qatar: The importance of public-private cooperation and partnerships was stressed in connection with the National Strategy.	Use of public-private partnerships represents implicitly a rejection of neo-liberal ideas of how the state in a modern society acts most effectively in managing the economy.
Some emphasis placed on importance of implementation, monitoring and evaluation	Oman: Talal al Rahbi, Deputy Secretary General of the Oman Supreme Council for Planning, said (Al Nasseri 2015): "We need to focus on implementing plans and learn from them." Saudi Arabia: Long-Term Strategy 2025—"The third pillar [of the Strategy] consists of follow-up and implementation mechanisms . . . This pillar operationalizes the old adage: what gets measured gets done." Bahrain: Sheikh Mohammad bin Essa Al-Khalifa, Bahrain's Economic Development Board chief executive,	In recent decades there has been much discussion of strategic learning. Within a strategic planning process this learning might be encouraged during the monitoring and evaluation phases.

(*Continued*)

Table 6.4 (Continued)

	Examples	*Comments*
	"It's all well and good, and probably easy, to come up with a vision ad strategy for executing that vision. But actually getting this done—having enough people with the appropriate abilities, experience and skills—is difficult."	
Economic challenge perceived as reliance on oil—strategic intent to achieve economic diversification	Oman: 1995 Muscat conference—the country would no longer depend on the oil sector and non-oil sources of national income (industry and services) would become more important than oil income. Bahrain: Bahrain's Our Vision—aspiration to achieve economic diversification.	The identification of reliance on oil as a problem—at least in the future when the oil runs out—is common to all the six countries. And the interest in economic diversification appears to be common to all of them.
Strategic investment in National human capital	Qatar: The vision statement of 2008 offered this analysis of oil dependency: "Hitherto, Qatar's progress has depended primarily on the exploitation of its oil and gas resources. But the country's hydrocarbon resource will eventually run out. Future economic success will increasingly depend on the ability of the Qatari people to deal with a new international order that is knowledge-based and extremely competitive." United Arab Emirates: "A diversified and flexible knowledge-based economy will be powered by skilled Emiratis and strengthened by world-class talent to ensure long-term prosperity for the UAE." Vision 2021 highlighted the importance of education to the country's future.	Investment in the nationals of a country not only meant that s country's workforce could have a higher composition of nationals (and less reliance on foreign workers) but also that a new type of productive, innovative and knowledge-based economy could replace an oil-based economy.
Better living standards	Oman: Better living standards were featured in five-year plans steered by the Socio-economic Strategy 1975.	The tone of many of the vision statements and plans of the Gulf states is one of concern for, and service to, the nationals of a country.

	Examples	*Comments*
	Bahrain: Bahrain's Our Vision articulated aspirations for better living standards. United Arab Emirates: Vision 2021 saw Emiratis in the future enjoying the highest standard of living.	
Reduction of poverty	Saudi Arabia: In 2002, HRH Crown Prince Abdullah, Deputy Premier, Commander of the National Guard and Chairman of the Supreme Economic Council, declared a war on poverty in the Kingdom. This resulted from a visit to poor citizens' homes in Riyadh. Saudi Long-Term Strategy 2025 then identified reduction of poverty as one of five challenges and it was included in the Eighth Development Plan as one of the strategic bases.	It is, of course, possible for poverty to persist even when GDP per capita rises, because this economic indicator is an average that may be associated with widely differing patterns of income and wealth distribution.
Environmental protection and sustainability	Qatar: Qatar's 2008 vision statement saw environmental development as one of four lines of national development. The vision statement stressed the need to manage environmental development "such that there is harmony between economic growth, social development and environmental protection." Saudi Arabia: The Eighth Development Plan included the following as one of the strategic bases—"Sustain care for environmental protection, promote environmental regulations, protect and develop wildlife, and conserve natural resources and rationalize their utilization". United Arab Emirates: According to Vision 2021, there was to be action on climate change, carbon dioxide emissions, and fragile ecosystems. And Government	Qatar's conceptualization of four lines of national development (human; social; economic; and environmental) represents an evolution of the socio-economic conceptualization of development. Elsewhere is the world there is reference to sustainable growth, which represents a combination of at least two challenges.

(*Continued*)

Table 6.4 (Continued)

	Examples	Comments
	would ensure clean air and water for future generations and protect citizens from environmental health hazards.	
Women's greater participation and empowerment	Qatar: The Qatar National Vision 2030 (launched in 2008) included the following desired outcome: "Enhance women's capacities and empower them to participate fully in the political and economic spheres, especially in decision-making roles". Saudi Arabia: The Eighth Development Plan included as the second of its strategic bases the following—"Place emphasis on the welfare of women, upgrade their capabilities and remove the constraints that impede their participation in development activities, in line with the Islamic values and teachings." United Arab Emirates: Vision 2021 looked forward to women gaining greater opportunity for full participation in active life	At the end of the 1990s the emir of Kuwait tried to enfranchise women but Parliament rejected the initiative when it first met again after dissolution in May 1999. This experience suggests that greater participation by women is an aspiration that may prove challenging from the point of view of reconciling the old and the new.

to focus on implementing plans but also mentioned the need to learn from implementing.

The Vision 2030 produced in 2016 by Saudi Arabia and the UAE Government Strategy 2011–13 are both worth special comment in this summary. In the case of Saudi Arabia's Vision 2030, it referred to two institutional innovations: involving the setting up a Center for Performance Management of Government Agencies and the setting up of a strategic management office, with responsibility for coordinating government and sectoral programmes. These together with the intention to work in partnership with the private sector, the commitment to engage with everyone, and the interest in government responsiveness, accountability and transparency, all suggest a desire to create a reformed system of governance based on strategic state capabilities and an enabling relationship with citizens. The actual and practical realization of this in the years ahead would be a new and important episode in the governance story of this Gulf state.

Likewise, the strategic framework advocated by the OECD (2013) appeared evident in features of the design for the delivery of the UAE Government Strategy 2011–13. The delivery of the strategy should have been made more effective by the following features: (i) alignment of financial resources to strategic priorities, (ii) a culture of accountability, (iii) joined-up policy-making, (iv) evidence-based decisions, (vi) consultation of stakeholders, (vii) improved inter-government integration and coordination mechanisms, and (viii) strategic partnerships within adequate regulatory frameworks. All of these elements of a government system would be consistent with the strategic state framework promoted by the OECD. So, providing the strategy itself was right, doing these eight things right should have led to greater government effectiveness in national development.

It appears from assessments and data provided by ministries in some of the Gulf governments that there have been trends and changes in desired directions. Less clear is whether they can actually be attributed to the Development Planning and strategic visioning that has taken place. In respect of the economy particularly, the data provided is not conclusive of the proposition that the strategic visions, strategies, and development plans were delivering a decisive transformation from oil-based economies to more diversified economic bases, or that they had delivered a private sector that was in the driving seat of economic development. For example, the non-oil private sector massively increased its contribution to Saudi Arabia's GDP, but it is not clear to what extent this was influenced by the Saudi Long-Term Strategy 2025 or by the Eighth and Ninth Development Plans.

Reference List

Al Nasseri, Z. (2015) Singaporean Experience to Enlighten Oman Vision 2040. [online] [6 June 2015]. Available from: http://omanobserver.om/singaporean-experience-to-enlighten-oman-vision-2040/

Bahrain (2008) Our Vision: The Economic Vision 2030 for Bahrain. Available from: www.bahrainedb.com

Bahrain Economic Development Board (2013) Economic Vision. [online] [27 January 2013]. Available from: http://www.bahrainedb.com/en/about/Pages/economic%20vision%202030.aspx#.UuYcrXmCroA

Elbanna, S. (2013) Processes and Impacts of Strategic Management: Evidence from the Public Sector in the United Arab Emirates, *International Journal of Public Administration*, 36(6), 426–439.

General Secretariat for Development Planning (2008) *Qatar National Vision 2030*. Doha, Qatar: Qatar General Secretariat for Development Planning.

General Secretariat for Development Planning (2011) *Qatar National Development Strategy 2011–2016: Towards Qatar National Vision 2030*. Doha, Qatar: Qatar General Secretariat for Development Planning.

Kingdom of Saudi Arabia (2016) Vision 2030. Available from: http://vision2030.gov.sa/en

Kuwait (2010) Vision 2035. Available from: http://www.da.gov.kw

McKinsey & Company (Autumn 2008) Bahrain's New Vision: Conversation with Sheikh Mohmmed bin Essa Al-Khalifa, *Transforming Government*, 24–29.

Ministry of Development (1995) Vision 2020. *Vision for Oman's Economy Towards a Better Economic Future*. Sultanates of Oman: Ministry of Development, June 1995.

Ministry of Economy and Planning (2004) The Eighth Development Plan 2005–2009. [Publication date assumed]

Ministry of Economy and Planning (2004) *Saudi Arabia: Long-Term Strategy 2025*. Available at http://www.mep.gov.sa [28 October 2016].

Ministry of Economy and Planning (2009) (Kingdom of Saudi Arabia) Brief Report on the Ninth Development Plan. 1431/32–1435/36. 2010–2014. [Publication date assumed]

Ministry of Economy and Planning (2014) Achievements of the Development Plans (Facts and Figures). Thirty-First Issue. [online] [24 October 2016]. Available from: http://www.mep.gov.sa/en/knowledge-resources/

Ministry of National Economy (2008) *Oman: The Development Experience and Investment Climate*. Sixth Edition.

OECD (2013) *Strategic Insights from the Public Governance Reviews: Update*. GOV/PGC(2013)4, *Public Governance and Territorial Development Directorate. Public Governance Committee*. Paris: OECD.

Oman (2008) Trade Policy Review. WT/TPR/G/201. Report to World Trade Organization. 21 May 2008.

Oman Observer (2015a) Oman Vision 2040 Panel Reviews Steps to Prepare Strategy. [online] [5 June 2015]. Available from: http://omanobserver.om/oman-vision-2040-panel-reviews-steps-to-prepare-strategy/

Oman Observer (2015b) Workshop on 9th Five-Year Plan Concludes. [online] [6 June 2015]. Available from: http://omanobserver.om/workshop-on-9th-five-year-plan-concludes/

Peterson, J. E. (2005) The Emergence of Post-Traditional Oman. *Working Paper*. Durham: University of Durham, Centre for Middle Eastern and Islamic Studies.

Reuters (2015) S&P Cuts Oman Credit Rating as Budget Deficit Widens. [online] [21 December 2015]. Available from: http://www.arabianbusiness.com//s-p-cuts-oman-credit-rating-as-budget-deficit-widens-612959.html

Reuters (2016a) Kuwait Sees Budget Deficit Jumping by 50% in 2016–17. [online] [7 February 2016]. Available from: http://www.arabianbusiness.com/kuwait-sees-budget-deficit-jumping-by-50-in-2016-17–620146.html

Reuters (2016b) Oman to Cut Budget Deficit 27% This Year, Minister Says. [online] [7 February 2016]. Available from: http://www.arabianbusiness.com//oman-cut-budget-deficit-27-this-year-minister-says-616918.html

Sabah Al Ahmad (2014) Amir of Kuwait Statement on Executing the Development Plan. [online] [27 January 2014]. Available from: http://www.da.gov.kw/eng/festival/vision_his_highness.php

Secretariat (2014) Trade Policy Review: Kingdom of Bahrain. WT/TPR/S/294. 18 March 2014. Pages 1–78. Available from: https://www.wto.org

Shaalan, S. (2015) The Vision 2040 and the Ninth Five-Year Plan: International Experience and Community Consensus/Oman . . . Economic Step towards "Leadership".

[online] [6 June 2015]. Available from: http://www.businesstendersmag.com/en/26-english/investigation/974-oman-. . .-economic-step-towards-leadership

Staff Writer (2015) Bahrain Subsidy Cuts 'Insufficient' to Offset Cheap Oil, Says Fitch. Sunday 6 December 2015. [online] [21 December 2015]. Available from: http://www.arabianbusiness.com//bahrain-subsidy-cuts-insufficient—offset-cheap-oil-says-fitch-614275.html#.VnfYmISWHQM

Townsend, S. (2015) Greening the Desert: How the UAE Aims to Change Its Carbon Footprint. [online] [13 March 2016]. Available from: http://www.arabianbusiness.com/greening-desert-how-uae-aims-change-its-carbon-footprint-599849.html

Townsend, S. (2016) Oman to Publish Strategy to Boost Industrial Sector. [online] [20 February 2016]. Available from: http://www.arabianbusiness.com//oman-publish-strategy-boost-industrial-sector-620945.html

Trenwith, C. (2015) Focus—Bahrain's Fiscal Tightrope: The Island State's Battle to Regain Lost Ground. [online] [19 August 2015]. Available from: http://www.arabianbusiness.com//focus-bahrain-s-fiscal-tightrope—island-state-s-battle-regain-lost-ground-602661.html

UNDP (2011) Country Programme Document for Bahrain (2012–2016). July 29, 2011. Available from: http://www.arabstates.undp.org/content/dam/rbas/doc/CPD/Bahrain%20CPD.pdf

United Arab Emirates (2010a) Highlights of the U.A.E. Government Strategy 2011–2013: Putting Citizens First. Available from: http://planipolis.iiep.unesco.org/upload/United%20Arab%20Emirates/United%20Arab%20Emirates_Government_strategy_2011-2013.pdf

United Arab Emirates (2010b) Vision 2021. Available from: https://www.vision2021.ae/en

World Trade Organization (2014) Qatar. Trade Policy Review. Report by the Secretariat. 18 March 2014. Available from: https://www.wto.org

7 Governing for Results

Introduction

This chapter could be seen as largely about the impact of governments in the Gulf and a trawl of the available published data to see if there is evidence that Gulf states with more strategic capabilities have done better. As will be seen, the findings are not conclusive, although they are suggestive – and the following questions indicate a range of factors that need to be considered in explaining effectiveness:

(i)   Is government trying to do the right things?
(ii) Is the government, and all its partners, really committed to the strategic priorities and associated strategic goals and working hard to deliver them?
(iii) Does the government have, and is it using, the necessary strategic capabilities that can turn national strategic aspirations into reality?
(iv) Are the circumstances of government strategic action favourable or hostile?

By government trying to do the right things we mean has it got the right strategic priorities and are the chosen strategies intelligent ones? The fourth factor, circumstances, is a really serious complicating factor. In very adverse circumstances maybe the best that can be hoped for is very slow progress in the right strategic direction or even not slipping back too far. (We have in mind here an analogy of a sailing boat moving fast when it is running before a strong wind that is filling its sails and a sailing boat that has to keep on tacking to sail in the opposite direction to the wind—and thus bound to make only slow progress in the direction it is going.)

In this chapter and in the conclusions we have found it useful to use two concepts of strategic management, which are the concept of a resource-based strategy and the concept of strategic capabilities. We think both are very helpful in understanding the Gulf states' visions and plans and their attempts to become more effective in their implementation and successful delivery. They each attract a different question for strategists:

i) What are our best and most important national resources and how can they be used in strategic action or strategic programmes to help the country and its people flourish?

ii) What strategic capabilities do we have and what strategic capabilities do we need government to develop to help us become more effective in delivering the long-term strategic visions and plans we have made?

As we have seen (in chapter 6) and will argue again in this book, the Gulf states have as the kernel (Rumelt 2011) of their stated strategies, the idea of moving from a government strategy which is based on oil as the key strategic resource to one where the strategy is based on the country's national human resources. The new strategy is linked to ancillary ideas of putting more emphasis on exporting, foreign direct investment, skills, innovation, and so on. It is summed up in some plans using the phrase of moving to a "knowledge economy".

It is interesting to note that the private sector management literature on strategy coming out of the United States really got interested in the idea of resource-based strategy in the 1980s, especially the late 1980s (Hamel and Prahalad 1994). Up until that time, the tendency, in the business literature and in the business schools, was to think about strategy in completely the opposite way, to begin with a thorough analysis of industries and markets, to identify where the profit potential was at its greatest and to identify the competitive pressures and only then begin to think about making the organization fit the requirements of strategy. In other words, until the resource-based strategy gained a following, many considered strategy to be first and foremost about strategic positioning—meaning, what industry should we be in, and where in the markets of that industry should we place the firm? Should we position it as a producer of standard products or services charging standard prices or should we position ourselves as being different in some way from other businesses, such as the design of our product or the service, or our after-sales service, or some such thing. Finally, should we be operating in the whole industry or should we find a segment of customers and concentrate on them? And only after the desired strategy was identified did the strategist think through what this meant in terms of organizational design and other organizational characteristics.

It is difficult to prove the next point, but arguably one of the hardest things to do when an organization uses a positioning strategy is to develop the organizational capacity needed by the chosen positioning. Changing organizational structures, reallocating budgets, developing new skills and capabilities, and changing organizational cultures to match the requirements of a new strategy are challenging things to do. It may well be the same in the public sector. It is interesting to think about the lessons learned by public sector organizations using quality management tools to improve their effectiveness: in the UK in the 1990s they found evidence that resources and partnerships and society results were the least amenable to the planned improvements sought though the EFQM Excellence Model. Obviously, we are underlining here the issue that resources were among the most difficult things to improve (that is, change) on a planned basis.

So, a chief executive could approve a new strategy for a business based on a positioning approach and then find that developing the new skills and capabilities was a big barrier to successful implementation. We can imagine, therefore, a pragmatic response to this lesson, along the lines of: if developing new resources is generally difficult, what strategies could we pursue using either our existing resources or resources we are confident we can acquire or develop? Strategic positioning would be consciously and deliberately constrained by resources. The business could start with thinking about resources and then think about its positioning options.

Culture and skills may both be seen as examples of resources. Skilled human beings may be seen as resources—human resources. Capabilities as bundles or complexes of skills lodged in people can also be seen, therefore, as resources. In this chapter, and for the special purposes of this book, we want to concentrate on the idea of strategic capabilities as concerned with strategic management processes rather than the design of strategies. We will define strategic capabilities as capabilities available to a government that it can use to interact with citizens and other stakeholders, that it can use in long-term thinking and planning, and that it can use to ensure strategic visions and plans are delivered. So, we are restricting our use of strategic capabilities in this chapter to the concept of capabilities needed for the processes of making and delivering strategies. In recognition of this special definition, we might give the concept of strategic capabilities an extended name—strategic process capabilities.

In this chapter we assess the development of strategic capabilities in the six Gulf states. We use this assessment to look for relationships between strategic capabilities and important national outcomes. These outcomes are generic outcomes (GDP per capita, happiness, and environmental performance). This will allow us to place the situation in the Gulf states in a more international perspective. Then we look at the outcome of reducing dependence on oil resources, which is an outcome with great meaning for the visions, strategies, and plans of the Gulf states. At the end, we will return to the topic of resource-based strategies in the Gulf states and introduce a point about time-pressures in the assessment of feasible strategic options.

Four Strategic Process Capabilities

We do not have the satisfaction of being able to present empirical data on all the capabilities conceptualized in the OECD's strategic framework (OECD 2013). What we can do is operationalize a set of strategic capabilities that do roughly approximate to key aspects of the strategic state framework for which there is published data.

Our four strategic process capabilities are:

  (i) long-term strategic visioning;
 (ii) ensuring government coordination, integration and coherence;
(iii) mobilizing public authorities, and public and private stakeholders behind the long-term strategic vision; and
(iv) evaluating strategic action (policies) and adapting.

We think all of these are consistent with the OECD thinking on strategic states, although there is much more in the OECD framework than these four capabilities (see Figure 7.1).

Our data source on these capabilities is the database created by the Hertie School of Governance, as featured in the Governance Report 2014 (Hertie School of Governance 2014). Table 7.1 presents the values based on 12 variables extracted from this database with the value for each process capability being based on an average value for the variables included in that capability.

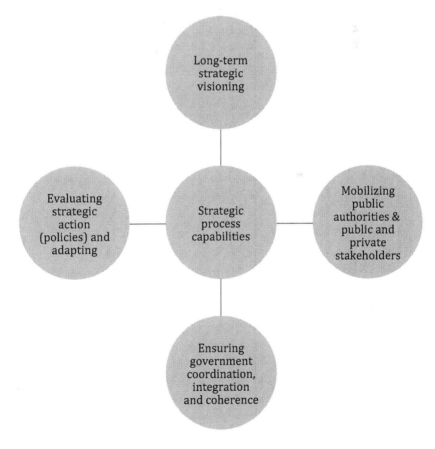

Figure 7.1 Strategic Process Capabilities

Table 7.1 Strategic Process Capabilities (Hertie School of Governance 2014)

Country	Ranking	Total score	Long–term strategic visioning	Ensuring government coordination, integration and coherence	Mobilizing public authorities, and public and private stakeholders behind the long–term strategic vision	Evaluating strategic action (policies), and adapting	Government Effectiveness Estimates (–2.5 to +2.5) (World Governance Indicators for 2010)
Denmark	1	6.56	1.32	1.71	1.64	1.89	2.1
UK	2	6.55	1.07	1.95	1.64	1.89	1.6
Germany	3	4.96	1.57	0.90	1.64	0.85	1.6
Sweden	4	4.76	1.07	1.14	0.66	1.89	2.0
Singapore	5	4.62	1.11	0.95	1.15	1.41	1.8
United Arab Emirates	6	3.96	1.57	0.38	1.64	0.37	0.9
Oman	7	3.15	1.57	–0.43	1.64	0.37	0.4
Qatar	8	3.05	0.59	0.38	1.16	0.92	0.9
Japan	9	2.97	0.83	0.14	1.15	0.85	1.5
China	10	1.74	0.33	–0.11	1.15	0.37	0.1
Bahrain	11	1.19	0.02	0.14	1.15	–0.12	0.2
Venezuela	12	0.94	0.58	1.44	0.15	–1.23	–1.1
Brazil	13	0.24	–0.15	0.35	–0.33	0.37	0.0
United States	14	0.20	0.11	0.07	–0.83	0.85	1.5
Turkey	= 15	0.00	–0.15	0.11	0.16	–0.12	0.3
South Korea	= 15	0.00	0.10	–1.14	1.16	–0.12	1.2
India	17	–0.53	0.08	–0.59	0.65	–0.67	0.0
Saudi Arabia	18	–2.82	–0.87	–0.94	–0.34	–0.67	0.0

Russian Federation	19	-3.10	-0.87	-0.17	-0.83	-1.23	-0.4
Kuwait	20	-3.51	-0.88	-0.65	-1.30	-0.67	0.2

Notes: The 12 variables in the Hertie School of Governance data set were identified as follows:

a5031 Do the authorities have a long-term strategic vision for territorial/urban planning?
a5032 Do the authorities have a long-term strategic vision to protect the environment?
a5030 Do the public authorities have a long-term vision for the development of human capital (education, health, etc.)?
a5033 Do the authorities have a long-term strategic vision relating to international or regional integration?
a5074 Overall coherence of public policies
a5010 Degree of coordination/collaboration between ministries
a5011 Degree of coordination/collaboration within administrations
a5081 Is the capacity of national public authorities hampered by divisions within the state apparatus?
a5020 Are the actions of the public authorities in line with a long-term strategic vision?
a5022 Do the public authorities have the capacity to encourage public and private stakeholders to work towards that vision?
a5071 Is the evaluation of public policies a common practice?
a5072 Authorities' capacity to adapt policies to changes in the economic and social contexts

The government effectiveness estimates from the World Governance Indicators published by the World Bank are shown in the final column of Table 7.1. As can be seen, there is a very approximate, indeed very rough and ready, correlation between the total score for strategic process capabilities and the government effectiveness estimates. The highest estimates tend to be associated with higher scores for strategic process capabilities and the zero and negative estimates appear to be associated with lower scores for strategic process capabilities. If government effectiveness is a function of strategic effectiveness and operational effectiveness, it is possible that some of the countries with a low score on strategic process capabilities are relatively better on operational effectiveness than they are on strategic effectiveness.

Based on this table, we can present a league table of the Gulf states in terms of their strategic process capabilities. This is shown in Figure 7.2.

Table 7.1 also suggests that the United Arab Emirates and Oman both scored highly on two of the strategic process capabilities—long-term strategic visioning and mobilizing public authorities and public and private stakeholders. Qatar also scored well on mobilizing (but less well on the long-term strategic vision than the United Arab Emirates and Oman). Bahrain's scores for long-term strategic visioning and for ensuring government coordination, integration and coherence were mediocre. The scores for Saudi Arabia and Kuwait suggested weaknesses in all four capabilities, with Kuwait being weakest of all the six Gulf states in respect of a strategic process capability for mobilizing public authorities and public and private stakeholders.

Strategic process capabilities

1: United Arab Emirates, Oman, and Qatar

2: Bahrain

3: Saudi Arabia and Kuwait

Figure 7.2 The Gulf States' League Table of Strategic Process Capabilities (Hertie School of Governance Database)

Generic Outcomes

If we turn now to some comparisons of how well the six countries have done over the last decade or so, what emerges? Our preference is to follow the current fashion in public governance and look at outcomes in relation to the economy, social well-being, and the protection and improvement of the environment.

In terms of economic outcomes, it is now quite common to examine trends in GDP per capita. This may be preferred rather than GDP growth because it enables us to look at a measure of economic growth that has been adjusted to take account of the different size of populations when comparing countries or to take account of population growth for a single country. Sometimes there is almost an assumption that GDP per capita is useful because it gives a rough indication of income averages. However, this can be misleading because societies vary significantly in terms of income and wealth inequalities and average figures may, therefore, tell us little about the incomes of actual people. In fact, many commentators in recent years have noted that income inequalities have really increased in many countries during the 1980s and since the 1980s. It seems, therefore, doubly unwise to use GDP per capita data to draw too many conclusion about how well off and prosperous ordinary people are.

We think it is perhaps better to use GDP per capita for an entirely different purpose, which is as a measure of macroeconomic productivity since it represents an output (GDP) divided by an input (population). Obviously, it is only one of a number of different possible measures of productivity of a society, but it does provide one dimension of global macroeconomic productivity.

In Table 7.2 we can see that the countries accruing the biggest proportionate benefits from oil (Kuwait and Saudi Arabia) do not have the highest

Table 7.2 Strategic Process Capabilities and Generic Economic Outcomes for the Gulf States

Country	Strategic process capability ranking	GDP per capita (economy's productiveness) (PPP— constant 2011 international $) 2014	GDP per capita—change between 2005 and 2014	2015–16 Global Competitiveness Index (score)
United Arab Emirates	= 1	64,563	−32%	5.2
Oman	= 1	38,855	−11.2%	4.3
Qatar	= 1	134,182	+16.8%	5.3
Bahrain	2	43,408	−2.8%	4.5
Saudi Arabia	= 3	49,619	+27.9%	5.1
Kuwait	= 3	69,878	−25.7%	4.6

Notes: The GDP data was sourced from the World Bank. The 2015–16 Global Competitiveness Index data is from Schwab (2015).

GDP per capita among the six countries in 2014. The runaway winner is Qatar and the United Arab Emirates does very well by exceeding the GDP per capita of Saudi Arabia and coming close to matching Kuwait's GDP per capita. There must be other factors at work apart from the (possible) effects of strategic process capabilities of government because while both Qatar and the United Arab Emirates appear to possess a lot of such capabilities, so does Oman, and yet it does not match the GDP per capita of either of them. It seems possible that the 32 percent drop in the United Arab Emirates GDP per capita between 2005 and 2014 could be down to the economic difficulties Dubai ran into during 2008 and 2009. These difficulties included a massive slump in the stock market of Dubai in late 2008 and problems in early 2009 in servicing its debt renewals (see Chapter 1).

We turn now to another economic variable included in Table 7.2, which is global competitiveness. In the publication by the World Economic Forum in 2015, three of the Gulf states came out slightly ahead of the rest in terms of judgments about global competitiveness. These are the United Arab Emirates, Qatar, and Saudi Arabia. The other three—Bahrain, Kuwait, and Oman either stood still or saw their score for global competitiveness drop slightly. It is not easy to draw simple correlations between the extent of strategic process strategic capabilities and competitiveness. Both the United Arab Emirates and Qatar have high scores for the strategic process capabilities, but Saudi Arabia scored poorly on the four capabilities. Saudi Arabia's strategic process capability profile looks a very weak one. Yet, Saudi Arabia's global competitiveness score went up a lot between 2008 and 2015, from 4.7 to 5.1, whereas Kuwait's competitiveness was 4.6 in 2008 and 4.6 in 2015. So, there is certainly no obvious link between the strategic process capabilities of government and the global competitiveness of the economy. Of course, it might be argued that given that the first major strategic management initiatives of most of the Gulf states were only occurring in 2004, 2008, and 2010, perhaps it is too soon to be seeing changes induced in competitiveness of the economy as a result of strategic visions and strategic and development plans.

Turning now to social well-being, we might note that the national citizens of the Gulf states tend on the whole to emerge from international surveys as relatively satisfied with their lives. The average life evaluations (that is, happiness scores) of people in Bahrain, Kuwait, Qatar, Saudi Arabia, and the United Arab Emirates in 2013–15 were far greater, for example, than average life evaluations of people in China, India, Japan, Russia, South Korea, and Turkey. There was a reduction in the average life evaluations of people in Saudi Arabia between 2005/2007 and 2012/2014 and very slight increases for people in Kuwait and the United Arab Emirates over the same period. The data in Table 7.3 shows the average "ladder score"—that is, the average answer to the Cantril ladder question asking people to evaluate the quality of their current lives on a scale of 0 as the worst possible life to 10 as the best possible life. According to Helliwell et al. (2015, 4):

Table 7.3 Strategic Process Capabilities and Generic Social and Environmental Outcomes for the Gulf States

Country	Strategic process capability ranking	Happiness—average life evaluations 2012–2014	Happiness—average life evaluations 2013–2015	Environmental Risk Exposure (2013)	2016 Environmental Performance Index 2011	10-year % change Environmental Performance Index—scores (2016)
United Arab Emirates	= 1	6.90	6.57	0.67	69.4	26.3%
Oman	= 1	6.85	No data	0.53	60.1	27.3%
Qatar	= 1	6.61	6.38	0.68	69.9	30.1%
Bahrain	2	5.96	6.22	0.61	70.1	7.5%
Saudi Arabia	= 3	6.41	6.38	0.65	68.6	25.4%
Kuwait	= 3	6.30	6.24	0.64	64.1	45.3%

Notes: The values for Happiness in the table are national averages for life evaluations of life satisfaction. The higher the score is, the more positive the evaluations. The samples for World Happiness Reports were nationals and Arab expatriates, except that the 2013–15 sample for the United Arab Emirates was changed to include non-Emerati population. The data for Oman was only collected in 2011 and so there is no data for 2013–15. The data source for the happiness data was Helliwell et al. (2013) and Helliwell et al. (2015). The data source for the Environmental Performance Index was Hsu et al. (2016). The Environmental Risk Exposure data was downloaded from http://epi.yale.edu/downloads. The data was downloaded on 24 May 2016.

There is also evidence that broader measures of good governance have enabled countries to sustain or improve happiness during the economic crisis. Recent results show not just that people are more satisfied with their lives in countries with better governance, but also that actual changes in governance quality since 2005 have led to significant changes in the quality of life.

They also remark that the most improved countries in terms of government service delivery had much better average life evaluations than countries with much worsened government service delivery and that the scale of this difference is equivalent to a massive increase in GDP per capita.

Can we find any relationship between a governance variable and average life evaluation in Table 7.3? Arguably, there is a hint of a relationship for 2012–14. We can see that the three countries with the highest ranking for strategic process capabilities (United Arab Emirates, Oman, and Qatar) have higher average life evaluations than Saudi Arabia and Kuwait, which have much lower strategic process capability ratings. But Bahrain appears to be a bit of an anomaly. It has a slightly lower score than the rest even though its strategic process capability score is not the lowest. In other words, based on strategic process capability scores, happiness is less than we might have expected.

Table 7.3 also reports the Environmental Risk Exposure and 10-year percentage change in Environmental Performance Index. The Environmental Risk Exposure is an indicator of hazards to human health posed by unsafe water, unsafe sanitation, and so on. The table shows the values for 2013 (and the lower the values the better.) There is a rather complicated picture for this indicator. The risk lessened in Bahrain for the years 2010–13; they lessened for people in Oman over the period 1990 to 2013; and they got moderately less in Saudi Arabia over the years 1990 to 2013. But in Kuwait the risk worsened in the period from 2000 to 2013. They worsened in Qatar from 2000 to 2010. And they worsened in the United Arab Emirates between 1990 and 2010. There appears to be no obvious connection to government strategic process capabilities.

We would emphasize the relatively good happiness scores of the nationals of all six of the Gulf states (ranging from the United Arab Emirates at the top end to Bahrain at the bottom end). However, a possible inference from a recent study attempting to link governance and happiness might be that political unrest in Bahrain has been a factor depressing its citizens' happiness score. The study used data for 14 countries in the Middle East and North Africa, which included Kuwait, Saudi Arabia, and the United Arab Emirates. The study did not include Bahrain, which is why we say that there is a possible inference that political unrest may be a factor in explaining the lower score on happiness for Bahrain compared to the other Gulf states. The governance data used in the study was the Worldwide Governance Indicators of the World Bank. The period addressed was 2009 to 2011, and thus was a very interesting period in the light of the Arab Spring's occurrence in 2011. The researchers used statistical analysis and summed up the results of their study as follows (Fereidouni et al. 2013, 1036):

> Unhappiness has been recognized as one of the main factors that cause political unrest in the MENA region in recent years. The aim of this paper is to assess the role of governance indicators on people's happiness in the MENA region. The results show that political stability and absence of violence, government effectiveness and rule of law have positive and significant impacts on happiness in the region.

Obviously, their study period has added significance because of its inclusion of the year of the Arab Spring. They drew out the following implication from their statistical results for the governments of the region (Fereidouni et al. 2013, 1036): "governments, for example, should create favorable political relations with other countries and try to settle internal conflicts as well as religious agitation in order to reduce tension and lower risks and uncertainty for their citizens." Could we infer from the findings and from this stated implication that internal conflict within Bahrain is an issue in the happiness data of its citizens? We can only say, maybe. The issue of internal conflicts is picked up again briefly in the final chapter.

Finally, in Table 7.3, there is trend data on the Environmental Performance Index, which is an index made up of a large number of individual items and is intended to provide a holistic assessment of environmental matters in a country. The compilers of the Environmental Performance Index claim that poor performers on the Environmental Performance Index have broad governance problems. According to Hsu et al. (2016, 111):

> The Index's bottom third, composed mostly of African countries with a smattering of South and East Asian nations, is a list of troubled states whose problems extend beyond their ability to sustain environmental and human health. These nations show that environmental performance is an issue of governance—only well-functioning governments are able to manage the environment for the benefit of all.

Essentially, the scores on the Environmental Performance Index are generally lower than the United States, Singapore, Northern European countries (for example, Sweden, Denmark, and Germany), about the same order as China (or slightly better), and much better than India. They are all much the same in the case of the Gulf states, although Oman and Kuwait are slightly worse. With the exception of Bahrain, they have all substantially improved their Environmental Performance Index score over a ten-year period.

It is very evident from looking at Tables 7.2 and 7.3 that there is no general relationship between these economic, social, and environmental variables and the strategic process capabilities, although there are hints of something in respect of GDP per capita and average life evaluations. It is tempting to argue that strategic process capabilities may be having a positive impact on macroeconomic productivity and average life evaluations (happiness), although it would also be necessary to suggest that Bahrain is a special case in these respects. In fact, Bahrain also appears to be a special case in respect of changes in the Environmental Performance Index over a ten-year period. It would be speculative for us to suggest what might account for Bahrain being different from the other five, although we can note that there have been some internal tensions within Bahrain since 2011.

Economic Diversification

In the previous chapter we saw that a constant theme in the strategic thinking of the Gulf states was an intention to reduce the dependence of the state on oil revenues and to create a more diversified economy in which non-oil industries and non-oil exports were of growing significance. If these strategic intentions were being successfully implemented, we might expect to see the oil rents of the Gulf states decline as a percentage of GDP. The evidence on oil rents is shown in Table 7.4 and Figure 7.3, where it will be

Table 7.4 Oil Rents (% of GDP)

	United Arab Emirates (%)	Oman (%)	Qatar (%)	Bahrain (%)	Saudi Arabia (%)	Kuwait (%)
1995	17	29	27	16	32	40
1996	19	34	35	19	35	42
1997	17	31	32	17	32	40
1998	11	19	23	10	23	30
1999	13	26	27	14	27	34
2000	20	41	37	18	42	49
2001	16	33	30	15	35	43
2002	14	31	27	14	33	36
2003	17	31	30	15	39	41
2004	20	36	34	17	45	48
2005	24	42	38	20	53	57
2006	25	40	34	21	53	56
2007	23	38	31	20	51	54
2008	27	38	33	23	59	60
2009	18	29	24	15	39	42
2010	21	34	28	17	44	51
2011	25	40	30	21	49	59
2012	24	36	26	18	46	58
2013	22	34	24	18	44	55
2014	19	28	20	15	39	53

Notes: This oil rent data was obtained from the World Bank. Oil rents are the difference between the value of crude oil production at world prices and total costs of production.

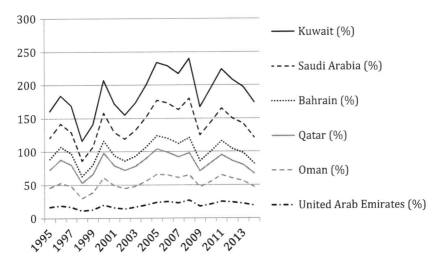

Figure 7.3 Fluctuations in Oil Rents in the Gulf States, 1995–2014

seen that the movements up and down of oil rent seemed to be more or less synchronized. For example, oil rent as a percentage of GDP seemed to peak in 2000 before falling again, and then started rising after 2002 until 2008, representing a boom period in terms of oil rent. Arguably, the movements reflect the state of the global oil market. It is also obvious from Figure 7.3 that there are very big fluctuations in the oil rent over time but between 1995 and 2014 these fluctuations do not appear to be occurring around a sharply falling trend line. There is, as yet, no sign of a move away from economies based on oil, and thus no signs as yet of a move away from rentier economies.

One other thing that is interesting about Table 7.4 is the possible implication that strategic process capabilities are in some way related to oil rent as a percentage of GDP. Specifically, the two countries with the worst showing in terms of strategic process capabilities are Saudi Arabia and Kuwait and they have had relatively high percentages of oil rent, whereas United Arab Emirates, Oman, and Qatar have had relatively lower oil rents as a percentage of GDP and yet appear to be much better in terms of strategic process capabilities. The same might be said about the World Governance Indicator estimates for government effectiveness: the countries with a higher percentage of oil rents (Saudi Arabia and Kuwait) have lower estimates than the United Arab Emirates, Oman, and Qatar that have lower oil rents as a percentage of GDP. At first glance, Bahrain seems an anomaly. Because of its low value of oil rent (as a percentage of GDP), we would expect its scores on strategic process capabilities and its estimate for government effectiveness to be higher.

Strategic Contradictions that are Very Time Dependent?

The kernel of the government economic strategies being pursued in the Arabian Peninsula seems clear enough. Replace dependence on oil by investing in National human resources, diversify the economy, build up non-oil industries and exports, and create a knowledge economy for the future. In essence, go from a strategy in which the key resource is oil to a strategy in which the key resource is the innovative and productive power of the people in the nation. But is it easy to do?

One issue that was evident from looking at national development planning by the Gulf states is the difficulty of turning aspirations into reality. Good intentions are not enough. Clarity of goals is not enough. The commitment, for example, to economic diversification to reduce dependence on oil was very evident in speeches, statements, and in plan documents. But dependence on oil means in part dependence for economic growth and dependence for government revenue. It was not going to be politically and socially acceptable, therefore, to reduce dependence on oil by simply opting out of the oil industry if this meant reverting to lower standards of living and fewer public services. The wealth creation of the oil sector needs to be replaced by something new. And the ability to find and develop this something new depends on circumstances.

Moreover, circumstances generally prove to be quite powerful in shaping government action and results. This can be illustrated by the example of the fall in oil and natural gas prices from the middle of 2014. This fall hurt government finances. By December 2015 all the Gulf states—including Qatar— were being forced by this nosedive in oil and natural gas prices to restrain or rationalize public spending and reconsider government subsidies. Qatar's Ministry of Development Planning and Statistics reported that the foreign trade surplus had shrunk by just over 50 percent in the year to September 2015. It appeared that in that same month of September 2015 the wealthy Qatar government still wanted to finance planned government spending on economic development projects and subsidies (Staff Writer 2015):

> In September, Qatar's finance minister Ali Sherif Al Emadi said the Gulf state would not scale back economic development projects or cut state subsidies for fuel and food in response to low oil and natural gas prices, because government finances remain strong.

By December 2015, with the Qatari government announcing an expected deficit in 2016, the first in 15 years, there was also a statement by a minister that the government was rationalizing public spending (Reuters 2015):

> "On the fiscal side, the government is taking measures to rationalise expenditure. Still, markedly lower hydrocarbon revenue will narrow the surplus in 2015 and is expected to lead to a modest deficit in 2016 of around 4.8 percent of GDP," Development Planning and Statistics Minister Saleh al-Nabiy said in the report by his ministry.

Sometimes the circumstances prove to be too powerful for government: in the battle between circumstances and purposeful interventions by government, circumstances may well win out. This can be illustrated by the situation of Oman from the middle of 2014 and into 2015 and 2016. The key feature of the circumstances was the precipitous decline in international oil prices. The government decided it had to put money into its oil sector to counter a drop in oil production because the economy was not yet in a position where the non-oil sector could sustain the growth of the economy and sustain government revenues if there was a shrinking contribution from oil.

In the knowledge that delivering national priorities and strategic goals for national development is far from easy, and in the knowledge that circumstances can slow up delivery of plans or even block them, what can be done? One answer is to recognize that strategic changes in national economic and social affairs are rarely easily "programmable"—you cannot just decide on goals and actions and then think that the next bit of implementing them will be easy to design, and just a technically and politically easy matter to bring about. If strategic change is not easily programmable, the planning of implementation has to be taken very seriously. Risks caused by changed circumstances in the external environment have to be identified, assessed, and planned for. Contingency plans may be needed if the attempts at de-risking the plan are not successful or not possible. Implementation itself has to be taken seriously, and so there needs to be the creation of necessary information systems, the creation of reporting systems so that key decision makers can decide in good time if a corrective action is needed to keep the plan on track. In short, there need to be capabilities in monitoring the implementation of strategic plans. Sometimes this monitoring and correcting of the actions taken under a plan will call for deeper evaluation and learning to understand why the hoped for results are not materializing. So, there need to be capabilities for evaluation and learning. And in overall terms, there needs to be organizational capabilities for the government machinery to work in a unified and integrated way if there is to be government agility and responsiveness to changing circumstances. They are also needed to cope with implementation challenges that will be encountered during effective execution of long-term plans.

It is quite possible that governments that are poor at visioning the future are also poor at evaluating policies and adapting to changes in context. Table 7.1, based on the Hertie School of Governance data, seems to show this when a bivariate table is produced. See Table 7.5.

It is possible that among national leaders in the Gulf states the experiences of national development planning had been leading to a growing realization that the delivery of goals is not easy and that capabilities for implementation have to be increased. In the Long-term Strategy 2025 of Saudi Arabia it was, for example, remarked that people in Saudi Arabia who thought about issues in relation to national development agreed that the record of converting good ideas into actions and results was uneven.

Table 7.5 Long-Term Strategic Visioning and Evaluating and Adapting

	Visionary	*Not very visionary*
Good at evaluating and adapting	Denmark, UK, Germany, Sweden, Singapore, Japan, China, **United Arab Emirates, Oman,** and **Qatar**	Brazil United States
Poor at evaluating and adapting	Venezuela	Turkey, South Korea, India, Russian Federation, **Bahrain, Saudi Arabia, Kuwait**

Source: Based on Table 7.1 above

Planning, therefore, has to become strategic planning, with its attention to monitoring and evaluation to enhance the impact of planning. Was there such a growing realization? Saudi Arabia did manifest a concern for more plan impact in the development of its planning methodology for the Eighth Development Plan (2005–09) and the new emphasis that was given to monitoring and evaluation. And as we noted in the case of Oman, in 2015 the Deputy Secretary General of the Oman Supreme Council for Planning was quoted as emphasizing the need to focus on implementing plans and learning from them.

Variations in strategic capabilities such as those for implementation, for monitoring and evaluation, for learning, and for government machinery to act in unified and integrated ways (to achieve levels of agility and adaptability needed to cope with changes in circumstances) could be evident both over time in a single country or could show up as national differences between the six states. Either way, the existence of variations in capabilities could be a critical variable that makes the relationship between having a national strategy for economic and social development and the success of national development slightly more complicated. A strategy may be important for faster and more effective economic and social development, but strategic capabilities may be necessary if strategy is going to have an impact. So, we might expect that a country needs a strategy plus strategic capabilities in order to have successful government-led national development.

But all that said, do the Gulf states find themselves confronting a massive strategic issue in their chosen strategy to overcome their dependence on oil? Is there a special problem facing them because they need the oil revenue to build a new type of economy based on human resources, and because of the volatility—the boom and bust—of world oil prices? Is this special problem that the periods in which income is flowing from oil at high prices is soon followed by prices falling? As we saw in Figure 7.3, an upswing began in 2002 and was nearly over by 2008, and really over by mid-2014. How does the strategic thinking and planning deal with this issue of relatively short windows of opportunity to take advantage of high prices to build a new type of economy? And is it right that it is harder to motivate the development of the necessary strategic process capabilities in the societies where the dependence on oil is greatest (as measured by oil rents against GDP)?

Summary

It looks as though the recent moves by Gulf states since 1995 to become more strategic have not yet transformed their economies away from being dominated by oil. Arguably, the move to becoming more strategic is retarded by bigger oil rents (as suggested by the data for Saudi Arabia and Kuwait). It might be said that the six countries are on a learning curve regarding the use of strategic management to reform public governance and become more activist states in the economic sphere so that dependence on oil is lessened.

The essence of the government economic strategies in the Arabian Peninsula is generally to replace dependence on oil by diversifying the economy, building up non-oil industries and exports, and creating a knowledge economy for the future. This makes human resources the critical and most important resources. It is a resource-based approach to strategic thinking.

In terms of strategic capabilities it has been found that, based on the Hertie School of Governance data, that these capabilities do matter for both the productiveness of an economy and the happiness of the public. However, the Bahrain government seems to constitute a special case: it does not seem to fit precisely the pattern of results characterizing the other five Gulf states. As we saw in the chapter, there has been a statistical study of happiness of the citizens of countries in the Middle East and North Africa region that suggests internal conflict may be related to levels of unhappiness.

Reference List

Fereidouni, H. G., Najdi, Y. and Amiri, R. E. (2013) Do Governance Factors Matter for Happiness in the MENA Region? *International Journal of Social Economics*, 40(12), 1028–1040.

Hamel, G. and Prahalad, C. K. (1994) *Competing for the Future*. Boston, MA: Harvard Business School Press.

Helliwell, John F., Richard Layard and Jeffrey Sachs (editors) (2013) *World Happiness Report 2013*. New York: UN Sustainable Development Solutions Network.

Helliwell, John F., Richard Layard and Jeffrey Sachs (editors) (2015) *World Happiness Report 2015*. New York: Sustainable Development Solutions Network.

Hertie School of Governance (2014) *The Governance Report 2014*. Oxford: Oxford University Press.

Hsu, A. et al. (2016) *2016 Environmental Performance Index*. New Haven, CT: Yale University.

OECD (2013) *Strategic Insights from the Public Governance Reviews: Update*. *GOV/PGC(2013)4, Public Governance and Territorial Development Directorate. Public Governance Committee*. Paris: OECD.

Reuters (2015) Qatar Slashes 2015 GDP Forecast, Raises Fiscal Surplus Projection. [online] [21 December 2015]. Available from: http://www.arabianbusiness.com// qatar-slashes-2015-gdp-forecast-raises-fiscal-surplus-projection-615624.html

Rumelt, R. (2011) *Good Strategy Bad Strategy: The Difference and Why It Matters.* London: Profile.

Schwab, K. (editor) (2015) *The Global Competitiveness Report 2015–2016.* Geneva: World Economic Forum.

Staff Writer (2015) Qatar's Foreign Trade Surplus Halves to $3.3bn from Year Earlier. [online] [21 December 2015]. Available from: http://www.arabianbusiness. com/qatar-s-foreign-trade-surplus-halves—3-3bn-from-year-earlier-611059. html#.Vne_MYSWHQM

Part II
The Supranational Level

8   The Gulf Cooperation Council

Introduction

The Arabian Gulf states for centuries have been the centre of commercial trade flows, being located just where Asia, Africa, and Europe meet. In January 1968, after the announcement of the withdrawal of the British Empire from the Arabian Gulf countries, the rulers saw that they would be more powerful if they were united as a group. The first step was the creation of the United Arab Emirates. The second step, finally taken in 1981, was the creation of the Gulf Cooperation Council.

The Gulf Cooperation Council was 35 years old in 2016. Its total population in 2015 was around 52.69 million. According to OPEC estimates in 2015, its crude oil reserves were 40.7% of the world's total reserves.

Gulf Cooperation Council formation

In May 1976, Sheikh Jaber Al-Sabah the Crown Prince and Prime Minister of Kuwait announced the need for a union of all the Gulf countries. During Sheikh Al-Sabah's visit to the United Arab Emirates in May 1976, Sheikh Zayed gave his approval and support.

It took several years to form the Gulf Cooperation Council. During the Arab summit in Jordan in November 1980, the ruler of Kuwait suggested to Sheikh Zayed Al Nahyan, ruler of Abu Dhabi, and Sultan Qaboos, ruler of Oman, the need to create a body that led to the legal framework of establishing the Gulf Cooperation Council.

The Reasons for the Establishment of the Gulf Cooperation Council

The idea of blocs and alliances became influential in the twentieth century after the end of the Second World War, and it has become commonplace for groups of countries to be linked by common interests in an entity. That is what actually happened with the Gulf countries. The Gulf Cooperation Council was focused on three goals:

1   To create bloc forces to fill the security vacuum resulting from the British withdrawal from the Arab oil kingdoms;
2   To establish a barrier against strong regional ambitions to control the oil resources in the Gulf;
3   To deepen and strengthen relations, links, and aspects of cooperation between Gulf Cooperation Council citizens, especially the residents of the six nations who were descended from common ethnic origins.

A meeting of foreign ministers was held in Riyadh, Saudi Arabia, on 4 February 1981. Following this, the Cooperation Council for the Arab States of the Gulf—referred to as the Cooperation Council—was established. The agreement was signed in the Arabic language at Abu Dhabi, United Arab Emirates, on 21 Rajab 1401 corresponding to 25 May 1981 between Bahrain, Kuwait, Oman, Qatar, Saudi Arabia, and United Arab Emirates. Its headquarters were to be in Riyadh, Saudi Arabia.

The Gulf Cooperation Council was established in accordance with their special relations, common characteristics, and similar systems, which were founded on the creed of Islam, which binds them. It is said that that coordination, cooperation, and integration between them serves the sublime objective of the Arab Nation. It was seen as being in conformity with the Charter of the League of Arab States which calls for the realization of closer relations and stronger bonds and which calls for service to Arab and Islamic causes.

Its primary objective is to effect coordination, integration, and interconnection between member states in all fields in order to achieve unity between them; to deepen and strengthen relations, links, and areas of cooperation now prevailing between their people in various fields; to formulate similar regulations in the fields of economic and financial affairs, commerce, customs, communication, education, and culture and, finally, to stimulate scientific and technological progress in the fields of industry, mining, agriculture, water and minimal resources; to establish scientific research; to establish joint ventures and encourage cooperation by the private sector for the common good of their citizens (General 2016).

Gulf Cooperation Council structures

The main organization of the Cooperation Council is composed of the following:

1   The Supreme Council
2   The Ministerial Council
3   The Secretariat General

The Supreme Council is the highest authority of the Cooperation Council and was formed of heads of member states. Its presidency was to rotate based on the alphabetical order of the names of the member states. The 2016 President of the Gulf Cooperation Council was Saudi Arabia.

The Supreme Council was to hold one regular session every year. Extraordinary sessions were to be convened at the request of any member seconded by another member. Its sessions were to be held in the territories of member states. A Supreme Council's meeting was to be considered valid if it was attended by two-thirds of the member states.

The functions of the Supreme Council were to realize the objectives of the Cooperation Council and lay down the higher policy for the cooperation council. The Ministerial Council was critical to its workings; it provided recommendations and reports to the Supreme Council. Voting in the Supreme Council was to be on the basis of one vote for each member.

The Ministerial Council was to be formed of the Foreign Ministers of the member states or other delegated ministers. The Council Presidency was to be for the member state that presided at the last ordinary session of the Supreme Council. It was to convene every three months and could hold extraordinary sessions at the invitation of any member seconded by another member. Its key functions were to propose policies and prepare recommendations, studies, and projects aimed at developing cooperation and coordination between member states in various fields.

The Secretariat General completed the main structure of the Gulf Cooperation Council. This was to be composed of a Secretary General, who was to be assisted by assistants and a number of staff as required. The Supreme Council was to appoint the Secretary General, who had to be a citizen of one of the Cooperation Council States. The Secretary General's period of office was a period of three years, which could be renewed once only. Dr. Abdul Latif Bin Rashid Al Zayani was appointed the Secretary General of the Gulf Cooperation Council from 1 April 2011.

As might be guessed, the Secretary General was to be directly responsible for the work of the Secretariat General and the smooth flow of work in its various organizations. He was to represent the Cooperation Council with other parties within the limits of the authority vested in him. The Secretariat General could, among other things, prepare studies and integrate plans and programmes for member states' action.

The Gulf Cooperation Council Budget

Member states contribute in equal amounts to the Secretariat General's budget. The Saudi government built its headquarters in Riyadh, Saudi Arabia. Its initial budget was about SR 80 million ($21.33 million). The budget has grown to about SR 500 million ($133.33 million).

Disputes between Members of the Gulf Cooperation Council

When disputes arise between members of the Gulf Cooperation Council, rulers have solved the dispute on a private level. But a formal procedure for dispute resolution was envisaged. The Gulf Cooperation Council was to have a commission called "The Commission for the Settlement of Disputes" which was to be attached to the Supreme Council. The Supreme Council was to establish the composition of the Commission for every case on an "ad hoc" basis in accordance with the nature of the dispute.

Security Issues

Aggression against any member of the Gulf Cooperation Council is deemed an aggression against the entire set of member states. As we noted at the beginning of this chapter, a big impetus to its formation was a perception of the existence of an external threat and a desire to strengthen collective security. According to Held and Ulrichsen (2012, 6):

> The Gulf Cooperation Council was formed in May 1981 as a defensive bulwark against the Iranian revolution in 1979 and subsequent Iraqi invasion . . . it suffered from lingering suspicions among the smaller Gulf states, particularly Qatar but latterly also the UAE, of perceived Saudi hegemonic designs in the Arabian Peninsula . . . The Saudi-led intervention to restore order in Bahrain in March 2011 demonstrated some of the motivations (but also tensions) driving policy-making at the GCC level. Nevertheless, the fact of its survival over three turbulent decades sets it apart from every previous attempt to create a durable inter-state organisation in the Arab world.

Until 1971 British-led forces maintained peace and order in the Gulf, and British officials arbitrated local quarrels. After the withdrawal of these forces and officials, old territorial claims and suppressed tribal animosities rose to the surface. The concept of the modern state introduced into the gulf region by the European powers—and the sudden importance of boundaries to define ownership of oil deposits—kindled acute territorial disputes.

Iran has often laid claim to Bahrain, based on its seventeenth-century defeat of the Portuguese and its subsequent occupation of the Bahrain archipelago. The Arab clan of the Al-Khalifa, which has been the ruling family of Bahrain since the eighteenth century, in turn pushed out the Iranians in 1780. The late shah, Mohammad Reza Pahlavi, raised the Bahrain question when the British withdrew from areas east of Suez, but he dropped his demand after a 1970 UN-sponsored plebiscite showed that Bahrainis overwhelmingly preferred independence to Iranian hegemony. In fact, the religious leaders of the Iranian Revolution revived the claim to Bahrain primarily on the grounds that the majority of Bahrainis were Shia Muslims, but Iranian secular leaders subsequently renounced the claim in an attempt to establish better relations with Bahrain.

There have also been issues in relation to Iran and the UAE. In 1971 Iranian forces occupied the islands of Abu Musa, Tunb al Kubra (Greater Tumb), and Tunb as Sughra (Lesser Tumb), located at the mouth of the gulf between Iran and the UAE. The Iranians reasserted their historic claims to the islands, although the Iranians had been dislodged by the British in the late nineteenth century. Iran continued to occupy the islands in 1993, and its action remained a source of contention with the UAE, which claimed authority by virtue of Britain's transfer of the islands to the emirates of Sharjah and Ras al Khaymah. By late 1992, Sharjah and Iran had reached agreement with regard to Abu Musa, but Ras al Khaymah had not reached a settlement with Iran concerning Greater Tumb and Lesser Tumb (Congress 2016)

The Peninsula Shield Force was established during the third Gulf Cooperation Council summit held in Manama in 1982, with member states agreeing to establish a "Peninsula Shield" made up of joint military forces from member states. The Peninsula Shield Force established its headquarters close to the city of Hafar Al-Batin in the Eastern Province of Saudi Arabia in 1985. The Peninsula Shield force represents an important defence against social and political instability and security threats in any of the member states.

According to Asharq Al-Awsat (2011) the Peninsula Shield Force undertook its first mission in 1986, after Iranian forces invaded Iraq's strategically crucial Faq Peninsula during the Iraq-Iran war. Initially, the Peninsula Shield Force was made up of 5,000 troops, and was increased to approximately 40,000 troops from all member states. The Peninsula Force sought to build up the Gulf Cooperation Council's defence capabilities, with member states establishing unified operational procedures, training, and military curricula. In addition to this, the Peninsula Shield Force began to carry out joint military exercises and maneuvers with all Gulf Cooperation Council states' military forces. The Peninsula Shield Force holds joint training exercises every two years with the Gulf's militaries (Al-awsat 2011).

Iraq's invasion of Kuwait in August 1990 was a shock to the Gulf Cooperation Council states. Kuwait was a major supplier of oil to the United States. The Iraqi takeover posed an immediate threat to neighbouring Saudi Arabia, another major exporter of oil. If Saudi Arabia fell to Saddam, Iraq would control one-fifth of the world's oil supply. All eyes were on the White House, waiting for a response. President Bush, who succeeded President Reagan, stated simply: "This will not stand."

In the last months of 1990, the United States participated in the defence of Saudi Arabia in a deployment known as Operation Desert Shield. Over 500,000 American troops were placed in Saudi Arabia in case of an Iraqi attack on the Saudis. The US further sought multilateral support in the

United Nations Security Council. Traditionally, Iraq was an ally of the Soviet Union, who held a veto power over any potential UN military action. Looking westward for support for their dramatic internal changes, the USSR did not block the American plan. The UN condemned Iraq and helped form a coalition to fight Saddam militarily.

Bush, remembering the lessons of Vietnam, sought public support as well. Although there were some opponents of the conflict, the vast majority of Americans and a narrow majority of the Congress supported the President's actions. When all the forces were in place, the United States issued an ultimatum to Saddam Hussein: leave Kuwait by 15 January 1991 or face a full attack by the multinational force.

January 15 came and went with no response from the Iraqis. The next night Desert Shield became Desert Storm. On 24 February 1991, the ground war began. Although the bombing lasted for weeks, American ground troops declared Kuwait liberated just 100 hours after the ground attack was initiated. Concerns were raised that if Saddam's regime were toppled, the entire nation could disintegrate into a civil war. Iraq agreed to terms for a ceasefire, and the conflict subsided (USHistory.org 2016).

The Syrian Civil War came out of the unrest of the 2011 Arab Spring protests. Escalation to armed conflict came after President Bashar al-Assad's government violently repressed protests calling for his removal. The war is being fought by the Syrian Government, a loose alliance of Syrian Arab rebel groups, the Syrian Democratic Forces, Salafi jihadist groups (including al-Nusra Front) and the Islamic State of Iraq and the Levant (ISIL). All sides receive substantial support from foreign actors, leading many to label the conflict a proxy war waged by the regional and world major powers. In 2016 the Gulf Cooperation Council member states were still standing behind their declaration of solidarity not to recognize the Assad regime.

The Yemeni Civil War began in 2015 between two factions claiming to constitute the Yemeni government, along with their supporters and allies. Houthi forces controlling the capital Sana'a and allied with forces loyal to the former president Ali Abdullah Saleh have clashed with forces loyal to the government of Abd Rabbuh Mansur Hadi, based in Aden. Al-Qaeda in the Arabian Peninsula (AQAP) and the Islamic State of Iraq and the Levant have also carried out attacks, with AQAP controlling swaths of territory in the hinterlands, and along stretches of the coast. A coalition led by Saudi Arabia with other Gulf Cooperation Council member states became involved in military operations by using airstrikes to restore the former Yemeni government and the United States provided intelligence and logistical support for the campaign.

The Arab Spring of 2011: Poverty and Governance

It has been suggested that the Gulf Cooperation Council governments may have tended to respond to the Arab Spring in a way that compromised the government strategies of diversifying the economy and reducing dependence on oil (Held and Ulrichsen 2012, 18): "Moreover, initial reactions to popular demands for reform in the 2011 'Arab Spring' only complicated longer-term strategies of economic transition." The reactions are said to have been ones of giving pay rises in the public sector, increasing benefits, and job creation (Held and Ulrichsen 2012, 19):

> regimes preemptively announced public sector pay and benefit increases and additional job creation in government ministries. These short-term policy decisions exacerbate the challenges of reformulated dual and imbalanced labour markets, streamlining and incentivising national workforces and strengthening private sector development.

The 2011 Arab Spring was unrest that began in Tunisia and spread to various countries elsewhere in the Middle East and North Africa. Some of the countries most affected were Tunisia, Egypt, Libya, Yemen, Syria and Bahrain. Tunisian Mohammed Bouazizi, a 26-year-old fruit vendor, set himself on fire in the town of Sidi Bouzid in a protest against police abuses. This inspired a popular uprising. The unrest in Tunisia was soon being replicated in a number of countries.

Before the January protests that ended his 30-year-rule, the fiercest unrest to challenge Egypt's Hosni Mubarak was not inspired by politics, but by a lack of bread. In the summer of 2008, the country experienced a shortage of subsidized bread; being the world's largest wheat importer, the impact was felt immediately. Dozens of riots touched off across the country, and to contain the violence, Mubarak actually ordered the army to bake loaves of flatbread for the masses.

The Gulf Cooperation Council member state most affected by the Arab Spring was Bahrain. Forces from other member states went to Bahrain to maintain order and security and to protect strategic facilities at the request of the Bahraini government. The decision to send Gulf Cooperation Council troops to neighbouring Bahrain came after Bahraini police clashed with Shiite protestors in a violent confrontation. The troops included more than 1,000 Saudi soldiers, who were part of the Gulf states' Peninsula Shield Force. There were also 500 police from United Arab Emirates. This deployment was in accordance with the agreement of the member states that any threat to the security of any member state is an act of aggression to the security of the rest of the member states (Arabiya 2011).

Why did the Arab Spring happen? There are a number of possible explanations. Some commentators think that poverty encourages mass demonstrations and civil wars to overthrow governments. Others suggest that weak governance and the lack of participation of the civil society make such things more likely.

Development of Economic Institutions

The Gulf Cooperation Council economic agreement covered a Customs Union, Common Market, Economic and Monetary Union, Development

Integration, Human Resources Development, Cooperation in the Fields of Scientific and Technical Research, Transportation, Communications and Infrastructure (Council 2001).

The first phase of the Gulf Cooperation Council customs union was launched in January 2003. Its full implementation has taken 12 years because of issues such as how customs' revenues would be shared by member states. It became fully operational from 1 January 1 2015. The customs union basically refers to a free trade bloc with a common external tariff— five percent duty is to be levied on goods imported from countries outside the Gulf Cooperation Council. Air, sea, and land ports anywhere in the Gulf Cooperation Council area that have direct connection with the outside world can be a single point of entry for imported goods meant for any member state. As part of the customs union, products manufactured within the member states are considered national products and their movement within the region is free, attracting no customs levy (Peninsula 2015). It was a step towards a full-fledged regional common market.

On 1 January 2008, the Gulf Cooperation Council common market was introduced. The common market gave citizens from each of the six member states the same rights and entitlements. Under the agreement, citizens have the same rights in areas such as employment, healthcare, education, social security, and residence, as well as in economic activities such as trading in stock markets, setting up companies, and buying and selling properties (Reuters 2008).

The planned establishment of the Gulf Cooperation Council monetary union in 2010 did not happen due to technical difficulties. The monetary union would eliminate transaction costs that citizens must endure due to having several national currencies in one regional bloc. A common market and common central bank would also position the Gulf Cooperation Council as one entity that would have great "influence on the international financial system" (Khan 2014).

Economic Integration

A resolution of the Supreme Council (22nd Session, Muscat, Oman, 30–31 December 2001) addressed the setting up of a Standardization Organization for the Gulf Cooperation Council for the Arab States of the Gulf (GSO) in preference to transforming the Saudi Arabian Standards Organization (SASO) into a Gulf organization.

The GSO aims at helping the Gulf Cooperation Council achieve the objectives set forth in its charter and in the Economic Agreement by unifying the various standardization activities and following up application and compliance of the same in cooperation and coordination with the standardization bodies in the member states in an endeavor to develop the production and service sectors; foster the member states' inter-trading; protect the consumer, environment, and the public health; and encourage industries and agricultural production that would enhance the member states' economy, maintain the achievements of the member states and minimize the technical trade barriers as envisaged by the objectives of the customs union.

The member states have progressively lowered nontariff barriers, both as part of integration efforts and in response to commitments under the World Trade Organization (WTO). Significant progress has been made in establishing unified technical standards (currently covering some 3,000 products) and harmonizing and reducing customs administrative procedures and clearance requirements.

With open borders between member states, improvements in infrastructure, especially roads and telecommunications, are generating benefits. According to Arab News (2016), a road connecting Saudi and Oman is ready to open; it will shorten the distance between Oman and Saudi Arabia by 800 km. There had been a two-year delay, but the road, which runs through the Empty Quarter desert, or Rub Al-Khali, received its first trial operation by the Royal Oman Police. The Gulf Cooperation Council Railway, running from Kuwait City to Muscat, should link the six member countries of the Gulf Cooperation Council by 2018. The 2,117-km railway is estimated to have cost $15.4 billion.

In summary, the economic integration of Gulf Cooperation Council member states has been happening, albeit slowly, and even though there are some aspects of the integration still to be accomplished.

Environmental Issues

In May 2015, Doha hosted the thirty-fifth meeting of the undersecretaries responsible for environmental affairs in the Gulf Cooperation Council. The meeting considered a study to establish the Environmental Monitoring Center and developments related to the United Nations Convention on Climate Change, the Kyoto Protocol, the Vienna Convention for the Protection of the Ozone Layer, and the Montreal Protocol on Substances that Deplete the Ozone Layer, as well as the Gulf Cooperation Council environment and wildlife award.

The Qatar Assistant Undersecretary for Environmental Affairs, Ahmed Mohammed Al-Sada, emphasized that one of the GCC's achievements was the "patronage of Their Majesties and Highnesses the leaders of the Council to the process of joint environmental action, and their wise directives to protect the environment in the GCC countries and to maintain the sustainability of natural resources in order to meet the aspirations of the peoples in achieving sustainable development and promoting economic and social progress and stability" (QNA 2015).

Summary and Conclusion

The Gulf Cooperation Council was officially set up in May 1981. It was initiated by the Kuwait government and supported by the United Arab

Emirates in the late 1970s. The main drive for establishing the Gulf Cooperation Council was to protect the national security of the Arab Gulf states. The Gulf states will need to depend on their own capacity and improve their strategic management capabilities (Nixon 1990).

Progress on economic, social, and environmental cooperation has been somewhat slow. The Gulf Cooperation Council countries are facing many challenges internally and externally. Their youth is demanding more from their governments. Social media is empowering people. It enables members of society to complain and make their opinions heard. Governments of member states in the Gulf Cooperation Council are trying to meet public expectations.

Reference List

Arabiya, A. (2011) *Al Arabiya*. [online] [28 July 2016]. Available from: http://www.alarabiya.net

ArabNews. (2016) *Arab News*. [online] [9 July 2016]. Available from: http://www.arabnews.com

Asby, P. (2012) Culture Change is Needed in the Civil Service as well as in Banks. *The Guardian*. [online] [20 April 2016]. Available from: http://www.theguardian.com

Asharq Al-Awsat (2011) *Asharq Al-Awsat*. [online] [28 July 2016]. Available from: http://www.aawsat.com

Congress, L. O. (2016) *Country Studies*. [online] [July 2016]. Available from: http://countrystudies.us/persian-gulf-states/94.htm

General, G. S. (2016) *GCC Secretarial General*. [online] [26 July 2016]. Available from: http://Gulf Cooperation Council-sg.org

Held, D. and Ulrichsen, K. (2012) Editor's Introduction: Transformation of the Gulf. In: David Held and Kristian Ulrichsen (editors) *The Transformation of The Gulf: Politics, Economics and the Global Order*. London and New York: Routledge. Pages 1–25.

Khan, G. A. (2014, June 29). GCC Tries to Persuade UAE, Oman to Join Currrency Talks. [online] [19 April 2016]. Available from: Arab News: www.arabnews.com

Nixon, R. (1990). *Leaders*. Second Edition. New York: Touchstone.

Peninsula, T. (2015, January 3). GCC Customs Union Fully Operational. [online] [19 April 2016]. Available from The Peninsula: http://thepeninsulaqata.org

QNA, Q. N. (2015). *Qatar News Agency*. [online] [29 July 2016]. Available from: http://qna.org.qa

Reuters (2008, January 3). GCC Common Market Comes into Effect. *Arabian Business*. [online] [19 April 2016]. Available from Arabian Business: http://www.arabianbusiness.com

USHistory.org (2016) Operation Desert Storm. USHistory.org. [online] [28 July 2016]. Available from: http://www.ushistory.org/us/60a.asp

Part III

Commentary and Conclusions

9 Summary and Conclusions

Introduction

Public Governance in general, at supranational level as well as national level, places a priority on economic, social, and environmental issues. One thing we learn when studying public governance in the Gulf states is that the national leaders have to build governance institutions and governance capabilities that can create some kind of moving equilibrium that additionally encompasses the cultural, religious, and political dimensions of these countries. This does not make them simpler or less complex governance systems than those of other countries. We can see in long-term visions produced by GCC countries starting in 1995, and coming right up to 2016, not only statements about their economic, social, and environmental priorities, not only about the aspirations to values aiming to uplift living standards of their citizens, but also statements about the importance of their cultural and religious frameworks.

Academic discussions in universities and analysis in international policy circles (for example, policy circles based on the OECD and the World Bank) have been very concentrated on government networks and democracy and on government effectiveness, respectively. Anyone looking seriously into the context of the Gulf states will soon appreciate that there is also a discussion to be had about government resources and their use to maintain social cohesion by genuinely trying to meet the aspirations of national citizens. This last statement is another way of introducing the idea of the rentier state, to which we return in this last chapter. It is clear to us that the relationships between government resources and citizens' aspirations provide a pivotal dynamic at the heart of governance in the Gulf states at the present time. It is also at the heart of the meaning of this next quote from Held and Ulrichsen (2012, 4) that concerns the reconstruction of the state in the Arabian Peninsula in a period when government resources are based on oil revenue:

> Redistributive mechanisms of socio-political control emerged within a highly stratified economic framework encompassing nests of rentiers flowing downward from the state at its apex. New bureaucratic

structures integrated existing (merchant) and new (middle-class) groupings into emergent politics as ruling families co-opted support and
acquired support through the spread of their wealth to their citizenry.
Moreover, the influx of oil rents enabled the monarchies to manage the
scale and rapidity of their socio-economic transformation in the 1960s
and 1970s with minimal social upheaval.

The changes in public governance and the nature of the state and economy
coincided with very fast population growth. Take the case of Saudi Arabia:
its population quadrupled over the past four decades to nearly 30.7 million
in 2014. The population was expected to total 35.7 million by 2020, at a
compound annual growth rate of 2 percent since 2014.

In this concluding chapter we want to do three things. First, we want to
revisit some of the discussions in the book, although this time providing
more of a commentary (that is, more judgment) whereas before we have
tried to be as descriptive and analytical as we could be. Second, we want
to think about what we have learned about the attempts, through public
governance and the application of long-term strategic thinking and the use
of strategic plans, by leaders of the Gulf states to break out of the systemic
nature of the rentier state and their countries' dependence on oil resources.
This could be seen as attempts to reinvent the rentier state as a strategic state
and shift the centre of gravity of these societies from oil to human resources.
Third, we want to think about what generalizations we can offer from this
study of the Gulf states to the generic literature on public governance and
its reform and modernization.

Challenges

The list of challenges facing the Gulf states seems endless, although their
urgency and importance varies over time and from one country to another.
To name a few that we think are important:

1 Government decision-making and the need for more transparency
2 Corruption
3 Justice—distribution of income and wealth, distribution of opportunities
4 The empowerment of women and their active participation in national
   development activities
5 What to do about the development and employment of young people
6 Unemployment and participation rates of nationals (and the problem of
   the "rentier mentality")
7 Weak civil society and the need to increase citizen "voice" through engagement and participation in the national development agenda
8 Continuing to make reforms—legal, political, social, and economic
   reforms

9   Developing a smart government strategy to deal with the constraints on government success because of the fluctuations and business cycles in oil prices

10 Reforming public governance and developing a strategic approach to national development

According to Transparency International Corruption Perception Index (CPI) 2015, a country or territory's score indicates the perceived level of public sector corruption on a scale of 0 (highly corrupt) to 100 (very clean). A country's rank indicates its position relative to the other countries in the index. The recent index included 168 countries and territories (see Table 9.1).

It is interesting that Qatar and the United Arab Emirates score so highly on the index since they also scored highly on strategic process capabilities and the government effectiveness estimates published by the World Bank. It seems to suggest that more capable government (including more strategically capable government) is more honest government. (Although we note that Oman ought to be alongside them in the scoring of the CPI based on its capabilities and reputed government effectiveness).

Issues of justice are neglected by academic studies that privilege statistics on the GDP per capita of a society. From the point of view of looking at the tensions in society, it is not a good index. As we noted earlier, the Greek philosopher Aristotle in ancient times believed that all societies—in his days city-states, mainly—had the rich and the poor, and also those in the middle. International experts have been pointing out for a long time now that inequality got worse in the 1980s and stayed worse. Some observers believe inequality has ratcheted up another notch since the international financial crisis of 2007–09. People have begun to talk about the super-rich one percent of populations and the 99 percent who individually have very little. Public governance has to deal with the effects of such inequalities and somehow achieve social stability. This means finding how to create social justice and a sense of fairness; it means addressing the risks of social resentment among the mass of people. This was all recognized 100 years ago

Table 9.1 Transparency International Corruption Index

Country	Rank	Score
Qatar	22	71
United Arab Emirates	23	70
Saudi Arabia	48	52
Bahrain	50	51
Kuwait	55	49
Oman	60	45

Source: Transparency International. Retrieved from http://www.transparency.org/cpi2015 (14 August 2016).

when sociologist Max Weber wrote about public administration in the new age of bureaucracy and the need to handle the pressures for "compensation" from what he described as the "propertyless".

It was noted in Chapter 6 that poverty was an issue highlighted in the Saudi Long-Term Strategy: Crown Prince Abdullah, Deputy Premier, had declared a war on poverty in the Kingdom in 2002 following his visit to poor citizens' homes in Riyadh. It was still an issue in 2009 as can be seen from Saudi Arabia's Ministry of Social Affairs reporting in April 2009 that there were about three million Saudis living below the poverty line.

The Saudi unemployment rate fell to 11.5 percent in 2015, mainly due to fewer Saudis joining the labour force rather than higher employment. According to Arab news reports, there were two incidents in 2016 involving the destruction of academic degree certificates by jobless youths: an unemployed dentist burning his certificate in April 2016 and a young Saudi woman tore up her master's degree certificate because it did not help her land a job. In the context of unemployment it may be an issue that the GCC countries have migrant workers from South Asia and Southeast Asia.

Local Saudi newspaper, the Saudi Gazette, reported on 6 June 2016 that around 50 percent of mobile phone shops are up for sale and another 20 percent are shutting down in reaction to the move for total Saudization in the telecommunication sector. Saudi nationals' have higher salaries—around SR 4,000/month against expatriates with salaries of around SR 2,500/month.

The Minister of Labor, Mofrej Al-Haqbani, said on 10 May 10 2016 that the ministry had failed to implement Saudization in some sectors. He attributed this mainly to the lack of coordination and non-involvement of some.

Rentier Mentality

After the Arab Spring in 2011, the governments in the GCC spent billions of dollars from their high oil price revenue to make society calmer and less likely to join in the protests. Did this counter social grievances and the danger of protests by entrenching a rentier mentality in the population?

Distribution of Opportunities

All six GCC governments have almost the same dreams and aspirations for their citizens. In order to be achieved the governments will have to meet and address some severe challenges and offer opportunities. Will the strength and effectiveness of their systems of public governance be enough? Meeting some of the challenges (for example, the young population) could also be seen as creating opportunity, especially if the governments and their partners in the business world together create attractive, high value-added employment opportunities for the young. The drive for diversification as well as the challenge of a burgeoning population delivers a greater need for GCC countries to educate, train, and develop their people through the public service systems for education, training, and development, and healthcare.

Becoming Visionary and Strategic

The Gulf states have embraced the notions of government setting long-term visions, being selective and focused, and working in partnership with private businesses. For example, in Saudi Arabia there was the vision statement for 2020. And now there is a new Saudi Vision 2030, which is to be the heart of the Arab and Islamic Worlds, become a global investment powerhouse and a transformed Saudi economy to be a global hub for Asia, Europe, and Africa.

In the 1990s and later, GCC governments looked for external help with this more strategic approach and contacted numerous consultants to work on planning. It seems the feasibility studies and consultancy led to an almost "one size fits all" concept of the GCC states' visions and economic strategies. International consultants conducted most of the feasibility studies and these appear to have been done without getting sufficiently involved with stakeholders to better understand the main challenges of each of the GCC states. The consultancy groups tend, we suspect, to see all the GCC states having the same situation in terms of governance.

The Problem of the Strategy to Achieve Economic Diversification

OPEC nations enjoyed a period of 10 years of high income. It took only one year of a big drop in the price of oil to create major crises in the OPEC nations. This was not just in the Arabian Peninsula. Venezuela and Nigeria were also in trouble: Nigeria lost 75 percent of its income and half a million Nigerians lost their jobs in the first four months of 2016 and millions more are suffering.

The drop in the price of oil from the middle of 2014 affected the Gulf governments' financial budgets, making expenditures higher than revenues. The governments of the Gulf states still greatly rely on oil revenue. To illustrate the effect of the financial strain placed on the Saudi government, we can note that public debt reached 30 percent of economic output in 2016, and the government planned to reduce the public sector wage bill as well as subsidies by 2020. Saudi government targets in April 2016 included reducing public-sector wages to 40 percent of spending by 2020, from 45 percent in 2016. The obvious question from the sidelines is: what will reducing the state spending do to the "conditional consent" that underpins political loyalty in the largest Arab society in the Arabian Peninsula?

Globalization, Rentier States, and Strategic States

It seems that most informed opinion has believed for 20 years now that we live in a globalizing world. The need for integrated, agile, and strategic governments can be linked to the perception that government effectiveness is needed to cope with the impacts of globalization and that effectiveness is demanded by the pace and complexity of globalization. A report by PUMA in 1996 made this point (PUMA 1996, 6): "By blurring institutional and policy boundaries, globalization is challenging governments' capacities to provide effective and coherent policy responses". This was just one of many reports that has advocated improved government management. It called on governments to develop strategic direction to guide government work and to achieve internal coordination and integration. At that time, the emphasis was more on policy coordination whereas today the tendency would be to urge that the various strategies of different government ministries be aligned to the long-term vision and priorities of the government and to be integrated and coordinated on a cross-ministry basis. Very often, too, there is now a call for a prominent role to be taken by a high-powered centre of government equipped with suitable capabilities to facilitate the delivery and coordination of long-term vision and long-term strategies of government.

In recognition of this we can suggest that increasingly there is a need to think about the strategic state as the end result of the reform of public governance and that this is taking place in circumstances defined by globalizing processes and the changing global situation. We have depicted this in Figure 9.1:

Figure 9.1 Modernizing Public Governance—the Strategic State in a Context of Globalization

Looking to the future, we can ask to what extent the Gulf states actually buy into what Held and Ulrichsen called the Washington consensus of economic development. And does the recent economic malaise of America and Europe partly create a climate in which suggestions that the GCC states could learn more from countries like Singapore become more credible? But, if so, will learning from the East problematize the desirability of democratization at the same time as boosting support for state-led economic development? That is, has the Washington consensus underpinned the idea of democratization as part of a modernization project, or has it just been about economic policy?

At this point it is worth noting that this is not a New Public Management agenda, which particularly engaged academics in the 1990s (and by which some academics are still fascinated). The New Public Management probably can be best seen as having some links with the neo-liberalism doctrine that was applied in the United Kingdom, the United States, and elsewhere in the 1980s. New Public Management was not really concerned with public governance since it believed efficiency and management hierarchy might be increased in order to streamline and make government cheaper without asking for any significant change in the relationship between government and public. We can think of New Public Management as taking place inside the systems of public service delivery and with little formal impact on the service delivery interface with the public. In contrast, the reform and modernization of public governance is concerned with government effectiveness and not simply with government efficiency. As a result of this change of focus, the modernization of public governance ends up wishing to see the active engagement of citizens and private stakeholders by government. Government is an enabler and not just a provider of public services.

Likewise, we can also distance the public governance reforms from the Washington Consensus, which we just referred to, and which was a set of policy prescriptions promoted by bodies that included the International Monetary Fund and the World Bank. Whereas some saw the Washington Consensus as concerned with fiscal discipline, reduced spending on subsidies, and more spending pro-growth, pro-poor services (for example, the World Bank supported governments investing in primary education rather than spending on subsidizing university education), and so on, others described it in terms that sounded very neo-liberal.

Of course, we should note, as the OECD accepts, that whatever the consensus (Washington Consensus or the need for a set of public governance reforms), the view that now prevails is the need for governments to tailor reforms to suit the circumstances of individual countries and not to slavishly follow model patterns of West or East.

It looks as though the Gulf states have not broken out of the system of rentier states, but it also looks like some of them are building up quite significant strategic state capabilities, which we have referred to here as "strategic process capabilities"—these are United Arab Emirates, Oman, and Qatar. And it looks as though this development of governance based on strategic state capabilities is something that citizens appreciate as shown by the average life evaluations as well as correlating with more productive economies as shown by GDP per capita

If our earlier conceptualizing of the new public governance is correct—leadership, institutions, and strategic state capabilities, then leadership will be the critical dimension for breaking out of the rentier state system.

It should be noted that a strategic state approach is neither a state-dominated approach nor a minimalist state approach. The quality of a strategic state might be judged using a number of criteria. These criteria concern the development of: focus, integration, coordination, coherence, and persistence. Some of these words seem to be closely related in meaning and may at times be used almost interchangeably. We have in mind the following three words: coordination, integration, and coherence. However, from the point of view of the development of new public governance we can define these words to bring out important differences between them. Coordination could be defined as work of aligning the work of ministries. This work may be done by a centre of government. The coordination of the activities of ministries could produce an integrated approach to government problem-solving. So, if there was, for example, a desire to improve the health of the nation because there were concerns about peoples' life expectancy, then the coordination of activities by a number of ministries may contribute towards tackling the problem as defined by the government. So, integration relates to the effective coordination of government activities to address a problem.

Which then leaves coherence as being a judgment or perception by government insiders or outsiders that the various actions of government makes sense (looks coherent) and are not contradicting each other. Incoherence would be when people judged that the actions of various government ministries, or of various levels of government, are not making sense. So, that would give us coordination of activities, integration of the effects of those activities in producing solutions, and judgments by observers that the actions make sense and don't seem to impede each other.

At the end of this book we have come to the conclusion that the six Gulf states have proceeded at different speeds down the road to the strategic state. As we discussed in Chapter 7, we think it is reasonable to interpret comparisons of data for the six countries as showing that the United Arab Emirates, Omar, and Qatar have gone furthest in developing strategic (process) capabilities needed to be an effective strategic state. We also think that it is possible that Saudi Arabia and Kuwait may struggle more to develop strategic-state capabilities because they have a bigger reliance on oil. We think it is not surprising really; it almost seems in keeping with common sense views about human nature that a context of munificence is not conducive to striving to make progress.

There was evidence from our comparisons that the citizens of the United Arab Emirates and Qatar experienced living in a higher productivity economy (but we note again the issue of uneven distribution of the benefits of economic growth within a society) and reported on average higher life evaluations (that is, they were more satisfied with their lives). It was interesting in Chapter 7 to read of the suggested benefits for happiness of living in societies with good governance—benefits that some think may matter more than high GDP per capita.

We have also concluded at the end of this book that as far as we can tell from the data, none of the six states have escaped the constraints of a rentier state framework. This is based on the evidence about the oil rents expressed as a percentage of GDP. To this can be added the comments that there has not been the breakthrough in foreign direct investment that was seen as part of the post-rentier economy. The foreign direct investment was very low (as a percentage of GDP) in 2014. Even the United Arab Emirates was reporting that foreign direct investment was only 3 percent of GDP in 2014 and for Qatar it was 0 percent in 2014.

Breaking out of the rentier state framework has been shown by events such as the Arab Spring in 2011 and the crash in oil prices in 2014 to be very difficult both in terms of the need for rulers to maintain conditional consent and for reasons of government spending and investment being supported by the Gulf state's oil sectors.

Assuming that the Gulf states continue to see their future based in human resource development, innovation, and knowledge-based economies, as Saudi Arabia is continuing to do with its Vision 2030, then efforts will need to continue in building effective institutions of governance and building strategic-state capabilities. This will be the responsibility of the national leaders in the Gulf states.

One very specific leadership challenge is to develop a more credible strategy kernel for the governments' economic strategies, one that learns lessons in relation to the relatively short time periods in which there is an upswing of oil prices (maybe 6–10 years) before the brakes on public investment and spending have to be applied.

It might also be helpful to recognize that despite the similarity of the long-term visions, there are in fact quite different de facto economic interventions by governments. Some countries—such as the United Arab Emirates—have invested in diversification. The investment led by Abu Dhabi was invested, or was planned to be invested, in nuclear power, industrial infrastructure, state-owned export-oriented heavy industries, and high tech heavy industries. But it also made a side-bet in long-term overseas investment. And, of course, even as far back as 1976, Kuwait has been pursuing international investment. In 1976 it set up the Fund for Future Generations with $7 billion and this organization was mandated to provide Kuwait with a foreign investment vehicle. Does this indicate that there really is the possibility of very different long-term visions and strategies between the six countries? Have the vision statements and strategies been based on too much imitation of one another's strategic thinking (or too much reliance on external consultants who have put forward one-size-fits-all strategies and intentions)? And has there consequently been a failure to capture the real strategic intentions in the vision statements and strategies produced to date? One challenge for leaders in the Gulf states is to ensure that the strategic thinking is really owned within government and that vision statements and strategies are energized by the will and determination of the leaders—and with this being done on the basis that each country needs its own strategic direction suited to its situation, its resources and capabilities, and its goals and options. The new few years could be a moment of truth for the development of the strategic state in the Arabian Peninsula and the prospects for escaping from a rentier state.

Some Last Words on the Implications for the Gulf States

It might be hoped that the quality of national government and national leadership in the GCC countries has been improving over the last decade. Public sector leaders appear to be becoming more accountable for their performance. In Saudi Arabia, for example, in 2016 King Salman issued a royal order relieving Ahmed bin Aqeel Al-Khatib, the Minister of Health, of his responsibilities.

Over the same period it can be argued that the rise of social media means that citizens in GCC countries have a louder voice in national life. Possibly as a product of both of these trends, the GCC countries have moved, albeit slowly, into social and political reforms of their institutions.

High calibre and credible leadership is needed for the big responsibilities of transformation. Leaders carry the fate of these six countries on their shoulders in the years ahead. They will no doubt continue their efforts at maintaining social solidarity. Every successful nation must have social solidarity. If the individual believes in the excellence of the social solidarity of their society, he or she will be ready to offer "conditional consent" which is the basis of political stability and the legitimacy accorded to rulers.

Connecting Back to Concepts and Theories of Governance

At the beginning of this study we considered that our theoretical concerns included weighing up the usefulness of the concept of a "rentier state" when trying to understand the predicaments as well as the essence of the six Gulf countries and gauging how much descriptive and explanatory power the concept of a strategic state might have for changes that were occurring in the Gulf states. We also wanted to know if the types of characteristics attributed to a strategic state by the OECD might be relevant to the understanding of the Gulf states as strategic states. We have ended up with a judgment that the Gulf states are still functioning within the confines of a rentier state. The evidence we considered in Chapter 7 on the extent and the pattern of fluctuations in oil rent (as a percentage of GDP) was an important consideration in that judgment, showing the impact of world oil prices on the oil rent as a percentage of the economy. Another consideration was the evidence of the rapidity and severity with which governments' public finances were compromised by the drop in oil prices in 2014. This showed that the governments were vulnerable to a big drop in oil prices and that they were reliant on oil revenue for public spending. The governments were still dependent on the oil sector for both the state of the economy and for their own revenue.

As we bring the book to a close, it is time to think about how the evidence we have looked at might relate to the governance literature in the social sciences, and what we think might be some important conceptualizations developed in this study that could be useful in wider debates on public governance throughout the world. Therefore, the following comments represent our effort to generalize conceptually as a contribution to the bigger theoretical debate on public governance.

It should be noted that the writers in the public governance literature and practitioners do have a variety of ends in mind and a variety of ideas of what good governance looks like. For example, in the early 1990s it was suggested that,

> For the policy statements now emanating from other aid donors, especially governments of major bilateral donors, tend to be relatively militant and provocative in asserting that (multi-party) democracy and civil liberties are essential components of 'good government', and conditions for aid.
>
> (Moore 1993)

We have made a clear choice to focus on government effectiveness. We could have focused on many other things, most notably democracy. We were aware we could have explored governance in relation to democracy, but we were interested primarily in governance as a public management issue and so chose to focus on government effectiveness. This puts us theoretically alongside the concerns of the World Bank (1997) and the OECD (2013), as well as Levi (2006) who made the same choice when introducing her article on a new theory of government. The development of the public governance literature could be well served by having clarity about the distinct ends that may be important in theoretical formulations. It is also important to be clear about public governance being concerned with government, and thus the distinctness of concerns of the public governance literature from the use of governance to denote a different set of social relationships from those implied by concepts of hierarchy and contracts, even if these are being investigated as public sector phenomena (Johanson 2014). In fact, the writing on governance as a non-hierarchical and non-contractual way of organizing activities overlaps with the public governance literature to the extent that modern public government might make use of networks of service providers and will need to understand how to get the best results from them in the public interest (Milward 2015).

Our first generalization is that the effective strategic state has at least three components: strategic leaders, good strategies, and good strategic process capabilities. The strategic process capabilities include four (at least):

(i) long-term strategic visioning;
(ii) ensuring government coordination, integration and coherence;
(iii) mobilizing public authorities, and public and private stakeholders behind the long-term strategic vision; and
(iv) evaluating strategic action (policies) and adapting.

In our study of the Gulf states we have found some evidence that governments that scored highly on long-term strategic visions also tended to score highly on evaluating policies and adapting to changes in their context. This might be seen as suggesting that the two correlated sets of capabilities (visioning and evaluating/adapting) formed a higher-level or more generic type of strategic capability—which we think could be usefully generalized as a capability for being purposeful and conscious. The remaining capabilities were, arguably, organizing capabilities—achieving integration and coordination within the government machinery and organizing in the sense of mobilizing public authorities and mobilizing public and private stakeholders. So, perhaps governments need two high-level strategic process capabilities in order to be effective in public governance terms, which we will label here: capabilities for being purposeful and organizing capabilities.

It is possible to make connections between these statements and the government/governance literature. We suggest two such connections here. First, Deutsch (1966) put forward the interesting proposition that there were two types of leaders in government. There were, he said, 'prophetic leaders' who put forward new ideas, and 'continuing leaders' who exercised real power. We would suggest that the prophetic leaders do not have to generate the new ideas all by themselves. (As has often been suggested about leaders generally, both public and private sector leaders, they do not have to dream up a long-term vision in isolation—by themselves—they often find good ideas though discussions and conversations with others.) Deutsch's continuing type of leaders accepted some of the ideas of the prophetic leaders and applied them. We could link this duality of leaders to a duality in strategic process capabilities. We might say, therefore, that governments need to be able to lead (capability for being purposeful and conscious) as well as manage (capability to organize government for integrated and coordinated action and mobilize others both within the public sector and beyond government). This could, therefore, be seen as similar to proposals made about the need for leadership and management in private sector organizations (Kotter 2001).

The second connection is with the ideas of Barber (2007), who might be seen as offering yet another conceptualization of the strategic state. He presented a model of national government in which strategic direction was combined with a number of things that we might see as creating effective organization (performance management and development of capability, capacity, and culture). Strategic direction could be seen as corresponding to the idea of a capability for purposeful and conscious action, and performance management would correspond to the capability for ensuring integrated and coordinated action within government (and for ensuring partnership working was productive). His model is more comprehensive than the scope of our study—for example, his reference to capacity and culture and also his underlining of the differentiation of government domains (command and control, devolutions and transparency, and quasi-markets); see Figure 9.2.

Strategic process capabilities is (probably) an important factor in creating overall government effectiveness, a generalization we base on the empirical

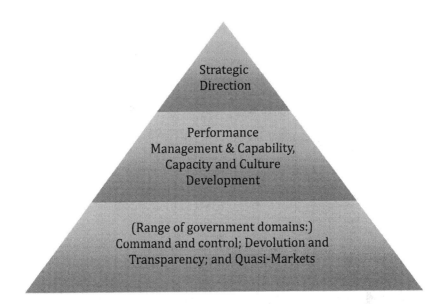

Figure 9.2 Barber's (2007) Model of Effective Government

co-variation of the estimate for World Governance Indicator for government effectiveness and an overall score for strategic process capabilities reported in an earlier chapter.

Other things being equal, strategic process capabilities in a strategic state can be expected to bring benefits not only for the economy (higher productivity) but also for the happiness (life evaluations) of members of the public.

The Gulf states provide a simple example of how a government strategy for the economy may be resource-based in contrast to a strategy based on analysis of the strategic situation and an attempt to position the economy in global markets. (See D'Aveni [2012], for an example of the latter positioning approach to the design of government economic strategy). In the case of other countries, the application of a resource-based approach to government strategy may have to be more complex than a simple argument that an oil-based economy needs to become a human resources based economy, but the idea of seeing the government as strategizing by means of a resource-based model of strategy is clearly the point that might be generalized from this study.

The next point we want to discuss is whether government strategy can be totally reduced to strategies for linking national resources and public aspirations. This arises from thinking about why the Bahrain state seemed to be a special case. Why did it not seem possible to totally assimilate it within the analysis that seemed to work for the other five Gulf states? Why did it seem to deviate from attempts to link strategic process capabilities and the productiveness of the economy and the happiness of the public?

We speculate that a fundamental aspect of a strategic state is how it relates to the public. A strategic state is not a strategic state simply because it uses long-term strategic visions and strategic plans. It is also a strategic state because of its relationship to citizens, the business community, and others in civil society. The strategic state is not self-sufficient. It works at catalyzing the activity of others in problem-solving and even in co-production of public services. A strategic state is defined by its catalyzing of societal action and by its interactive relationships with others, both at the formulation stage of strategic planning and the delivery stage. It is, in fact, important to see the strategic state as both an enabling and a strategic state.

We think the idea of the state enabling the public to achieve its aspirations goes quite well with an assumption that the public is best understood as being bound to, or supportive of, government through contingent consent (Levi 2006). We would emphasize this assumption rather than an assumption that the public identifies with government based on loyalty that is primarily emotional, moral, or principled in nature.

The experience of Bahrain might show one of the problems with Aristotle's assumption that the only cleavage in society that matters (and the only one that is reflected in the different types of governance that exist) is the cleavage between rich and poor. (In fact, maybe Aristotle should have paid more attention to another differentiation in the societies and constitutions of his own day—the differentiation between slaves and citizens. He discussed them at length and then ignored the significance of slaves in his core political analysis.) In the case of Bahrain, the issue has been not so much the tension between rich and poor as between different religious communities. There has been official concern about the influence of religious leaders based outside Bahrain, who might have influence over the Shia population. This leads us to suggest that governance has to be concerned with fears as well as aspirations—yet another duality!

According to Levi (2006), security dilemmas are motivated by fear, and this fear arises where individuals come to expect threats by others. She notes at one point that ethnic conflict is a major component of state failure. We would suggest that, building on Levi's point, fears might develop between religious groups as well as ethnic groups. Add into this a fear that one of the groups in society are being influenced by external voices, especially if these external voices are people living in countries with whom there is some degree of tension with the country in question, and you have a potent source of tension between government and a section of society.

We probably have to go back to the seventeenth century ideas of Thomas Hobbes (1962) to find any commentator interested in the interplay of opportunity (aspiration) and insecurity. One reading of Hobbes's arguments was that there is a simultaneous existence of a desire for power and a fear of oppression within society. The desire for power was associated with aggression, competition, and the wish to "live well". According to Hobbes, fear of oppression led to people seeking the aid of society to secure their life and liberty. Of course, we would suggest, if the competition and aggression is occurring between two sections of society, one side or both sides may seek security from aggression by asking for the aid of government. The challenge for government in the face of internal societal conflicts is how to build confidence in the different parts of the society that they can think and act in social solidarity with each other and that they will be safe from aggression and not exploited.

Where internal conflict within a society is not resolved, and where a sense of insecurity and threat is a big problem, it must damage the attempts by a strategic state to mobilize society behind national goals for development. Thus, it is possible that unresolved internal societal conflicts seriously limit the ability of strategic states to act effectively. In effect, unresolved conflicts are limits on public governance in the national interest. Or to express a related Hobbesian idea, government effectiveness is needed for the citizens' sense of security as well as for the realization of citizens' aspirations.

Finally, we offer the generalization that a movement towards a strategic state is full of collisions of strategic visions and associated strategic plans with contingent events. In our study one of the main contingent events was the Arab Spring in 2011, when a response was evoked that involved Gulf state governments taking decisions and actions to bolster internal security and stability even if at times this meant taking a step backwards in terms of changing from being a rentier state. Another big contingent event was the drop in oil prices in 2014. It could not be argued that this event in 2014 was an unanticipated event, because it was explicitly perceived by the governments of the Gulf states as likely to happen, but the exact timing of a future fall in oil prices was not predicted. This event, when it occurred, created a "critical juncture" (Levi 2013) because governments were still very dependent on oil revenue (and not tax revenue) and thus still embedded within a rentier state paradigm. Cutting public services and cutting subsidies might seem like a dismantling of the rentier state and an assault on the hold of a rentier mentality among national citizens. However, it also could spell the weakening of regime legitimacy if the extent of conditional consent among the public was eroded by these cuts. This would be destabilizing for a strategic state that seeks engagement and participation of the public. In other words, it was a critical juncture because its effect on the trajectory of the nations could be decisive (Acemoglu and Robinson 2012)—in this case either consolidating a country's rentier state model or helping to liberate a country from its grip. This would have been at a time when the Arab Spring event was still fresh in the minds of national leaders and they were sensitive to issues of public consent to being governed. The collisions of vision and strategy with contingent events are not an invalidation of the concept of the strategic state but the normality of the strategic state. Presumably, this reveals that capabilities in handling critical junctures are also part of a set of strategic state capabilities.

Reference List

Acemoglu, D. and Robinson, J. A. (2012). *Why Nations Fail: The Origins of Power, Prosperity, and Poverty.* New York: Crown.

Barber, M. (2007) *Instruction to Deliver.* London: Politico's.

D'Aveni, R. (2012) *Strategic Capitalism: The New Economic Strategy for Winning the Capitalist Cold War.* New York: McGraw-Hill.

Deutsch, K. W. (1966) *The Nerves of Government: Models of Political Communication and Control.* New York: Free Press.

Held, D. and Ulrichsen, K. (2012) Editor's Introduction: Transformation of the Gulf. In: David Held Kristian Ulrichsen (editors) *The Transformation of the Gulf: Politics, Economics and the Global Order.* London and New York: Routledge. Pages 1–25.

Hobbes, T. (1962) *Leviathan.* Collins.

Johanson, J. (2014) Strategic Governance in Public Agencies. In: Joyce, P., Bryson, J. and Holzer, M. (editors) *Developments in Strategic and Public Management: Studies in the US and Europe.* Houndmills, Basingstoke, UK: Palgrave Macmillan. Pages 268–284.

Kotter, J. P. (2001) What Leaders Really Do, *Harvard Business Review*, 79(11), 85–96.

Levi, M. (2006) Why We Need a New Theory of Government, *Perspectives on Politics*, 4(1), 5–19.

Levi, M. (2013) Can Nations Succeed? *Perspectives on Politics*, 11(1), 187–192.

Milward, H. B. (2015) The State and Public Administration: Have Instruments of Governance Outrun Governments? Introductory Perspectives, *Asia Pacific Journal of Public Administration*, 37(4), 217–223.

Moore, M. (1993) Declining to Learn from the East? The World Bank on 'Governance and Development'. *IDS Bulletin*, 24(1), 39–50. Institute of Development Studies.

OECD (2013) *Strategic Insights from the Public Governance Reviews: Update. GOV/PGC(2013)4, Public Governance and Territorial Development Directorate. Public Governance Committee.* Paris: OECD.

PUMA. (1996) *Globalisation: What Challenges and Opportunities for Governments?* Paris: OECD.

World Bank (1997) *World Development Report 1997: The State in a Changing World.* New York: Oxford University Press.

Index

accountability 115
active industrial policy 30
Advisory Council (Qatar) 66
alignment 52
Arabian Peninsula 4
Arab Spring (2011) 12, 14–15, 68, 159–60

Bahrain's crown prince 12
Basic public services 91
benchmarking data 80
better governance and happiness 142
budget cuts 122
budget deficits 116
budget transparency 53

capabilities 45
capacity development 10–11
central agencies, strengthening of 48
Centre for Performance Management of Government Agencies 111
centre of government 10, 111
challenges 8, 11, 19
circumstances 147
citizens: citizen opinions 52; citizens involvement in development planning 99; engagement with citizens 52, 111
civil service training 115
civil society strength 53
coherence 30
competitiveness rankings 89–91
compliance 33
conditional consent 169, 173
constitution: Bahrain 67–8; Kuwait 75; Oman 69–71; Qatar 66; Saudi Arabia 62–6; United Arab Emirates 72–3
constitutional change in Bahrain 13
consultation 114

consultation and partnership with civil society and the private sector 113
Consultation Council (Oman) 70
Consultative Assembly (Saudi Arabia) 62
consultative style 74
context 54
coordination 52
credibility of the state 47
credible leaders 35
crisis management 52
cultural and religious dimensions 165

democracy and economic growth 50–1
democratic culture 73–4
democratic government 33
demographic changes 5–6
differentials of wealth and income 27
diversification, success of 107
diversification of the economy 17, 97, 103, 113, 114, 115, 118, 144
dynastic elites 41, 62, 63, 78

East Asia 49, 51
East Asia's economic successes 30–1
economic ambitions 5
economic growth rates 6–7, 42
economic problems in Dubai 16
Economic Vision for 2030 (Bahrain) 114
Eighth Development Plan (Saudi Arabia) 9
electoral process 75
enabling government 171
escaping from a rentier state system 173
export projections 103
exports (Qatar) 113

factions 11–12
fall in oil and gas prices in 2014 146
financial strain
five-year development plans 94
foreign direct investment in 2014
    172–3
foreign workers 15–16

GDP per capita
global competitiveness 140
globalization 3, 170
good policies 50
governance: definition 21; governance
    indicators may be related to each
    other 84–5; governance problems
    and poor environmental performance
    143; governance processes 4;
    perceptions of governance in the
    Arabian Peninsula 85–8
government effectiveness 21–2, 33, 46,
    81–4, 138
government executive 61, 68
government finances 146
government intervention in the
    economy 91
green growth 33
Gulf Cooperation Council 72, 76, 153,
    154–5
Gulf Cooperation Council and issues:
    the Arab Spring of 2011 159–60;
    economic developments 160–1;
    environmental issues 161; security
    156–8

happiness 140–2
horizontal organization 29
human agency 21, 35
human resource 119
human resource development (HRD) 16

impact of state capability on income per
    capita 50
implementation and monitoring 101
implementation problems and the
    Kuwait parliament 121–2
incentives in a market system 27
individual freedom 25
individualism 25
industrial conflict 23–4
inequality 28, 57, 167–8
institutional approach 44
institutional restraints on leaders 36
integration 30
international crisis (2007–9) 32
investment 102–3

Iraq invasion of Kuwait 12
Islamist ideas 14

Keynesianism 26
knowledge economy 133

labour markets 16
leadership 22, 35, 45, 174
learning 122
learning from other countries 99–100
learning process 33
liberal-pluralism 40
life evaluations 140–2
long-term national visions 31, 48
Long-Term Strategy 2025 (Saudi
    Arabia) 101

management consultants 169
market forces 26
merchants 67, 71, 74
middle class elites 40–1
minimalist state 60
modern government 94
modernization 105
monitoring and evaluation 9, 148
municipal elections (Saudi Arabia) 64
munificence 172
Muscat Conference 95

National Action Charter
National Agenda (United Arab
    Emirates) 119
National Assembly (Kuwait) 75
National Development Strategy
    (Qatar) 113
National Economic Strategy (Bahrain)
    114–15
nationalist ideas 14
nationalist rulers 41–2
neo-liberalism 28
neo-liberal philosophy 24–5
networks 30, 52
New Public Management and
    neo-liberalism 170–1

oil: dependence on oil 94, 116; (oil)
    economies 6; exports 74; prices 17,
    98–9; (oil) rents 7, 144–5, 166
open political system 4

parliament 13–14, 75–6
partnership with the private sector 31
perception data 81
personal power 78
personal sacrifices 35

pluralist perspective 63
political barriers to implementation 116
political institutions 22–3
political leaders 48
political societies 68
poor are ill-served by public policies 46
population growth 5
poverty 46
poverty reduction 103
power struggle 68
predatory behavior 34
private sector investment 108
private sector share of the economy 108
protecting the dynamism of the
    market 28
public debt 169
public governance: definition
    3; generalizations on 174–9;
    institutions 65; modern 29; OECD
    reviews 31; personalization (Oman)
    69–70; reforms 52
public management reforms 45
public sector corruption 167
public spending 26

quasi-voluntary compliance 33

regulatory quality 81–4
reinventing the rentier state 167
reliability 35
rentier economy 145
rentier mentality 18
rentier state 5–6, 7–8, 61, 62, 74–5,
    78, 165–6
reporting on implementation to the
    public 102
resource-based strategy 132
revolutionary intellectuals 41

Saudi Long-Term Strategy 2025 9
Saudi vision in 2016 110
security 72
security dilemmas 34
security issues 12
Shia community in Bahrain 12–13
social democracy 23, 24
social inclusion 33
spread of wealth 166
state's capacity 51
strategic intent 8
strategic management office (Saudi
    Arabia) 11, 111

strategic planning 96, 102, 103–4, 114,
    116–17, 119, 120, 121
strategic planning approach 9
strategic planning impact in the UAE's
    public sector 117
strategic priorities 31, 117
strategic process capabilities 134–7,
    138, 176
strategic state 30, 51–2, 65, 66, 170,
    171–2
strategic-state capabilities 3, 111,
    128–9
strategic-state capacity 29, 30
succession process (Saudi Arabia)
    62–3
sustainable environment 118,
    119

Third Way 25
trade unionism 27
tradition 101, 118
transparency and accountability 73,
    110–11

UNDP 8–9, 10–11

vested interests 46
vicious cycle of government spending
    26–7
violence 34
vision statements 93, 101, 112,
    114, 116
voice and accountability 81–4

war on poverty (Saudi Arabia) 168
wicked issues 52
women councilors 64
women's contribution to society and the
    economy 110
women's empowerment 112, 115,
    118
women's enfranchisement 76
women's participation in national
    development 109
women's participation in political
    life 15
women's participation in the
    economy 105
World Bank assessment of MENA 31
World Bank model for effective public
    sector 49
world wars 25–6